No **Time**

for

Commas

D. Steven Russell

Booklocker.com, Inc.
2014

Second Edition

Prologue

Three small figures sat along the cortex of their changing world, sharing ideas of reality, and knowing that they might again soon be thrust into a structure, a sea, a sky, or a desert of uncontrollable dreams.

None spoke their common fear as each night's opening doorway nudged a shared oblivion closer toward the final sleep of infinity's indiscernible beginning and end. If they prayed, it was likely selfishly symbiotic and hidden from honesty; they probably prayed only for the dreamer's continued existence...for his heartbeats and breath.

A fourth man sat calmly nearby, with an unfiltered cigarette drooped loosely between his left thumb and index finger, looking at growing flashes of blue and purple lightning approaching. His legs dangled over the edge of a pink rocky cliff, and a canyon of rolling valleys and hills unfolded before him. Storms were building in the distance and a moist breeze rose from the valley to make his cigarette glow orange and to warn of the dreamer's deepening slumber.

The middle being became nostalgic. "Remember how he used to roll over a bale of hay before he would pick it up, because he was afraid a live rattlesnake might be baled into it?" He chuckled and shook his arm dramatically, as though a snake had bitten him, looking to the others for approval. They ignored his performance, and so, he blushed.

It was this sort of careless chatter that attracted the dreamer's boundless rakish compass.

"Yeah," continued the tallest of the group, "He acquired that behavior after seeing only one bale with a live snake in it—a harmless blue racer garden snake. He hauled thousands and thousands of bales and I don't think we ever saw a baled rattlesnake. Yet, after the blue racer snapped at him, he would never pick-up a bale of hay without looking at all sides of it first. It is amazing how

delusional fear alters a boy...and ultimately, a man. He wasted a lot of time looking for boogie snakes, but given the possibility, WAS it irrational behavior...or just inefficient prudence?" He winked to underscore his dangling riddle.

"Ever stop to think that women affected him the same way," mused the wiry looking man? "Think about it...he managed relationships based on false learning and fear. Hell, if I weren't here to guide him, he would have likely been stuck with the same woman his whole damn life. We would have missed all that other adventure, including this one. Now THAT'S scary!"

Thunder rumbled, and then cracked like a gunshot, as lightning arched across the multicolored, layered canyon walls below. It was getting closer and darker.

"What do you think a bullet would do to our universe," queried the man who had started the snake dialogue? "HE thought about that until it made him sick, and he has yet to find an answer. Would it destroy us, or simply place us all in eternal sleep? Would we all make it, none of us, or just the dreamer? You know what I'm asking." He squirmed uncomfortably. He could never leave the tough questions alone, and failed to see the rough ride he would put his mates through if that thought became a flashing arch...and so it would.

Lightning hit where the three had been engaged in discourse and, so, they were blasted into a blended drama of memory, reality, and dream; they became players: One a father, one a dying son, one a spinning bullet and the deluge of pain unleashed beyond its target.

The fourth man took a final puff of his cigarette, arose slowly and willed himself into the dream to guide only the dreamer.

As he tossed his cigarette, he became light, then lightning...first, he flashed to a future dream, and from there, into the dreamer's awakening now.

He knew that genius was not the essence of learning, but rather, timing, repetition, and context.

Unlike the others, each time he entered the dreamer's drama, he acted as a secret farmer and seeded lessons worth keeping. Each lesson was deliberately guided by divine caring and each caring was to make the dreamer believe himself less, while loving himself more. It was a slow growing process, invisible to all but one.

Waking and sleeping would eventually reverse roles and, with a final heartbeat and breath, would spark as the blue and purple lightning that takes all of our dreams and realities to the final incarnate and windless comma of appointed knowing.

Chapter 1
Violet awakening

A destined kiss blew from eternity and Doug awoke as though he had been whispered to by the New Orleans' night. It was 3:11 and he was keenly aware of the small, warm, gently curved, and beautiful woman beside him; he even knew that he loved her, though they had first touched only five days ago.

Doug wrestled to recall a fading dream, but could only remember that it dealt with violence...with children...with...Oh, God, he remembered it all.

He felt great pain, which surged an obligatory compulsion to recapture and rejoin the dream, but he yielded instead to embracing a sensory salve of the simple awakening *now*.

His mind spent a minute capturing random events and hours of telephone calls and laughter that led to this moment, and he felt a strained duplicity that was now welcomed as out of control.

Doug had only wanted to have a fling with her at a conference eight months ago and go home with detached memories. He knew he wouldn't; it was pure fantasy and by nature, he was shy and insecure.

Now, here they were, best friends and passionate lovers in a motel room near the French Quarter. Doug couldn't get enough of Violet's blue-green eyes, brilliant laughter, crisp mind, warm skin, thin neck, or designer-highlighted hair as they went about the town and then made love with impassioned "fit."

They laughed playfully each time they inventoried their clothing and found it strewn in mixed-gender about the room. Colorful twists of garments mapped the fury of their thoughtless heat and left a forensic trail of lovemaking.

Violet truly seemed to enjoy his company and gave herself so innocently to his touch. He had never known such emotional safety or openness before; not like this. It frightened him with adult vulnerability, yet also made him feel childlike and hopeful. Even now, however, his mind tried to tell him, "She's too good for you." He knew this to be the fatal end of all relationships for him, so, out of innocent hope and reckless fear, he ignored the warning.

He watched her sleeping and savored the warm, moist and sweet-smelling scent of her breath and her perfume as her black, silky camisole moved, predestined for this moment with the rhythmic patterns of her breathing in the room's filtered light. "Vivienne Westwood," he remembered. "*Boudoir.*"

He realized that this moment was something made possible only by the body's incredible gift of hearing, sight, taste, smell, and touch...without all of it, the moment would lack something and become two, or even one, dimensional. He could almost taste her.

Without her breathing added, even the perfume would be cold and alone, as when found on a test strip or on the wrist of a pale-faced, doll-like, cardboard-smelling sales lady. It was magical, so alive—Jesus, last year he was lucky to shake her hand and couldn't remember if he had even been allowed to do that.

As Doug's eyes studied the blue, gold, yellow and tarnished geometry of the old motel room, he could refocus his filters and smell living and long-dead elements of a 300-year old city. He could hear the random sounds of its energy being ground, kneaded, baked, and released into the starry night.

He ran his eyes along large cables and rusty bolts intermixed with peach and green refracted light and followed them to brush-painted yellow beams, where he realized the beauty of craftsmen holding together the past and the future with such temporal things. Any piece of it could unravel the whole in an instant and—even undisturbed—none of it would last forever. A great wind or rushing water from the nearby sea would leave it in ruins, or time, without effort, breeze, or dripping would eventually turn it to dust and another's lost memories would haunt this fading space.

But tonight it all existed and offered a refuse from the world's lonely ticking.

He felt full and eternal and, despite the *sin* of this existence, knew that, for the first time, he was being truly honest with himself and with his feelings. He loved this woman and her city—amazing for a farm boy. Amazing. If only the darkness would leave him alone.

Doug flinched and burned mentally as his auto-reminder mind told him: "BING: This is the morning that you will board a plane, return home, see your 2nd wife, take the yoke of your 11th job, resume a dozen AA meetings a week, and smile at the phony pretension that is now your chosen life.

How could it all get so off course, and take so long to get there? How could he find a renewal of spirit in a town that, a year ago, he wouldn't have spent a dime or a minute to visit? But, this city touched him.

"Life is a strange and curved little path, and in some way is bigger than our choices," he thought. "Perhaps there is indeed some higher plan that eludes our finest decisions, and, letting-go is the essence of seeing blind choice and of finally embracing grace. Perhaps it will find me now that I am broken and teachable. There are kind spirits and people who have always bridged the void."

As he gently sat-up in bed to avoid waking her, his mind generated memories and visions as though he were in a waking dream.

Suddenly and clearly, he saw and felt himself 200 yards from the finish line, exhausted and gasping for air, with a slight taste of blood in his throat, painfully thirsty, nearly done, and with the student body cheering.

On that day, he again drew a red ribbon, yet felt the glory of being popular for his ability to run. His time for this mile was 4-minutes, 49-seconds. He was second. He would shave-off another ten seconds, but never in a race that counted and never enough to be first.

Little Freddy Britton had crossed the line at least 20 seconds ahead and there were boys even faster in tiny towns with peeling nameplates just down the road.

But, in a young man's glory, the race was the cheering and not the ribbon. The student body liked him and, somehow, that filled the hole of his nameless shame. Doug was not popular, not invited to most parties, but was accepted...good enough for high school dorks and the shit-covered children of simple farmers.

Doug's cousin, Curt, was popular, and helped drag him into the popular crowd, though Doug knew he didn't belong there.

Curt watched over him like a brother. It was Curt who got him elected MYF President. It was Curt who got him invited to parties. It was Curt who helped him hang out with popular kids and cheerleaders as he and Curt endlessly trolled and *dragged Main in a '63 Chevy.*

Doug remembered Curt so fondly and vividly. Curt was solid, focused, athletic, taller, more confident, and likely smarter, yet always kept his 1st cousin close with love.

They were born only thirteen days apart and had been commonly perceived as twins until puberty began its alterations and each branched toward his destined paternal genetics, one a Thomas, and one a Russell. A mutation amplified as they went to college, joined the same fraternity, and began playing with alcohol. One would remain undefiled; one would become a powerless thrall.

Doug reflected that he had learned to put on faces, humor, and bullshit to keep people from looking too deep or too long. He did not want them to look, lest they see the shallowness of his being. The speed and brain of a youth can generate that sort of mask—quick answers, cute sayings, stories and tales, distraction, mania, car talk, girl watches, mirrored reflections, subtle nose-picking, nut scratching, and hormonal lies. This was how he kept them away while he found the strength to believe that he was good enough to be real, and someday, might be both good and real enough to be lovable. He falsely believed that this was an adolescent mask, not a distorted tumor with its own primeval staying power.

And, so, before New Orleans, he couldn't keep up, as the mask continued to outrun him.

It got thicker and even grew into his flesh as though it were a living part of him. The mask eventually *became* him, and fear of its removal left it growing with an intuitive life of its own.

He finally resolved that the mask would take care of him, and, when it didn't, he would leave the relationship or the job to avoid the shame of blank exposure. He was, after all, a runner, and it had served him well. Somehow, though, he knew that even now, this joined the ancient motel's brushwork as a temporal lie.

Sitting in the middle of the night, Doug's mind grabbed 40 years of experience and yielded an epiphany of the knower:

He was a B-student, a second-place miler, a third-place high jumper, and a person who couldn't pass IQ tests, yet, for some reason, he had lived his life as though he were brilliant, would finally win the blue, and might someday even fly.

He had likely convinced some people that he was blue-ribbon material—perhaps even this woman—but in the middle of the night, with pure and crystal thought and recollection, he knew the truth. He was a white-ribbon jumper and a red-ribbon runner trying to jump and operate in an A-student world...and he was tired. He could jump no higher and run no more.

Clarity was his for the moment, an acceptance and an awakening forever...humbling, yet freeing.

His life, as he had lived it, was over. He would play an A-student no more. He was done. He was exhausted by illusion and lie.

He prayed for a lasting quick fix, and hoped that revelation could undo his ruptured horror. He feared that residual, time released, damage might occur, but he prayed that it would not—to patch it.

"If anyone can love the undiscovered me, it is this woman, Violet," he assured himself. "She may just love me *for me*, and I may not even need to know who I *am* for her to discover me. Then, she'll share who I am with me and I'll *know* who I am. I am safe with this woman. She loves me deeply, so in that depth, I will find myself also for the first time in half a century. Damn, I'm sleeping with a cheerleader and she's too good for me, but I have to try. Perhaps I'm real...at least real enough to be loved by this blue ribbon woman for awhile longer, maybe even *forever.*"

"Ironically," Doug pondered, "it was death and trouble that opened this awakening and this place of vulnerability. In the presence of bland acceptance as a learned displacement for great pain, I intended, yet pretended, to be a Christian and a father, a husband, a lover, a leader. But I could not lead and I could not love. I gave so that they would like me and think me good. I created so that they would think me smart. But, I was a phony and I know it now for some umbilical reason in the quiet morning of a New Orleans pause."

He continued the logic. "My brother and his son gave me the gift of deep pain and from that has grown the inductive knowledge that I *can* love, because I loved them. From Bill's story, I can truly say that I understand the gift of life, for he had life and I watched it come full circle through Hell's shadow and Heaven's light."

The conclusion was simple. "I will take this gift and hang on to it with all my might. The season for hiding and lying is over for now, and I will seize life and live as long as God allows my existence. When I'm out of breath, I will simply end the race—this time without a ribbon at all—but having run as I must to keep up with this Violet awakening."

He breathed a silent prayer into the still night and floated again into her warm breathing, scent of *Boudoir,* then slumber.

The city crescendoed its groaning movements as they slept, dreamed of things beyond their control, and breathed separately mating layers of conscious existence.

Love offered a new hope, and a new day was about to dawn in New Orleans, where Violet would put Doug on an airplane and he would return to the golden-stubbled aftermath of wheat fields now harvested.

She would return to her world and they would resume secret telephone calls totaling 200 hours a month—filled with machine-timed disconnections, friendship, love, laughter, and boundless conversation. They would again shop for movies, laugh, read books, do laundry, and share the most intimate of loves across 726 miles.

Doug did not know that in a few hours he would feel pain as real as death's grieving, as he touched the spiritual tearing and ripping of her farewell hug. He would know then that this could not be over. Grace would be put to her benevolent test...a forgiveness that happens when man has done his best, but his path is no longer true.

Doug had experienced a moment of purity in the night, and no daylight, job, or marriage could drive that from his hope or his knowing. He might misunderstand its essence and source, but his course would have to change.

"Screw her and go home with the warmth of pleasure's moment," he reflectively smiled. How he would have cheated his heart with a conference fantasy.

Doug loved this woman and would do whatever it took to keep him on this path of the journey. The mask had suddenly vanished and he slept sweetly in spiritual nakedness, dreaming of the honesty in red ribbons and Violet's eyes.

Chapter 2
life's simple stage: a-long-and-three-shorts

It was one of those rare, windless days in western Kansas as Dollar came barking from the field. He caught something and played with it for a while, like a cat, but then hungered for some human companionship. His lop-ears flopped as his mix of mutant hound dog black, brown, tan, and white blended with the dust, weeds, shadows, and light, to seem like more than one being approaching.

Hank and Patsy were floating from the kitchen window into the yellow sun-baked yard, mixed only with butter churning, distant tractors, dusty summer morning smells, and meadowlark songs.

Billie was in the corral being tossed again and again from his Shetland pony, Willie, into the scented dust of fresh and crusting cow shit; yet, each time, he would defiantly beat the beige midget and jump back on, cussing: Billie and Willie. He was seven.

Dollar lay down by the front porch and Mommy threw some old chicken bones out for him to eat.

He ignored her and looked sideways down the snotty foam of his speckled nose at the chicken's thigh as though it were beneath him, but she knew he would eat it before the cats did and that he was just being predominate hound-dog coy.

Billie came and put his head on Dollar's belly and the two of them dozed from exhaustion in the late morning shade. Elm trees swayed gently to a gathering breeze, drowning-out 'This Ole House'...Windless in Kansas was a passing lull, subject to nature's fickle patterns blowing north, south, west, and sometimes even east to west as a gulf breeze touched and stirred Louisiana or Canada into the prairies.

We didn't have TV or air conditioning yet, and our telephone was a party line comprised of ringing a long-and-three-shorts. The phone hung on our west wall like a carved wooden breadbox with a little black metal right-handed crank.

Bernita Selfridge listened to every call to find gossip, but in an area that small, it was a matter of time before everyone knew what she had stolen anyhow:

Lynette Thomas is "going away," the little Martersdale boy is queer, Joey Deerslaw stole some gas from the Hartman farm, that good looking Bobbie Cardin is half-Mexican, and of course, Gerald Cartmaker is going to go *crazy* when he finds out—doctor or not—that his daughter is marrying a *nigger*.

"He's a doctor, sure, but...well, you know. She'll never be able to come home again and isn't that a horrible price to pay *just for love*—giving up one's family and all? She's so smart too...top of her class. I wonder if she's *thought* about what she's doing? And their children...why they'll be strangers to both *types* of people. They sure can't live down south. Why, those people are so prejudiced and all. And, speaking of doctors, isn't it a shame that we can't get another one here? Doctor V is going to get old eventually..."

These were our first impressions of life—simple, predictable, and without experience to measure its pain, correctness, or gratitude. Life was what one was told and what one did, nothing more. Irony was saved for consequence.

There was no stock market penetrating this farmer's world. There were no foreign cars, only trinkets in *Cracker Jacks* boxes, and a county fair with a pig roast every July.

Mental health was a secret if one lacked it, and those who needed it went *"to Larned"* to get *"the cure"* from pills or alcohol. Addictions and deep abuse were plentiful, but no one thought anything of it, and these were *private* things, spoken only in secret and shared on the party line.

Planes passed so high as to never be heard and one could usually count their white streaks against the crystal blue sky on two hands a day, with fingers to spare.

FM, what was that? Only two meaningful radio stations could be heard—Country music from KFRM in Cloud County, Kansas and

KOMA in Oklahoma City for rock-n-roll at night. There was some shit station from Garden City that one could hear when it decided to pierce the air, and of course KXXX in Colby, Kansas, with weatherman Snyder. Whenever he would say that the weather was gonna be fine in the winter, the ole man would say, "Let's bring in the cattle, put down straw and feed 'em. It's gonna blizzard." And, he was usually right. Snow it did.

I remember waking up one morning in late 1957 or early '58 to find that the house was *under* a snowdrift. Mommy and Daddy dug us out of the front door somehow and we went on a white-glacial search for cows and pigs. The pigs had simply walked over the fence on snowdrifts. We lured them back with food and dug out their fences to be a wall on the inside, trapping them in a giant white box, with rippled drifts sloping away into now hidden pastures.

We couldn't find the milk cows, and after some fretting, hot chocolate, coffee, hand-warming, and cold deduction, the ole man concluded that they might have gathered in a three-sided lean-to shed next to the barn.

Sure enough, we dug and dug and dug on the open side and suddenly a small deep toned hissing vacuum of air went past us. There were the cows! Their legs were wobbly, their eyes were spinning strangely, and they were gasping for breath. We had found them just in time.

The next two days were some of the greatest times of our youth.

We went up the drift that covered the barn and sled-rode down to its bottom, hundreds of yards away. For a normally flat geography, this was like discovering a new mountain in one's back yard. And explore it we did!

We built igloos half way down, threw snowballs, rode the sled, rode the washer lid, rode the grain-shovel, rolled down, rolled Billie down, carried Billie up, slid Billie down, beat each other up, drank hot chocolate, warmed on the open-grate floor furnace, and did it all again. We were exhausted at night, drinking a mixed hot toddy of lemon juice, a tablespoon of honey, and a shot of Jack Daniels to stop our coughing.

When a neighbor drove by the wonderland on his tractor, asking if he might get us something from town, we knew that all was well. I remember having a warm feeling about everything that day—nature, cows, family, God, and neighbors. It all seemed so good, cold, new, odorless, natural, unending, and interconnected by the white-induced, rare, farmer's vacation.

It was magical, but then it melted as if it were a vaporous memory that had never taken form. This somehow gave me a view that magical things do happen, that people create memories of God, and that God creates memories of snow. My faith was strengthened by this soon invisible pool of spiritual warmth coming from silent crystals of bitter cold.

This was the backdrop for the earliest memories of Billie. It seemed then that we would live forever and that life might threaten, but would never kill. We were those who killed.

We hunted sometimes, with cousins visiting for bonding sport, but ate what we killed and we killed our fatted friends, the livestock, for food. Nothing seemed incongruous. It was nature and we were its trusting servants.

Yes, we named our cows and then we killed them, but we would never die. Daddy would protect us, and we were *farmers*, cut from the earth and its chaotic cycles. We were a part of nature, and as long as we put back, the earth would give, including our lives.

It never occurred to us that life had a life of its own, that the smallest thing could harm us, or that we could die of our own hidden chemistries or from the earth that lived within.

Billie was walking in the yard one day and a rooster attacked him. He kicked at it, but slipped and fell on the rocks, whereupon the rooster viciously clawed into his head and began pecking at his eyes and forehead as he sat there screaming, waving his little hands at it and bleeding. I knocked the bird off and we got iodine and bacon for his wounds.

As we were having supper that night, our sister commented that the chicken tasted tough but the ole man growled, "Eat the fuckin' thing, it's not as tough as Billie." We were eating the attack chicken! *Farmer 100*: Don't fuck with the ole man and don't fuck with his family!

Milk came from two or three cows every day, morning and night. The milk was *separated* by turning a large cast-iron, wooden-handled, machine crank and gravity-feeding fresh cow-warmed milk from a formed chrome basin-pot on top onto a series of shiny inlaid funnels, where it was "separated."

The milk drained from a cast-iron spout into five-gallon buckets, while the cream was dribbled by another spout into a wide-mouthed gallon jar. The cream could be taken from the pump-house refrigerator and turned upside down the following morning without a *drop* of spillage. It just hung, thick as butter, upside down in the jar.

City cousins would visit, head straight from the car to the pump house, and gorge themselves with tablespoons of pure cream as a dairy luxury food.

I hated the taste of thick cream, but hated more drinking milk cooled with melting ice cubes, because it was lukewarm from our kitchen's refrigerator. Our pump house had the better refrigerator—a business decision.

We made buttermilk sometimes from sour milk and it was nasty. Butter churned from cream, and shaped with a wooden paddle, however, was delicious. I loved carving patterns onto the top of fresh butter after hand churning it. A churned cube of fresh yellow butter was the size of a soccer ball cut in half, though we had never heard of a soccer ball.

After *separating*, several gallons of milk were carried to the chickens and the pigs with some saved for the family and the cats.

The barn was about 120 child-paces from the pump-house and was the shit-filled staging area for white raw materials two times a day. It amassed, stored, and grew contempt.

The pump-house was a simple, gray, 10' square, flat-roofed concrete block building with a concrete floor that had a refrigerator, a sink for washing the separator's parts after each use, a small gas stove, a round metal tub for scalding water to remove chicken feathers, the milk *separator,* and a pile of farmer's shit for fixing unnamable strings of farmer's things. It was a place for beatings or solitude depending on the ole man's whereabouts and mood. I worked, always muttering to myself, and prayed to be alone.

I forcibly set my internal clock to the endless toil of morning and evening chores:

Milk the cows, feed the cows, make sure the cows had water, break 3" thick ice from the stock tank in the winter so the cows could drink, separate the milk, feed the cats, feed the chickens, feed the pigs, wash the separator, put the cream in the refrigerator in one-gallon glass jars, fill the metal *cream can* to be taken to the train station (each time five jars were filled), then get ready for school or play, study, and go to bed by nine. It seemed like a lot at the time.

Ironically, this churning of chores birthed both my type "A" work ethic and a conflicted hunger for laziness that could never be quenched. I looked for things that do nothing and learned from them—A storage tank sits for water as a manager sits for pay.

Somehow, nearly unnoticed, there was a huge round steel tank on top of the cube-looking pump-house that gravity-fed our house's plumbing. It was hooked to a 30' windmill tower which pumped clear, crisp, cold, perfect water year-around. A large garden was planted to the south of it each spring and the rest of its surroundings were a rural stockpile of dirt, prairie grass, scraggly trees, weeds, and rocks ... suitable for throwing.

The warm weather pump-house chirped with crickets. It smelled musty by summer, smelled like fresh milk twice a day, and wafted the inefficient, but welcomed flames of its cheap, open flame, propane gas stove by winter. If anything spoke to the simplicity of a farmer's core, it was this ugly, life-giving, concrete cube.

The storage tank didn't freeze in winter because of its mass and because of rising heat from the building beneath. But, sometimes the well itself froze from bitter cold nights of no wind (and therefore no pumping or *moving* of water). It, thus, broke a pipe beneath the ground, directly under the windmill tower. This was a chance to learn pain from the ole man. We would climb high above the ground, cling to the frozen windmill, pull pipes from the ground with log-chains and "wire-pullers," and *"pull"* the well from winter's grip to find and replace both its broken pipe and its deeply seated pumping *leathers*.

By then, a freezing north wind was oft blowing hard. There is no way to describe the synergy of Kansas "wind-chill," frozen metal, ice, and water's ability to accelerate cold—or to define one's deepest gratitude for pauses of warmth from the little propane stove in the pump-house—yet even I understood the role of water in keeping us alive.

Fixing the windmill could never wait. Cows swelled with milk yet died of thirst, so the farmer kept it all balanced. The well house was the life-blood, heart, and veins of our farm and the farmer's hand was the soul that drove itself as the keeper and physician of the precious blood.

Warm milk and stupid cows became a balance of cold justice and white judgment for me. I found that I hated milking cows, but became accidentally enchained to it when I was seven.

I meant well, but was incarcerated for the next eight years by one foolish act of early grandiosity, powered by an insecure need for daddy's unmerited approval.

I had watched the ole man milk cows every day for a couple of years, and had even tried my "hand" at the mechanics of milking, so I knew that I could accomplish it.

I thought spontaneously one night that I would "surprise" him and arise so early that the milking would be done before he arose. A dozen things could have gone wrong to foil my grandiose design, but they didn't. Sadly, as one of life's bitter lessons, I carried out my plan. I had them milked and was separating the milk when he got up. He came to the pump house and "caught" me succeeding.

In my fantasy, he would have hugged me, tossed me on his shoulders, and carried me into the house to tell Mommy and my sister, Dallas, what a good and wonderful child I was. He would have cried with joy and told me that he loved me for doing this amazing thing--and he would have known that it WAS an amazing thing—but that was not what happened.

He did seem unsmilingly pleased, but concluded quickly that if I could do it once, I could do it every day.

I don't know if he slept late, fucked the ole lady, or what, but he didn't milk the cows anymore. I did. This was part of my conflicted learning and I just never relearned "learning" properly.

On the one hand, I learned that, with vision, I could accomplish about anything on a given day...on the other hand, I learned to become innately and deliberately lazy and to seek out every chance in life to loaf. These luxuries were on hold for an eight-year decade now.

The milking process was simple, twice a day, every day, year-around: Put grain in the trough, call-in the cow. The cow was happy to have the food, so she would walk into the barn, put her head in the stall and begin eating. I would lock her head in by closing the wooden V-shaped stall, I would place a blue colored set of chain "kickers" around her back legs, just above the knees, to keep her from kicking me *too* hard, clean the dried wet and crusty shit off of her tits (routinely a wintertime job after she and her friends would shit a dinner plate sized runny pile and lay in it overnight to stay warm), spray her for bugs *if it was summer*, sit beneath her on a one-legged, crudely nailed, "T" shaped milk stool, with the bucket between my knees, and milk H-E-R with a boring, hand-strengthening, squeezing motion. When done, I would do the same to one, and some years, two more cows.

Sometimes I varied the boring sound and traded work efficiency for risky entertainment effectiveness. (If daddy caught me, I was in trouble. He demanded *only* efficiency).

Anyway, I liked the musical tones of milk hitting an empty bucket and, then, the muted, deep rippling tone of milk pinging and splashing in a bucket as it was filling. Each tone became duller and deeper as the bucket filled, so I could vary the tones by squirting the sides, the center, anywhere on the white liquid drumhead of steaming milk...or even the ground or the wall.

I likely was accidentally practicing some primitive form of white boy, milk barn, reggae-rap when one stirred my ensemble of milking tones together with the random sounds of slapping the cow for hitting me in the face with her tail and with endless cussing and muttering to myself in whole and broken persecuted low tones and syllables.

If the wind rattled the barn roof or door with its passing, that also joined the building chorus and the cow's giant nasal breathing and rhythmic chomping added a natural wooden trough background percussion sound. A moo was music lagniappe, though I did not yet know that word. It was all oddly beautiful, but definitely not top-40 material.

Different cows milked differently and had different personalities. The Jersey cow was brown, petit, had beautiful sad eyes and was amazingly attractive (farm boy issues aside). The Holstein was **gigantic**, black and white, coldly impersonal and could have served in Hitler's army as a Rommel tank ace, or even perhaps, as a tank. She was a milk-producing machine. Even with multiple stomachs, she must have pumped iron and worked overtime creating milk.

There were gallons and gallons per milking from this *single* four-digit, deliberate, mooing mammary machine. We were only business associates, never friends. She never kicked me, but pissed on me several times and refused to join my songs.

The cows would stand compliant for the milking, committed to the eating. It was symbiosis at its best, though I didn't yet know that word either. For context, I didn't really know many words, wasn't a good student, didn't listen well, and cussed a lot. I was ADD, if they had diagnosed it then. I chewed off the ends of my shirt collars in school, bit my nails to the quick, and hadn't a *clue* what was going on around me most of the time. Given these afflictions, I was caught by surprise, frequently, by normal acts of man or beast.

Sometimes, for whatever unstated reason, cow participants would kick me enough to spill the milk, whereupon I would cuss them loudly and beat them with the milk stool.

When they pissed, it was like a large garden hose of warm golden piss splattering on me, and it gave me firsthand knowledge of the farmer saying, "*It's rainin' like a cow pissin' on a flat rock.*" They rarely splattered shit on me, though it happened. It was stuporous and dully disciplined, so one had to find things to like about it...and so, I did.

Inside the captive fool is a dreamer, and so I recall learning that while milking in warm weather, I could squirt flies on the barn wall, ten or twelve feet away. I got so good at it that the wall became covered with flies and the more flies there were, the more targets I had. The more targets I had, the more I sprayed, and so on. The ole man beheld the white, dried forensics and beat me without mercy.

"That's not the GODDAMN bucket," he roared! "Quit it, you stupid little fucker." Damned if I know completely why, but I *just couldn't stop.* I have theories.

I actually loved TWO things about milking, and they were both warm weather sports:

One, I loved squirting flies on the wall...and after all, there were *gallons* of milk left over, beatings aside.

Intermittent reinforcement is most dangerous for me, and my dual reinforcement was that I normally only got a beating when he caught me with fresh WET milk on the wall; when he didn't catch me in time, it dried and became a part of the runny white splatter marks that were already there...and that only led to an ass chewing and a rare beating. A couple of times, though, he beat me when I had not been squirting flies, so I quickly reasoned that if it didn't matter, I might as well have some fun.

Herein was the duel reinforcement. That became my kind of logic, and it likely generalized to damage other normal learning.

Two, I *loved* filling the shiny blue sprayer with DDT and spraying the cows and the flies on the wall to watch bugs walk in circles and then fall to the floor...there were plenty of flies left over for squirting; the barn door was open...plus, I LOVED the smell of the spray, and I loved spraying from the hissing canister. I liked the sound of it!

Perhaps a frequent, joyful inhalation of DDT slightly tainted my logic regarding spraying other flies on the wall with milk, but I don't think so. Perhaps DDT also damaged my learning in other areas, though I am more akin to believe that it gave me some hidden, and yet to be revealed, super powers.

The sprayer was a sideways-turned, horizontal bean can looking thing with a long metal tube that had a wooden pump handle coming out of its back end and a spray nozzle on its front that sprayed vaporous clouds of perfumed death. It was, basically, a bicycle pump with a can of chemicals attached. Hell, its raw description is inadequate for its actual fun. It was simply a *GAS!*

A decade of hard time passed quickly, taking only eight years, with me marking the walls and hardening with each spring and summer that I spent in the joint. Several cows dried or died, but I got to know each bovine as we shared a cell under the warden's cruel pacing and unpredictable oversight of our daily milking. Solitary bovinement had its solitude.

Year around, a rusty fry pan with a broken handle sat outside the well-house door for our cats to get their milk. The cat herd swelled to around two-dozen each summer and then died-off to four or five as *nature* took her portion. Coyotes, runny-eye disease, fights, passing cars, hawks, snakes, territorialism, and harsh weather thinned them out.

Balancing two five-gallon buckets nearly full of milk made each easier to carry as one first fed the cats, then took a pig's portion to the pigpen 30-yards south of the garden. Carrying a lighter portion to the chickens 100-yards north of the pump-house gave time to look at the glistening starry sky or perhaps drift momentarily into the stirred golden and yellowing pinks and purples of a blue autumn or Easter Bunny sunset.

The ticking of the farm was so deliberate that only the sun was more constant, and even it lagged the farmer in its rising.

"Why was I born into this hard daily toil," I thought, back then, "when so many fortunate people are born warm, workless, and happy, in the city?"

My brother shared the farm with insufficient age to work. His nature helped me discover the farm's nature.

Yes...Billie was bouncing, constantly bouncing. He didn't move fast—in fact he moved slow—but was always moving towards something new.

We caught toads, turtles, and lightning bugs, fished with cane poles, and threw rocks at chickens and light poles. Occasionally, we would go to a 50-cent movie in town, eat pool-hall hamburgers, or hang out at the bowling alley. Three bucks would last all night.

Days were spent milking the cows before school or milking the cows and then going round and round a field on a tractor, looking for dust devils, and chasing, but rarely catching, an occasional rabbit that found itself frightened and exposed in the now-barren field.

Dust devils meant rain and rain meant a day off, so I looked for dust devils with the hope of a parched galley slave.

Rarely did they come, but sometimes the wind would blow from the east, fueling nature with a moist gulf breeze and—in the midst of a swinging pendulum of changing air—over several hours, *whirlwinds* would form. When they did, dust spiraled to heaven and magically grew rain.

When it rained, we always went to town. Town meant other people. Other people meant safety while daddy drank beer. Beer meant fun when daddy drank in those days...extra change, sacks of candy, no accountability.

On one of these summer sagas, I somehow found the nerve to ask a girl named Carla to go out with me, but I was so shy that it took me five months of steady dating to kiss her.

She was a petit brunette with sweet brown eyes, like the center of two nearly ripe sunflowers, and she had a spatula-sized blond bang where her cousin had bleached her hair while she was sleeping. I thought that she was beautiful.

We dated—usually double dated—with Ken and Virgie because Ken had a '64 Chevy Corvair.

I got to know Carla, and them, like no one I had known. We loved in some innocent way. We laughed at stupid things, played *"Down In the Boondocks"* era radio music in star-lit hayfields, and breathed heavily until I routinely went home with a 50-cent sized wet spot that smelled like Clorox on my jeans, from hot youthful passions.

Yet, for some insecure reason, I was afraid to intimately run my hands under her soft, firm bra and touch her bare flesh.

It was fear and not morality, so when I finally found the nerve, her breast was warmer to my fingers than anything I had ever imagined. My mind spun with euphoria and happiness.

Consequently, the day after, in the back seat of her brother's '53 Chevy, I wiggled my fingers gently into the pant leg of her cut-off shorts. Her brother played the radio, talked loudly about himself, and drove us home. The sound and moist warmth of this touch was unknowable beyond words and left me spinning, physically weak, and mentally floating. Boys normally built on this adventure.

But, the next day, Carla went off with the "harvest" and some sick, fear-filled forming jealous detachment inflicted me.

I wrote her a letter and told her that it was over. Then I sunk into the comfort of empty darkness and sensual life unknown. This was the beginning of my *mask of a blending countenance*. It suffocated and protected me with an involuntary and unnaturally shaped companionship in years to come, like evil clouds that resemble gods and beings.

I hurt me by not hurting them, and somehow felt like a hero because of it. This became a hard script to play-out as life went on, but I kept it subliminally sharpened, ready, and cloaked, nonetheless.

At first, I willed it into being. It gave me control over relationships and a door to exit them at any time. The deeper and faster I dove in, the more and faster I could save a woman from my unexplainable instability by leaving her just in time.

In some *sick* way, this made the same sense as shooting a cow in the head for food after you had named it and talked to it each day. It had a natural cycle to it and kept life distant, detached, physical, patterned, and fresh. Thank God for the refining of a man's path and for reshaping of his pathways.

This was unfolding as Billie turned eight—Farming, adolescence, surety, rain. It all happened as it must and life unveiled as it chose. We were along for the ride—I working and learning *slowly* about flesh, Billie bouncing from thing to thing, still cussing and beating his defiant little horse.

Then it happened.

Our daddy had a heart attack—his second in six years—and the family felt truly vulnerable for the first time.

Billie was afraid for his Daddy, but I laughed and told him that the ole bastard was too mean to die. 30 hours later, while I was out with a girl, my sister flagged us down and simply said, "Daddy is dead." This powerful, dangerous, roaring god, who injected, yet protected me with and from life's true responsibility, was dead. Just like that.

I have three clear recollections about the matter:

1) My brother crying and saying, "I want my daddy. I want my daddy. I want my daddy." 2) My mother falling helplessly into a deep and long-lasting pit of self-loathing darkness, and 3) Standing on the top of an irrigation dam at 3:11 in the morning, listening to a mile of invisible blowing leaves of growing grain, and thinking, "Who will take care of this land?"

I felt empty and afraid of life while for the first time, knowing that I was now comparing that not so much to death as to living without experienced power.

Just like that, I was powerless, beaten by something non-human. But, I intuitively sensed that this loss was mixed-up and overshadowed with the deliverance of being simultaneously humbled and free. God had granted the hidden evil of my unspoken prayers and spared me from the unquenchable growing anger of this violent man. I loved him, yet I was glad that he was dead.

I flashed back to the pre-dawn beating that he gave me in the pump house shortly after I had turned 15, perhaps six months before he died.

Something pissed him off; I never recalled what. He struck me with his fist and I fell into the pile of "farmer's shit" that fixes things. I recall a crystal moment of hate-filled resolve overcoming my reflexive fear, whereupon I yelled at him, "You can beat me to death, you son of a bitch, but I'll *never* fear you again. I *HATE* you! I hate you with complete hate! Go ahead...beat me some more, you chicken-shit ole fuck!" I braced for the beating. It didn't come.

He stepped back, red-faced and stunned. He looked as though I had landed a heavyweight cross to his jaw. He stared at me with deeply emotional flashing and piercing green eyes that first murdered, then forgave, and ultimately *perhaps* even respected me. He looked somehow broken. He turned without speaking and walked out. He became gentler. He never struck me again in his last living months on the Earth.

I knew that hour, but didn't yet realize, that he had given me the curse of defiance and the gift of never crawling again. My response to fear would relearn and seek out other methods of expressing itself, distorted methods...but never crawling. I loved and hated him with simultaneous fervor. He gave me so much energy.

I also recalled vividly, standing in the dark with his tender growing plants, seeing a black and white photograph that my mind took in color, of Daddy holding my baby sister, Mary Ellen, and looking so proud and so in love...she looking trusting, a complete and total daddy's girl. It was an eternal snapshot and the only pure love I ever saw in his eyes.

With female innocence, she accidentally gave what I deliberately never could and, from it, she would harvest his power without his rage, becoming beautiful, brilliant, focused, and wonderful.

Crops would grow, looking exactly like 100 fields before, but baby sister would be only five and thus unable to understand that, without warning, she was still photographed, but held by her Daddy no more.

Chapter 3
music, sports, and fear of dancing

I built a life on insecurity. I see that now.

I recall the horror of early dancing.

I was 13 and went to a dance where a small tan-colored record player echoed early, scratchy rock-and-roll from the corner of a sterile yellow-tiled January room, while I sat on a cold brown metal folding chair along a scuffed-up chair-lined cracked blue plaster wall and watched well-dressed popular people dancing and gliding with unbroken confidence and flirtatious bursts of chemically imbalanced sexual touching—poorly cloaked by quick looks, strategic detachments, and parent-chaperoned social laughter. They danced. I watched.

I watched their toes and feet carefully to map and learn the movements and steps, and then I tried to dance with some girl.

She could dance, but I only recall that I burned with shame and ignorance as the song dragged and as I tried to place my clumsy pigeon-toed feet with scuffed, ugly brown shoes into some pattern that matched what I thought others were doing.

Even when I got my feet seemingly "right" it was at the wrong time, because they had moved on to other toe-down, heel-up and leg-forward-leg-back patterns, with their arms and hands doing God knows what.

The more I tried, the more the song dragged and the more it dragged, the more I sweated and stunk with obvious, anxious befuddled terror.

One dance was enough. Later dances were only while drunk in college and only in large crowds where movement was squeezed and invisible, preferably obscured even further by black light and time-erasing strobes.

I never got complex things, and sports were no exception. I can ride, but I can't dance or rope.

I was 13 when I also decided to go out for football. I was *very* excited about joining the other boys in this bonding, girl-wooing, blood-sport, but knew that I was finished on the first afternoon when we got to the locker room and they handed out our green and white Bulldog uniforms.

Cousin Curt and the other boys were laughing, grab-assing, and joking-around as they seemingly automatically dressed and jogged out the door and onto the field; I was frozen in fear as I looked at the disheveled pieces of my assigned uniform and could *not* figure out how to put it together. I may as well have been handed a 500-piece jigsaw puzzle and given 10 minutes to assemble it.

I was spared this day from knowing the added horror of learning plays because I could not "assemble" the uniform. Plays would have been much worse, for me, impossible.

I waited until the other boys were on the field and simply snuck away, not returning again. No one noticed.

I loved basketball, but could not comprehend, even remotely, the requirements of a given position—guard, forward, whatever—much less the plays. I could comprehend the uniform, and it was there I was first introduced to the jock strap.

I went out several times in both grade school and high school, but recall only that basketball plays and dancing felt precisely the same to me.

It was like those tests where one has to mentally fold boxes. I cannot comprehend such things. Dancing, football uniforms, abstraction tests, basketball plays...all stand as triggers of stupidity, shame, and powerless horror. I was not destined to be a team-based jock.

Running...now, that initiation was funny. I was on the playground one evening and the coach told us all to run a lap around the field. It was perhaps half a mile and I easily outran everyone in that distance. That day led me to track and cross-country: Start at this line; finish at this same line—a simple uniform, no plays, no fancy footwork, count a few circles or hand a baton to someone perhaps, but really...just run. It was like driving a tractor around the field, but faster and without the tractor. I could do that.

Elmer Ringe was our track coach. He was a large, lanky, balding, leathery-looking old man with an egg-shaped, expressionless face and the cartilage surgically removed from his large nose. When he stood sideways, one could see the morning sun through the wood-paned glass of the classroom, yet shrunk into a small round, portrait like light tunnel through his nostrils. Long nose hairs refracted the light in an appropriate way.

This all took some time to get used to. Ok, actually, I never got used to it.

The nose peephole was ever-present and fascinating so I compulsively snuck peeks at the other side of Mr. Ringe through his nose hole whenever I thought he was not looking.

It was akin to looking at things through one's cupped hands, whereby one could see objects in a distant or focused perspective, almost telescopic, without the distraction of surrounding objects.

He was our driver's Ed teacher, so I saw moving pictures through Mr. Ringe's nose as we learned to drive. In the classroom, I took round, still shots of whatever was on his other side. I saw the world much differently through Mr. Ringe's nose.

He was harsh and quietly disciplined, yet seemed to take a liking to me. I recall his banging my head suddenly and without mercy against Jimmie Randecker's skull for our classroom horse-play, but he was not unfair, often gave me rides to track meets, and was silently gentle in his coaching disciplines.

When he banged one's head, it ached and rang for a while, and one wondered how such a large man could be so stealthy, but one did not worry about unwarranted or unprovoked attacks. He was, by *nature*, fair and kind.

Mr. Ringe liked discipline and order and I happily gave him that respect when my ADD imaginations left me this luxury. Mr. Ringe was my first recollection of a sponsor and a mentor, and in a strange way, he replaced the father that I sometimes desired. I was grateful, without yet knowing, for this balance in the life of a farmer's child.

Chapter 4
alternatives to dancing

Inability to dance gave me a social and emotional handicap.

God, however, being fair by nature, and strangely big, offered me an alternative to dancing that allowed me to truly enjoy music and attend many, many dances without dancing. It was surprising to me, and I was immersed in it completely before I knew. It was totally without a plan. It was called *"The Monsoon Winds,"* later *"The Regressions"* and finally, with time and seasoning, the *"'68 Reunion Band."*

I remained uninvited, but even popular people needed bands for parties, and they were so into themselves and their now developing sexualities that they didn't give a damn if the band was comprised of dorks or composers. They didn't even seem to care if the band was talented. They were there to show-off, drink, dance, fight, and fuck. These quality standards allowed us to learn and grow and so we became one of those little bands.

My first look at the Wendler boys was about 1963 when they moved down the street from my cousin Curt's house in town.

Curt and I were playing in the street that day, when Curt fell and ran a long, narrow, pointed piece of broken green bottle through the palm and out the top of his hand, like Jesus. Off he went to the doctor.

The Wendlers were moving in that day so I associate Curt's trauma with my first Wendler sighting.

The Wendlers were an eclectic group of people made up of an eccentric, angry, genius-level crop-duster named Clarence—the dad. His mate was a bright, warm, black-haired and cultured mother, Marjorie, who was an elementary school teacher. The sister, Susan, was very sweet and developmentally disabled. There were three brilliant, multi-talented and defiant boys, Lain, David and Jeff.

I got to know them when I was allowed to go to town because of their proximity to Curt's, house. They became my second family and after Daddy died, I spent all of my free time hanging out with the Wendlers.

My mind splices all years between the first Wendler day and the day I was first introduced to playing guitar, but I know I was 15. I had saved-up my money for some time and finally ordered a good looking, but really shitty-playing and sounding, fire-burst $30 acoustic guitar from Grandma's shit-house Sears Catalog. I now had a guitar and a desire, but not a tiny musical clue.

Like most things abstract, I spent some months fantasizing that I could play, banging on it and wishing myself into talent, but finally recognized that something was just not working.

It was the same theory I applied to the hobby of the times—assembly of model cars and model airplanes: Look at the instructions for 12 seconds, see a garbled blur of words and visual abstractions, feel frustrated and stupid, grab the glue, glue-on the wheels and any other big part that was required to "assemble" a car or airplane *looking* model, ignore the detailed parts and instructions, lick and paste-on the decals and let it dry...Wait a while, look at it, ascribe loosely that it "looked" like a car or an airplane, see a box full of small parts untouched, blush, feel stupid, see if "the car" or "the airplane" was dry, bend my elbow, freeze my face and throw or roll it against the wall to see how many things would fly off. Such was my self-taught guitar-playing discovery, minus a toss against the wall. But, then it was given, as a cosmic gift with magic instructions...Music found me.

I wandered into the Wendler's basement one evening and there were Lain and David playing electric guitars. It turned out that their dad, Clarence, knew about seven chords and had zero talent—BUT he had a deep love for instruments. As a crop duster, he would fly seven days a week, all summer, save his money, dabble in the stock

35

market all winter, and buy instruments and amplifiers as a collector's hobby.

Their basement was *filled* with six string electric guitars, amps, speaker cabinets, basses, record players, pianos, tambourines, harmonicas, and other musical "stuff". The dream basement had several Fenders, a Les Paul Gibson, Ampeg, and other dream instruments. It was like a musical toy store, and there I was…like family. It was a magical moment of desire and faith combining to give me a mustard seed of hope.

"Can you teach me to play," I asked timidly?

"Sure," said Lain, and he began to show me chords to songs that *he* esteemed were easy to play.

"Most rock songs really have only three chords," he smiled simply. "I can show you how to play dozens of songs with just three chords."

I thought, "Three chords…that's not many. I can do that. It's only three chords." And, so, I began to clank away at E, A and B with a little C, D, F and G thrown in.

Lain was a patient and wonderful teacher, unlike his brother David, who was impatient and arrogant and always played too loud. I learned from both of them, but became best friends with Lain, and later in life, with David. Lain was one year behind me in school and David was two years behind Lain.

Soon they taught me that by simply removing my "bird" finger from most chords, I could make the chord a minor, and my confidence grew.

They taught me to flatten my ring finger on the neck, squash that finger and hold it down with my "bird" finger, and magically create a chord five frets higher without even moving up the neck. They then taught me to pull that flat finger contortion up two more frets and I had all three chords of a rock pattern. It was amazing!

I was not a natural, but by watching them, I learned visually, and they offered me the added mechanics of it by grabbing my fingers and forcing them onto the right strings. It was the best of repetitive learning using sound, touch, and visuals. I found that, over time, I could actually do this as calluses replaced pain on my left hand's fingertips to show a modicum of discipline and progress.

The Wendler boys taught me enough that I learned to tune a guitar and even went to work "playing" my junky Sears acoustic while trapped on the farm. I knew for once that passion, walking with friendship, could overcome fear or stupidity, and I could see that, compared to these guys, I was not good, but that they didn't care. I loved being around them and the music, and, so, I spent windy and rainy hours, frosty and chirping nights, and cloudy and sunny days in their basement playing music.

Within a year, we jelled into a fledgling band. Our first "dance" was at their Catholic youth group on a Sunday night, and from there we were off and running.

Mr. Wendler was so proud of us. He hauled us around and kept the guitars strung and ready. We didn't have enough amplifiers or speakers, so we disassembled some old abandoned jukeboxes and used them to build speaker cabinets.

We ordered a 100-watt amp from an electronics catalog and ran wires until we were playing with three guitars, a bass, a piano and a PA system for singing. It was crude and perhaps even ugly, but it worked.

A buddy named Kerry Owens joined us by playing bass and a guy named Mark Shull played piano. Chuck Cochran played the drums. Lain and David could both play either lead or rhythm, and Lain also played the berry sax, allowing us to do songs like '*Tequila.*'

I had learned enough to hang around on rhythm guitar and thus we began our little group, The *Monsoon Winds*.

Our mothers made us look-alike, big collared, V-neck, hang down, black and maroon colored short-sleeved shirts and my sister,

Dallas, joined us as a dancer: *The Monsoon Winds & their Girl Tornado.*

This was the beginning of some of the deepest relationships and friendships possible, and I was blessed with being in the band. If only I had then learned to take these simple specifications for friendship into love relationships.

We played before crowds of one (1) in Grain Field, Kansas and before crowds of 300 to 400 people in Scott City, Dighton, Ness City, and other farm towns. We played wherever we could and as many weekends as we could. The money usually wasn't bad for a bunch of kids. Time is a blur to me and these were timeless times where the Earth's ticking stilled.

Ole man Wendler subsidized us for gas and dancehall rental when no one showed up, and helped us run the "business" side of the band.

Clarence only interfered with our music on one occasion and that was when we learned, but would not play, "The Green Beret" by Sgt. Barry Sadler.

Clarence's demands were simple: "You'll play that goddamn song or this band will *never* make another sound!"

We played it and I could see that he sometimes stood at the back of the room and cried. We were blessed in those days that we had not yet opened the door to drugs and alcohol. Those roads would come later, in and after about 1969 for most of us. Life was still innocent, hope-filled and alive.

I went away to college in 1967 after we had played for about three years. The other guys kept going. The band disintegrated when others went away to separate colleges a year later: Lain, Chuck and Kerry were all in the class of '68, but we were not yet "children of the 60's."

Chapter 5
growing up and defiance

Barring dementia, I will never forget the time that "the band" returned home from our various colleges and found our drummer, Chuck, with long hair.

Chuck had gone to Emporia State University, and somehow became a hippie. I was baffled and had not managed to intersect that culture yet, being an alcoholic frat guy at KU. Lain was not a hippie "type" no matter where he went. Kerry was in the middle. David later became not just a hippie, but also a cutting-edge hippie. He never operated on the path to normal, and was the real deal. I hadn't started down that road, *yet*.

One evening, some of the red-necked local boys walked out of the Corner Tavern and grabbed a set of tin snips out of their truck. They had spotted Chuck.

"Looks like this little girl needs a haircut," one of them scowled as they approached us.

"Not today," Kerry said firmly, as we all stared them down, leaning forward, looking tough, and quietly pissing our pants.

They decided against the battle and went back into the bar. We dodged a beating, yet our defiance and unity somehow took deeper root that day.

The innocence that we had lived was nearing an end as we left and returned, left and returned. Holiday breaks and summers found us more and more exposed to the world and its realities. Vietnam was raging and we were beginning to see that life was not Kansas and life was not fair.

I was a sophomore at KU and returned to Dighton for a holiday, whereupon we had a party at Chuck's house. He was now a full-fledged, longhaired, dope-smoking hippie and I was simply a drinking fool.

He challenged me to smoke pot that night, but I told him that I didn't want to get "hooked" on drugs. He laughed that I was calling weed "drugs" and taunted my fears until alcohol gave me additional courage and grandiosity.

Four of us drove into the country and lit a joint. I smoked and smoked and smoked and nothing happened. They said that they were stoned after the first half joint, but I had no concept of what they meant. I didn't know what being "stoned" meant.

On joint number three, while staring out the car's front window into a plowed field, I suddenly saw wagons circling in front of the car and Indians attacking them from the west.

I then began to chatter wisdom and read Mooner's mind, noting that I was following a series of yellow dots and dashes between his thoughts and mine, and so discerned that he was thinking about a stage play, specifically the theater's smiling and frowning masks.

Mooner naturally agreed with a bullshit "WOW, MAN" that I had described exactly what he was thinking and Chuck slowly announced, "Wow, Man. You're really stoned."

I liked it, though the two mile drive back was scary and I couldn't find the town of 1,000 people for about 40-minutes that seemed like a day.

I learned to spend college days stoned because college reality was worse than being stoned. Being stoned felt good. Not every reality could hide behind a joint, however.

I wondered why the university had sent me a *certified, return receipt requested,* letter. When I opened it, I was startled to find that I was being *accused of subversive activities,* specifically *SDS involvement in disrupting* a recent ROTC event in KU's football stadium...and that I would be *suspended from the university* on a given specific date if I *failed to appear* in the Chancellor's office by such and such a date and time. It was all *very legal* sounding and I was aghast. I had been doing laundry!

I immediately contacted the Chancellor's office, as the letter instructed, and appeared there at an appointed time.

Like pot smoking, I had no experience with subversive activity, or with authorities, and I didn't know what to expect. Hell, I could barely navigate the enrollment process! I explained that there was some mistake, that I was doing laundry, and that, "I'm neither a hippie nor a subversive." I thought "neither—nor" sounded intellectual, not hippie-like, and I needed every trick I could find. It didn't work.

"You can say whatever you like," I was told. "You can cut your hair and say that you were doing laundry, but I'll need you to meet with Professor Youngman of the Law School to determine what's true." I immediately made this appointment and showed up *very* afraid.

I was led into a small conference room covered with photographs. I saw that the table was covered by yet another panoramic photo of tiny protesters in the table-sized stadium.

"I don't understand why I'm here." I said, now terrified and with a shorthaired farm boy's most sheepish involuntary accent and look. "I haven't done anything."

Professor Youngman pointed at a list of names on an official looking piece of paper and then scrolled his finger to a name that looked like mine: Last name, comma, first name, comma, middle initial "S." "You *are* this person, are you not?" Dr. Youngman interrogated, staring at me firmly and without human compassion. "Yes," I gasped, still confused. "That is my name, but I cannot be that person! I...I...I was...doing *laundry!*"

He pointed at the tabletop picture to a red-circled, quarter-inch tall being with shoulder length, shaggy dog looking blond hair and said with pause, "Is that not you, young man?"

"No," I said. "It can't be. I was doing *laundry*. What *IS* this?"

"These are pictures taken by the FBI of demonstrators disrupting the recent ROTC event in our Stadium, and it appears that the leader is you. He smiled slowly, as with the joy of pulling wings off a lingering, fat, captured fly. He dragged his finger down the page and pointed again to my name on the official looking list, "… a Kansas City leader of the SDS".

He then, methodically, and with the tone of a closing argument, restated my first and last name. He stared coldly at me and pointed again to the "S"…"Middle name, 'Spencer'."

"But, my middle name is Steven…*Steven*…not Spencer!" I gulped with pale urgency, now grasping the full seriousness of this inquisition, locking-in on words like *FBI, demonstrators, SDS,* and *leader.*

"It's *Steven*…and I…I was doing my laundry on that Saturday. God, I'm just a farm kid!" I fumbled and fumbled desperately and, sweating profusely, grabbed my student ID, my driver's license, my birth certificate (YES, I had it and it said STEVEN!!), and my draft card and waved them all like a patriot's mix of American and white flags for him to examine. "Steven…see?"

"Steven?" He mused. "Ok, then," he said, copying the documents and talking unimpressed towards the green flashing copier glass. "Thank you for coming by, Mr. Russell. I'll check this out and if we determine that you are telling the truth, you'll get a letter from the university concluding this matter."

He offered neither apology nor comfort in his tone. It was transparent language, invisible. And what did "concluding," mean? I needed a beer, a pitcher of beer…no *two*…NOW.

I waited, but the letter never came. Nothing else happened though, and so, I went back to being a student as usual. Something in me hardened, though, and my innocence did not feel as protected or safe.

I began to listen from the parameters as students gathered and chanted on *the Hill,* as speeches were made about "the Man" and "the Establishment" and as people called Bob Hope "Nixon's jester."

Bob Hope...I LOVED that guy! Hell, I loved Nixon...a nice Quaker fellow.

It had all been a dull roar and a blur behind the parties, the pot, the study, and the music, until now, but somehow I felt vulnerable in my own country for the first time. I began to wonder if *any* of what these students were saying was true. I feared hearing it because the words were then undeniable to paranoid inquisitors. Such words waited to be discovered within my lie-detectable mind; but I feared not hearing it because it might be the great and indestructible democracy gasping for a final breath. I listened.

I found myself more and more smoking dope, drinking, listening to angry speeches, and, for the first time, resenting the stories that were emerging from a Vietnam that had already killed or taken the legs from good men I knew in western Kansas. Innocence was fading and I was becoming more jaundiced in some enlightened way.

I *felt* different and didn't trust people or institutions as much. Buildings were no longer magical backdrops carved from beautiful Kansas limestone, but rather were filled with educated, faceless old men, misinformation, division, paranoia, and fear. "The Establishment" now actually meant something to me and I knew that I had gotten an education that I did not come here for. This was KANSAS, for Christ's sake! Kansas. But was its middle name Spencer or Steven...and did it matter now?

For the first time I "felt" my education, and I didn't like its feel. I resented knowing what I now knew, and that resentment had no clear enemy.

This all faded over time as I drank more and more beer, listened to George Harrison songs and smoked hash, weed, and opiate-dope...green and reddish-brown three-finger bags from Thailand, Mexico, Hawaii, and Vietnam in the parking lot of an all American fraternity. It was the frat that Ronald Regan had belonged to, but I didn't see that irony, because history had not yet unfolded its future actors or their re-scripted scenes.

I know now that what I was feeling overall was passive-aggressive at least and defiant anger at best.

I began to grow my hair and claimed to be an atheist. I stopped feeling innocent and started feeling defiant about anything that crossed my path. It was easy to pour this anger into relationships. I had found that to be only an accountable outlet for a world where I no longer trusted or felt safe.

Life would no longer be linear as events became the metric for time. My youth was over. My next stop would be adulthood—without proper training or skills. Those would be provided by pain.

Chapter 6
17 bells

It was 4:30 when the phone rang in my office. Someone on the other end announced that they were with the Wichita Police Department and that my brother had requested that I meet him in the detective bureau, 5th floor, City Hall. This made no sense. I had no idea what had happened or why, but naturally dropped everything and ran to this unusual summons.

When I arrived, I found my brother, his girlfriend Laura, his ex-wife, Laurie and his two daughters, Ashley and Angel, somewhere between anxiety, terror, and tears.

Bill indicated that his son, Brendan, had gone to a shrink earlier that afternoon, that the session had gone particularly well, and that an hour later he had barricaded himself inside his mother's house with a 22-caliber pistol. He had stolen the gun from his brother Jason's safe, and now threatened to kill himself. I had arrived 55 minutes into the drama.

Police officers and blue-clad SWAT had barricaded-off the street, surrounded the house in full protective gear, and were using their *best-practice* SOP and chain-of-command to reason with my nephew.

Brendan insisted that they bring his girlfriend before he would talk or consider coming out. They, of course, following procedures and trading chips, indicated that this was not going to happen.

We sat anxiously and prayerfully around the edges of the bureau while a detective in the other room attempted to negotiate with Brendan via the house phone. Another detective on site tried to gain access to Brendan's constantly ringing cell phone.

Typical of teenagers, the cell phone was with a lowest-cost carrier that had no procedures for authorizing police access, or for handling this sort of emergency, so the officers were having no luck cutting off the phone and Brendan was conversing freely with a dozen giddy friends. For Brendan, it was a moment of real-world manic chaos and TV glory.

"The cops are crouching behind the bushes," laughed Brendan. "They think that I don't see them, but they're wrong. I'm pointing at them now, just 'cos I can."

He fired-off a couple of shots—into the ceiling—to appease his cellular listener and to show his sincerity. The police believed that he was sincere, child or not.

"If they try to get to me, I will shoot myself," he brazenly told his buddies. The more he said it, the more real it became. It was some mix of anger, drama, bipolar mania, and surrealism.

As any shrink knows, the more a kid tells other kids they will do something, the more they are forced to or they will lose face. Better to die than be embarrassed in the morning.

The police needed badly to control access to Brendan's phone, but they could not gain it. With each call, children were revving him up, feeding his madness, and encouraging defiance. One friend even told him about his girlfriend's recent affair with another common friend, no doubt thinking it might be helpful.

Months earlier, after jumping through a closed window on the second floor of his mother's house, Brendan defiantly told his girlfriend that if she wouldn't love only him, he would jump in front of a passing semi. And so he did.

Everyone reported that he was just being grandiose, and had not intended to be hit, but, he had hesitated an instant too long. He had his right foot amputated at the ankle that evening.

He was a beautiful child, 5' 11", blond hair, sparkling green eyes, filled with life and athletic ability. Now he had one foot missing to make a point.

"I'm a freak," he said one day bluntly, without apparent emotion or caring, yet perhaps trying to comprehend his body's new arrangement. "A freak." He smiled sadly and defiantly.

These events had been preceded by dozens of fights and outbursts at home, on school buses, in parking lots, wherever Brendan might explode.

He had broken his dad's nose a year ago. He had been to doctors and counselors and was supposed to take meds for manic-depressive disorder and ADD, but like most people new to meds, Brendan didn't want to take them, didn't remember, whatever...and the cycle of trouble continued to the evening of February 20th, where we waited in separate realities and a common time.

The movie ran, as it must. Several hours into the ordeal, the police announced that they were feeling better about their communications with Brendan. He was beginning to use the word "we" and even spoke of future events.

He asked if his dad might come and be with him, but the police quickly negotiated that into a later reward. My brother disagreed. This was all a good sign, the detective told us. Then, at about 9:20 p.m. the Lieutenant came and asked that "the mother and father" join him in his office. Horror chilled our hope.

"We don't know what happened," he said. "We were finally able to have his cell phone disconnected and had agreed that we would toss him a new one to communicate with us, but when we threw it through the window, per his instructions, we heard breaking glass, then a shot. Bill and Laurie, I'm afraid your son has shot himself. The ambulance crew wasted no time on entry, and had him in transport within seven minutes. He's on his way to the hospital now."

Our next scene was being escorted rapidly to Wesley Medical Center and being told eventually by an intern that the gunshot, "had certainly done some serious damage, but that we should not go into this thing with any preconceived doubts or concerns."

A salty old doctor, short of saying, "Hey, Fool," cut him off gently and indicated that in fact, "...the bullet was a hollow-point and did a great deal of damage when it entered point blank into his left temple, separating fragments and dividing into two spinning patterns through

Brendan's left brain. I frankly wouldn't expect a successful recovery from this sort of wound," he said, with that gift that only a seasoned country doctor can have.

It was clear to me and likely to others that Brendan was going to die. My brother was going to lose his son.

I flashed with recounting emotion and memories of Billie, and I ached to know even further that life was not a cycle; the earth owed us nothing for our labors, and now was not even a fair place to live. Sleeping dogs, defiant horses, breadbox phones, and crystal snow were suddenly punctured by the crimson seeping of innocent blood.

We sat two days later in a church where kids curiously looked for the hole in Brendan's temple, where adults with swollen eyes talked about his clutching a small cross in the last two weeks of his life, and where words of how good he looked were hollow points of their own for sisters to hear and family to pretend consoled them.

We slumped, stunned and saddened, as this young man's coffin seemingly glided silently and in slow motion up the aisle and the church bell hauntingly echoed 17 times.

Perhaps the dilatory chimes were for those of us who remained, or perhaps only for Brendan. I didn't know.

My brother half-smiled with a gentle gaze as his green eyes followed the coffin; then he sobbed and smiled again, sobbed and smiled, sobbed and smiled. I saw him as a small boy himself, sitting and crying, "I want my Daddy. I want my Daddy. I want my Daddy."

I felt great humility, but no freedom, in this death and knew that my brother would feel only guilt's bondage, though he would now be freed from the chaos of this reckless and troubled child.

I wished that I could hold him tight, until we were floating through the gentle snows and breezes of the past, blending with simple music and starting life anew with Dollar, attack chicken, mean horse, dust devils, summer rain, and new milk each day.

My thoughts wafted to a day when Brendan was running breathlessly out of the basement engaged in a child's dreamlike and borderless game.

"There was this guy down there," he shouted, with his eyes spinning like a suffocating cow, "and, and, I killded him and, then, he killded me and, then, I killded him again..."

I knew now that Brendan's mind had been both of those actors, even then, and that the outcome was prophesized by the mouth of a playful child. No matter who died in this battle, eventually, it would be him; he was both players in one mind.

We could separate cream from milk by turning a crank and running it across inter-connected funnels, but we could not separate the chemistry that battled life and death to death in this beautiful child.

"*...he killded me and, then, I killded him...*" my mind echoed. "*...he killded me and, then, I killded him again...*"

Chapter 7
...adventures make clear

My brother had gone far down the *"wall of oblivion"* when he decided to sober up.

He was doing his best to undo the wreckage of the past and to make amends. He felt a constant and lingering guilt, however, for the years that he had spent drowning his life and fueling his anger with drugs and alcohol. He had started before 13 and ran as far as he could into the chemical haze.

He knew that his kids had taken a great deal of the abuse.

There were times when they were unsupervised for days while he woke and slept through another binge of crystal-meth in Escondido. Kansas, Arizona, California, and other states—all the same.

Like the rest of the family, he roared and beat children without cause or warning for whatever was on his mind at the moment. He then lived remorseful at sunrise. His pain ran deep and his sponsor was working full-time to help him get through it. It was working; he was changing.

He had started his own carpentry and cabinetworks business and it was doing very well. He was hanging out with good people, had a half-dozen guys working for him, drove a brand-new truck, bought a powerful ski-boat, and took his kids and their friends out every summer weekend to enjoy quality time on the water.

Bill was replacing years of alcoholic darkness with chosen days of light.

The change in his countenance and in his children was phenomenal. It was visible to all. As Bill's sponsor ultimately told him, "The only trouble with being sober five years is you have to start *acting* like it." Bill was starting to act like it, but his son was trapped at the gates of bipolar hell.

I was battling my own demons, and had separated from my wife of 22 years to dive into work, isolation, fantasy, boxes of wine, appearance-sake jogging, and cartons of import beer.

Bill and I were half-brothers, but shared a common thread of genetics beyond our mother. Every male in our bloodlines had been a *raging* alcoholic, and it was indeed *the gift that kept on giving.*

We both tried to control our drinking, but found any occurrence to prove the adage: We drank to celebrate; we drank to forget.

We unknowingly created chaos to ensure that we were at extremes—never in the middle for long—and we added chemistry to enhance our alcohol and our extremes. The world eventually began to wobble. Our families were along for the demented ride.

Later, Bill would share the words with me: "*Cunning, baffling, powerful*" ... Old-timers would add: "*Patient* and *progressive.*" We did not drink as normal people.

At home, we generated chaos to unknowingly cause a reason for escape, and each reason led to yet others. Alcohol gave us a brief reprieve, then fueled a family fight, induced childish pouting, and became a reason to stomp-off cussing to the bar. We joined each other often. We did grandiose things and laughed loudly, but silently knew that we were both out of control.

I was well educated, high functioning, arrogant, and employed, so was able to watch my brother with some level of judgmental condescension for many years. My love for him made me watch him closely, and wish that he would get help. This did not stop me, however, from going to his house every weekend to smoke dope and drink beer.

I would find myself progressively driven home, passed-out and puking, in the back seat of my '49 Plymouth. Often, I drove myself home with one eye opened or a face out the window, because when not fully passed-out, I feared the law, and with that fearful motivation, esteemed myself to be a cautious driver.

We only exchanged harsh words a few times in life, and came to blows on only one occasion. Actually, we *meant* to come to blows, but failed because of our common affliction.

We were partying at a friend's house and began to have a clashed discussion on any random two of a drunk's recalled adventures. My brother got emotional and BARKED an answer at me in our daddy's voice with such tonal accuracy that I flinched and felt my eyes dilate with fear.

Given fear, and having sworn long ago that no one would treat me like that in my adult life, my anger instinctively exploded and I told him, "Don't EVER talk like that to me again, you fucking asshole, or I will slap you! I listened to that son of a bitch enough to know the ole man when I hear him, and YOU ain't gonna talk to me like that; not with *his* voice, not EVER. You may talk to your kids like that, fucker, but not to me!" That cut.

"Oh, yeah, fuck face," he roared, continuing in the ole man's voice. "Let's just step outside and see you slap me, bitch!"

He was much bigger than I, a perfect 6' 1" long-muscled carpenter, in shape, with an Eastwood shaped face and body, protruding veins, callused hands, and leather skin, handsome and, of course, younger.

I knew that he would hurt me badly and quickly, but didn't care at that *principled* moment I drunkenly reasoned that I might hurt him a bit first, so we rose to go outside, snarling, circling, and glaring like rabid dogs—he with stoned green eyes and daddy's voice, me with Ice House blue, and suicidal rage.

As we reached the door, and with God watching over little children, drunks, and fools, our friend's wife, Traci, walked in and nervously asked which of us might like to roll a joint?

She extended her trembling little arm and revealed a baggie with a forest-green bud in her opened palm. This was a no-brainer. War be damned!

Bill could roll a joint as smooth as a cigarette, and so he did. That was that, and we never argued again as drunks.

Within months, Bill sobered-up and I lost the drinkin' buddy of my life. All that remained was loneliness and isolation. I had no friends left, not really, and my marriage had *died with a whimper* as I watched her eyes look away and hide disrespecting sympathy for a now pathetic me.

My brother no doubt planned my sobriety as he had planned our drunks. He was a good planner and could build anything with scraps.

I woke-up that Friday from, not the worst drunk of my life, but from the most telling.

While living alone, I had been introduced to a woman who intrigued me. I kissed her with Tequila courage while her duplicitous boyfriend was off puking, and instantly began dating her: Blond, not redhead, business owner, not teacher, aggressive, not passive, passionate, not submissive. All was new.

Several weeks later, however, after only a few glasses of wine, I had burst into a fit of jealous rage, and had what some call "a moment of truth."

Here I was, living alone, new woman, new relationship, new everything…*same ole me*…angry, jealous, not fun while drinking after a brief dating period.

I would ponder briefly and, then, *pose* a twisted choice: Run, as I had learned, or sober-up, marry the babe, and live happily ever after—It was an easy choice for someone who bends every new truth. I would marry and because I was "sober," all would be well. All I needed was sobriety. Unfortunately, I didn't have a clue how to get it.

I had recently self-referred to our Employee Assistance Program for "depression," and the screening suggested that I might be an alcoholic. I believe the counselor said, "This instrument does not necessarily say that you have a current drinking problem, but rather measures your answers against tens-of-thousands of people who have taken the test and found themselves to be alcoholic. What it says about you is that you scored incredibly high in two of three major categories that indicate you may suffer from the disease of alcoholism...and you were on the *cusp* of the third category." In other words, I *aced* the alcoholic test!

I couldn't hear it, and I didn't know what that really meant until I had created the jealous conspiracy and blew-up over nothing with glasses of wine. Then it began to hit me that something really might be wrong. That was when the third component of my awakening came to pass.

My brother, who knew me better than anyone and whom I KNEW was an alcoholic, called me and said, "You know, you might want to go to an AA meeting with me, because only you can decide if you are an alcoholic, but I know you pretty well, and I'd bet that you'll hear something you can relate to."

I finally, yet still hesitantly, reflected: The Counselor's test, the jealous rage, and now my brother's *suggestion*...maybe I needed to consider a change...just for a while. I delayed it a night *or so* to ponder further, but knew the answer.

Three things turned the tumbler of truth, but because of the fist-sized hole of loneliness that I could now feel, stretching between my stomach and heart like a torn, chiasmic spider web, which caught and ate every drop of happiness and sunlight, every waking hour, I believed him. I knew instinctively that the hole was not my heart and was not my stomach ulcer, but was in fact my soul, and I knew that my soul was now running empty. I knew that if something could keep this insane man, who had been thrown in jail several times in several states, sober for 11 months, I had a *certain* shot.

I walked into my first AA meeting on Sunday, December 20th, like a lamb on a rope, proud to be led by my brother. I was done *fighting anything or anyone*, I thought...and for the time I was given a naïve, yet calming, *pause*.

It felt both humiliating and freeing to say for the first time *"...and I'm an alcoholic."* But Bill was there with me and so I felt safe and proud. I knew from watching him that we both had a chance at being both real and loved; it was now a matter of who and when; we had been freely given the *HOW*.

I didn't know yet what I would realize as I began to experience feelings and life again. I didn't know yet that not drinking was easy compared to having feelings.

I watched my now "older" brother intently, and clung to the hope that he gave me in our new and frightening adventure.

Chapter 8
cynicism, anger and life's terms

Now I know why AA says, *"NO RELATIONSHIPS THE 1ST YEAR OF SOBRIETY."* It is not just about the drunk; it is also about the sober drunk's *new* hostages.

Wet chaos and anger were what I knew drinking, so chaos and anger were what I knew dry. Each now cloaked itself better, transforming simple phoniness into inexperienced self-delusion and a shiny *new mask* of false humility, which experimented carefully and recklessly with new relationship politics and sly manipulations.

But, as an old-timer once told me, "Time takes time." Illusion and reality are necessary and kindred spirits who must learn together, each from its polar sibling, and then slowly battle for coexistence and peaceful balance within nonrefundable confines of their new human's soul.

God help the "normal" person who is there to spend each night with a newly recovering alcoholic. I speak for only me as a "we." We know all, see all, and are the new General Manager of the universe. We are suddenly filled with random deep humility, simple sayings, tears, and flip-flop arrogance as we know a new God and become His wise and able servants.

We think that we learn faster than all before us and are happy to discover and help with each of, what we believe are, *your* troubling character defects.

We confuse mania with serenity and are no longer inhibited from speaking "truth" by the blurs of alcohol. Truth, we believe, floods-in to fill the vacuum that was once our twisted knowing, and we judge those as *weak* who are having trouble 7, 10, or 20 years sober...they are just not *working a good program.* And, normal people? Why, they don't even have a program to help *them.* We discount all that does not suit the new day of our early walk.

We believe ourselves when we put on the learned face of our brother's keeper and carefully document lists and journals of the irrelevant, while lying to others and ourselves about pink elephants buried beneath the clutter in our hearts and in our *nature.*

We openly flail ourselves with past sins, publicly cry, and martyr ourselves with a bloody dragging motion for being forced to practice simple adult behaviors—the pain of meetings, the pain of life, the pain of emotions, the pain of being rejected by ex-wives and battered children...Don't they know who I am, NOW? Don't they understand what I have given up and what I am going through? Oh, the pain; oh, the suffering*!* I will resent them if they do not see it and more if they see it but do not congratulate my amazing progress.

We take on the badge of sobriety as though we had received a purple heart in a great war. Oh, the hell I went through being a drunk. Oh, the bodies and the carnage I have seen. Woe is that life.

This was my story for the first two years of sobriety, so my brother pointed me to old-timers and laughed me through it. "Don't take yourself too seriously," he gently chided.

Thank God for the mean-spirited ole bastards who reminded me simply, "That's bullshit! You're a selfish, self-centered fucker and you're putting personalities before principles!" My new wife said it another way: "You're acting like a two-year old!" Anger and chaos, chaos and anger, anger and isolation, isolation and resentment, resentment and self-justification...all bubbled and simmered into slow vengeance.

I moved-in with my new addiction two months sober and married her when I had been sober for only 10 months. Our animal attraction and intensity became a living hell as I dried-out so I escaped into work and meetings only to realize that she was glad to be rid of me.

I befriended her children and discovered that I was emotionally comfortable with teenage kids. It was quietly embarrassing, but aligned with the advice being given to me by my new shrink, so I followed it.

"Give her room," he counseled. "Spend time working your program and doing things with her kids."

Three years later, she still didn't seemingly notice that I was gone. Thank God for what we don't yet know and for what we refuse to see until it is revealed without mercy.

My brother hated my new wife because he thought her to be a meddler. She had conversations with his son, Brendan, and discovered that the boy had incredible amounts of anger towards his dad.

"I wish that he'd go with me to one of those damn counselors he sends me to," Brendan said bitterly. "He sends me to deal with my shit and does nothing to deal with his. I wish that we could talk about our anger together. But he won't. He doesn't think he has a problem now. He thinks it's all me."

My wife offered Bill tapes and books, as she had me, but he wanted neither, whereupon she noted that, "You'll have trouble learning new things if you don't listen and you don't read. How do you plan to learn new things?" He hated that and flushed with anger and defiance.

Then there was a sober Christmas dinner.

Side conversations, masked resentment, genuine love, laughter, anger, and recovery all mixed together as a new form of family gathering, but without alcohol.

As winter froze the salubrious waters of summer family fun, rage bubbled beneath the ice, oft engulfing posted signs. No doubt we thought that in the spring it would all be better, in a few summers, fine.

My then wife and Brendan would talk at length that Christmas about his passion for running a lawn-mowing business, and she reported that the child had a keen business mind.

She gave him self-help books and he read them, but when he quoted them to my brother, resentment grew towards his unwelcome "psychologist -wanna-be" sister-in-law.

Life remained an uncharted path and each of us walked it believing we were doing the best we could. Likely we were.

It was the cooking ingredients of a complex world that hampered the game plan...children wrecking cars, children demanding things, newly discovered alcohol and drugs, friends who betrayed them, girlfriends who were not faithful, fights, hidden evenings, broken bones, hormones, bipolar disorders. Complexity unfolded like travail, knowing its unraveled end and birthing its secret assassin.

Life began to strain at the players as each of them was doing what he could to deal with it in his own way. Work, meetings, school, sports, socialization, counseling, TV, movies, hanging-out, friends, therapy, retail therapy, painkillers, sex. The ticking of the Earth was again silent as the days crept by, and we were shielded from tomorrow's knowing. We could feel tomorrow, but we could not yet see it. By definition, all was well for *today*.

In a perfect linear world, the outcomes would be fair and each would have time to heal his wounds, repent for sin, and then care for his suffering brother. But this is not a linear world. It isn't even circular. It is alive, intertwined, and unpredictable, held together by the hidden bonds of physical strain, mental solutions, spiritual hope, chemical and cosmic randomness.

And so it was with my brother's program. He got better as fast as he could, but winter's evil pause and life's random acts of unkindness awakened the grim reaper, and my brother found himself drinkless in the starry fading of a February night.

Two months of winter, travail and pain had lapsed since Christmas dinner, and fate's secret mission was reaching an apex of harvest for the soul of its restless seed.

Chapter 9
recovering

Reflection is painful. I could not get Brendan out of my thoughts. I replayed the night over and over again.

I remembered that the calendar at the end of Brendan's hospital bed-sit on "20" when I knew it was now the 21st. It was as though the calendar refused to acknowledge that his night would come and so it refused to turn at eternity's midnight.

I recall that a compassionate nurse came and changed the blood-soaked bedding as an act of kindness to Brendan's mother, and I remember that as she did, I saw his naked, perfect body, with its missing little foot and a giant dick, and thought of the joy and pain that he would no longer know. I thought of the abrupt end to his flesh and his future. He had known pain enough and could no longer live in this world.

"I'm sorry," the young nurse said, blushing as she realized the exposure.

"It's fine," I responded whispering.

He lingered and the nurse kept saying, "He has a 17-year-old's heart. It's very strong. It will not let him go."

I asked her to explain the monitors and the 119 - 123 pulsating number. For us, *as I recall*, she said that number would normally be in the teens or low 20s, jumping to 30 when we sneezed. His brain pressure, because of the trauma of a gunshot, had reached the point where the spinal cord would likely have perforated the brain like a giant pin poking a swollen balloon.

I appreciated her honesty, and memorized his fading life *as* he *lay dying—h*eartbeats and breath, heartbeats and breath.

At sunrise, the monitors began to jump and the doctor stretched open Brendan's eyelids. I saw a black and yellowed emptiness with streaks of color, but no green and no light. His sparkling green eyes were gone.

"Pronounced," the physician said mechanically, "6:21 a.m."

I walked outside and stood smoking a cigarette, staring at a point of twinkling starlight in the black sky. I wondered if that same light had ever been captured in Brendan's emerald eyes. I wondered if he or I would retain memories after death.

My mind was manic. "Perhaps, because I have seen the light...when without flesh, I will become a part of the light, or the darkness, or only that indiscernible damp bleeding between some rock and its darkness beneath."

The poet in my brain tried to help. "What a thin layer it is between pond and air, farm and city, snow and melting, darkness and sky, flesh and air, skin and life, thought and action, finger and trigger, bullet and shot, wound and death...why was I ever given it: Precious, fragile, joyful, painful life? Why me and not my brother?"

"But it will go. My life will pass and become a parting instant, a brief ceremony, and then dust. Fighting to keep it or not, it will be taken from me, and a sunset or sunrise will find me no more."

My spiritual understanding was bleeding to cynicism as part of a natural process, and I was unaware of my emerging anger or the fact that my mind was now defaulting to an uncontrolled biochemical arcing between it and my decimated heart.

As I became more cynical to avoid eruption in social settings and at work, I suddenly realized that cynicism is anger disguised as humor—the drunk's premier sober mix.

"Vanity, vanity. All is vanity and vexation of spirit. Solomon," I reflected.

"For what is your life? It is even a vapor that appears for a little while and then vanishes away." James.

"And I will tear down this barn and build still larger barns...and I will say to myself eat, drink, and be merry...but the Lord said to that man, 'Thou fool, this night shall thy soul be required of thee.'" Luke.

My mind cascaded a vomiting backflow of scripture, anger, and sparking thought. I was nothing. I was only the spliced, interpreted exposures and programs in my head. I was replaying scenes without a change of perspective and I was tiring.

"God help me," I said humbly, and amazed by that. Involuntary humility gripped me with the smallness and bigness of it all, mixed, for one of the first times in my life, with honest sadness and reflex-compassion.

Thoughts continued unchecked. "Mormons aren't mean-spirited, like some fundamentalists. And when it's all fucked-up, and we lack enough faith, we act irrationally, and it's called grace. Jehovah's Witnesses...they live in repentant fear, and have a twisted view of Scriptures, but boy, can they quote them. I despise their religion, but their 'Bible' is my favorite. I can blend with them *all* as a mirrored reflection, a chameleon. *"A young man in want of heart,"* the Jehovah Witness' Bible says, and I now knew what that meant—me. My mind raced.

I had perfected by now that the trick—religion, friendship, love, it didn't matter—was to keep a relationship obscure enough, be a changing, yet strong and appropriate reflection, and be able to deliver a harsh ending by walking away at the height of someone's trust.

I bemused a moment for this *twisted* mask of *mirrored countenance*, felt a doubtful remorse, and thought again about mortality. "Death treats us that way when we most trust life."

I sought the answer in my roots. "When a plant completes its struggle and has fruit, we harvest it. When the cow trusts our daily feeding and grows fat, we feed it the plant's final offering as its final meal and then slaughter it as our food. Yet we think we're under different principles? Perhaps some cynicism is reality, not just anger, and the challenge is my acceptance of life's inhuman ways."

My mind raced. "Now I know that I will sometimes feel compelled to shoot myself in the left temple just to take the courageous, contagious, unknown journey. Then a tingling fear will grip me and I will think it better to wait and take chances on a slower judgment. Repentance, blood of Christ, wine, enlightenment, whatever...you might be fucked; maybe not."

"Faulkner carved the *wall of oblivion*. But you'll walk it without a *scratch*. I will ponder self-talk later, but for now, I'll feel the evil comfort of the ole man's voice barking belittlements: *'Shut up, you stupid fucking dolt!'* Oh, God, help me be still."

"I can feel detached accountability by yielding to long-dead guidance, and I can be still. Perhaps I don't need to seek the answers. Perhaps the answers will find me, or perhaps they are already hidden in me somewhere and need no finding. Perhaps someone will help me find them. For tonight, I cannot care." Through exhaustion, the racing became more reflective.

"Why did Brendan shoot himself in the left temple and not somewhere else? Was it a grandiose accident? He was leaning on his right handed crutch and forgot that the safety was on. It was an accident. I think so."

"And how was it that Bee had smiled before sunup, be it all so gentle and with that recognizable ornery green twinkle in the right eye, while his left eye drooped, gigantic, swollen with blood from the trauma of a gunshot, like a purple blood-filled baseball...death inevitable in knowing that it would have the 17-year old by dawn? Did he smile, or was it just the eye-strained blur of a bitter long day, too much hope in watching, and an unjust night of children dying?"

"Perhaps I had imagined it, but no...I'm sure...even with the bullet's spinning and churning as it weaved through the child's soft brain, somehow the right eye had smiled at 3:11 a.m. How? Why? Is it medically possible?"

"Fuck it, who cares! I saw it, but he's dead. It's all bullshit anyhow and in the certainty of a lightless eye, we'll all pass into the blank pages of unwritten history...another of the cattle turned in one flip of some church's Bible page or shot in an impersonal war started by some angry, well spoken and well dressed sociopath. Fuck it, you cynical asshole!" As my heart pounded, I became aware of my growing anger and so converted it easily to self-pity and compartmentalization: Another of a sober drunk's concoctions.

"I haven't done shit with my life and I know it. At least my brother lived on the edge. At least Billie had gone so far into the mist that people following him came back afraid. Brendan? The boy was simply manic-depressive—a bad moment of a bad day—and *poof*, no more." I was tiring beyond control.

My mind continued to hammer with resentment and growing anger as I calculated the zero game of it all—credit cards, plastic songs, flashbacks of abuse and abusing, colors, loves gone, sensualities, broken marriages, children who knew only the angry man, sponsors sharing AA sayings, car wrecks, toads, drugs, import cars, import beers, rebuilt houses, cheap trinkets, designer clothes, decaying clothes, fine wine, boxed wine…"But life ain't done with you yet," I knew, while searching for existence with mortal impatience and a resentment at living. Then the simplicity of a Spanish saying hit me.

"Estoy pensando en la immortalidad del sapo." I smiled to think of simple immortality. "I am thinking of the immortality of the frog."

A mix of conversations, self-talk, verses, poems, stories, life clips, movies, and fantasy began to flood my thinking and I knew that I was in for a wild ride of grieving insanity. I had felt this dark-thought-sparking-and-burning sensation much of my drinking life, and knew that, sober, it would hurt, but it could pass. Tonight I would go to a meeting.

I pondered sweetly that, after Brendan smiled with his eye, he sank into a state of REM sleep and never returned.

I watched his right eye moving up and down and side to side with dreams. I thought that perhaps it was just an eyelid's spastic response to gunshot trauma. Somehow I knew better. He was dreaming. I knew that we would never awake from the dream and realized that we are, thus, imaginary dust…tomorrow's whirlwind for posterity's rain.

I visualized that even a child could press a tiny handprint into forming concrete, yet in moments it sat, hard and cold, as solid stone, capturing the present as tomorrow's mirage.

He drifted away without even knowing that he was dreaming, and except for our memory, never knew that he had existed or passed.

In a thousand years, he would be in a still-timeless state of his last dream.

"May it be sweet," I thought. "And, God, please help my brother. If I feel this...he may die of a broken heart."

Chapter 10
my brother's keeper

I ran my fingers gently through Bill's silky, blond-and-graying hair and noticed that his hands were folded humbly, yet with the harsh and conflicting message of a crimson, heart-shaped nail-puncture scab on his upper hand between his thumb and index finger.

I knew that it was unnatural for him to fold his left hand over his right, but knew that it would not matter. Somehow, the soft feel of his thinning hair against my finger tips felt like the first time one touches a baby's head, and that newborn innocent euphoria and joy of life's marvel fills one's understanding.

It made me recall his being a newborn and the rancid smell of piss and shit in his diapers as they were washed in our farmhouse basement in a clunking round tub with a protrusion of simple black wringers. I smiled: Mom's first "automatic" washer.

I flashed to the time that Mommy had predictably monthly rage and an impatience that shook the farm because my brother had shit his pants beyond his time of "potty training."

With a combined, deep, multi-person, demonic sounding roar and screech that dwarfed daddy's greatest sound, my mother grabbed the giant brown turd out of Billy's pants and stood over the slow-moving boy waving it through the air like a 50s King Kong.

"I've had it up to my fuck hole with your shit," she screeched, and then she slammed the lumpy torpedo into the floor beside my brother with an angry stabbing motion.

It was the first time I had heard Momma use "*that* saying" and the first time that I knew she was to be feared beyond attack chicken, beyond the ole man, perhaps even beyond God.

My brother may have smelled like shit, lived in shit, given people shit, and even beat the shit out of people in his lifetime, but I don't recall him ever shitting his pants again as a sober child.

I knew that Bill could have the biggest heart I had ever known, yet could also roar without warning to frighten or hurt you like a cornered lion.

Whatever the mix, he was here now, rested-looking, muscular, slightly smiling, and so completely beautiful. I loved him more deeply than I had loved any other person on this Earth. He was my best friend and more. He was an anchor to my understanding of life's coming, and now he was an anchor to my understanding of its balance and brevity. I had watched him come and now, I had watched him go...leading me yet again with the courage that he thought he lacked. A broken heart had taken its toll.

The call had come on the morning of November 21st, the day before Thanksgiving at 6:05.

"Bill's dead," said the meek and shaking voice on the other end of the phone. "We think Bill's dead." It was Laura, his sweet true love.

Groggy and numb from a waking unreality, I stumbled around, threw on some mix of men and women's clothing and ran to my car.

I couldn't remember very well how to get to his house and the darkness made it even more surreal. I overshot a couple of small turns, but finally arrived to see Laura and Bill's two daughters standing outside of a neighbor's duplex. Their countenance blended perfectly with the still, gray, colorless and lifeless trees of winter's dawning, and I suddenly knew that it was not speculation or misunderstanding. My brother was gone.

The coroner's office and local PD had sent a team of investigators to examine the scene for foul play, but his daughter, Angel, told the dramaless tale clearly:

At about 9:00 she had gone to her room to talk on the phone after telling her daddy that she loved him. At about 9:20 she yelled "Goodnight" down the hall and, lacking a response, slid the phone to rest near her father's apparently sleeping body.

When she awoke to go to school, she touched him as he sat unmoving in the same chair and noticed that he was cold. The room was filled with the smell of urine and feces. He had shit his pants one final time.

She ran out the back door, leaving it ajar, to a friend's house and called Laura. Laura jumped in her car and called me. It was nine months to the day—and likely to the hour—that his son had died.

A flood of stark, colorful and unordered memories marched again uninvited through my lambasted mind and, beaten, I allowed it.

I silently knew that my life would never be the same. Something in me grasped that my heart had been given the precious gift of an eternal glimpse, and I knew that no amount of four-dimensional time, wisdom, theology, study, or conversation would convert it to sharable understanding. It was a gift from my brother and his son—the gift of powerless surrender and brokenness.

One of them alone might have only dented my calloused heart; together they had broken it.

I cried until I could not cry with the moistness of tears, knowing that it was a sadness-induced version of tear-drunken puking until there was nothing to regurgitate—empty, yet surging with pain...*useless till broken*.

A month before, I had met a beautiful, coy and illusive woman at a conference in Nashville, and had unnoticeably charmed her for days as best I could, attracting nothing.

As we ran into each other in parting at the airport, we exchanged numbers so that she might share some of her SAP computer wisdom with me and help us navigate an enterprise system installation for my employer. Her employer in Louisiana had one of the most successful installations known to date.

In the absence of lustful conquest, and with my mind clearing of hormones, I discovered for the first time that she was bright, intensely literate, creative, vigilant, honorable, and sober of mind.

My filters had not allowed this seeing in days and nights before. I resolved to get what I could from her mind now that I had failed to conquer her elegant body.

She had been rerouted by the airline so she was, *coincidentally*, on the same plane with my colleagues and me.

My last look at her then is the memory of a small, tired-looking woman sitting in the back row of the aircraft, reading a thick murder mystery, and looking fully intelligent and unapproachable.

Days of lust and attraction unreturned converted now to a brief clumsy chat and the professional confirmed exchange of e*ddresses.

Nothing could have told me then that she would soon become my next best friend because that chamber was to be opened by my brother's death in 30-days. Coincidence became infinite glimpse, unseen. I had found my Violet.

My brother would hand me the gift of broken surrender and thus the hidden key to a new ability to love and see love's beauty. Yet, in deploying this gift, I had more to learn and more broken fragments to shatter on my clumsy new path without him.

Chapter 11
with wisdom comes much pain

I visited my Violet and, then, flew away.

My chest felt as though I had somehow grown into the flesh of this woman, had become one flesh, and had then been ripped apart as a new wound when we hugged for the last time, parted, and I boarded the plane.

I could see a mural of Louie Armstrong draped behind her fading wave as I walked from the main terminal into my corridor. I had never felt this much pain for another *living* person, and it caught me by surprise. This was the daylight morning of a Violet awakening in the New Orleans night.

I deeply knew that there was not an ounce of pretense left in me—not for work, not for marriage, not for bullshit, not for life.

I had walked informed, but unknowing and accidentally, through a thinly coated cell of reality, into a new world of existence and into a knifelike awareness that my old life was now a dried cocoon. My every fiber knew that returning to New Orleans was all that mattered to *my* heartbeats and breath.

I had managed to visit the Crescent City after three months of growing friendship, followed by five months and 60,000 minutes of cell time with my now closest friend.

My 2nd wife, Leslie, had *apparently* not noticed that I was gone day and night on the phone any more than she had noticed it when I spent four years of this time with my AA buddies, smoking cigarettes, attending meetings, going for coffee, eating, and just plain bullshitting away entire weekends. How could she know?

My marriage had begun passionately, and, then, evolved with dropping temperatures, into a shared robotic reaching for self-improvement through books, tapes, therapy, and mind-based training dialogue. Self-improvement I drank of freely at the expense of relationship improvement.

I finally decided that, since Leslie did not miss me, I would not miss her. Resentment? Perhaps, but I recklessly poured myself into purchasing four cell phones at 3,000 minutes per month each, paying overage charges and spending every cellular minute in parking lots talking to Louisiana. I judged my heart to be a cheater, but in some theoretically Christless manner, I did not care.

In rain, in snow, and in hailstorms, I sat in my car and I talked with Violet. I flooded the dark void of my brother's memory with her brilliant light. I did this somehow ignoring that my life would inevitably hit a turning point of choice and literally lived in the *minute*. I never knew that another person, without touch, could offer me such mirrored joy.

In an interruption of the play, I ventured to Texas with my wife to visit her family. There, I again experienced the horror of their dysfunctional commune and carefully recounted family angers.

Each trip started with excitement and expectation for a resolution to 40 years of chaos, but each trip eroded (as it must) into untreated and resentment-filled anger, passive-aggressive shots, question-sculpted dueling, and finally, a silent stabbing death of the money-clad genetics that had cloaked and disintegrated itself with decades of masks and dozens of compounding secrets and lies.

At least my family had been openly violent. I hated this time and I hated Leslie's family. It was not for me.

Except for my step-kids, whom I loved deeply, and a disliking love for my wife, I could have cared less if the rest of her entire family cluster entered a Mexican bus and plummeted accidentally into the muddiest and darkest canyon of deepest Mexico.

The terror of dying peasants and the thrown reality of splashing mud, as they tumbled down rainy canyon walls that dwarfed the Grand Canyon, would have presented their first glimpse of true human beings and of the farmer's earth that had sculpted me.

Within this death-wish fantasy, I prayed each visit for Texas A & M to be beaten at football and even believed that one day, the

Kansas *Jayhawks* would again produce a football team to embarrass A & M, her father's alma mater.

Yes, this time was miserable for me, yet allowed me solace to recognize the battling reality of my own progressive alcoholic thinking; even dry...this infirmity really was *"progressive."*

Each return trip from Texas returned our shattered sub-family further into the head and further out of the heart, whereby we listened to self-improvement tapes all the way home, used the proper words and terminology on each other to avoid conflict, and pretended to be healthier, growing adults.

I did love her, but this growing lie was running against the grain of both my youth and "my" program and felt more and more like the alcohol-induced darkness that got me here. I became increasingly plastic and reflected in the midst of this chaos on my Violet light. This was before Violet and I had ever touched for the first time.

And now the ripping...As I flew home from New Orleans, I moved so far into my soul that I had no connection with survival logic or social reason. I was not even affected by the memorized and obligatory chambers of my heart, be they planted by scripture, be they learned from experience, or be they hard-wired by a modicum of innate character. I had somehow become primal, calm, and a stranger in my own body.

My wife and I returned in the same hour from Louisiana and south Texas, respectively—she amazingly "shocked" by her latest miserable trip to visit the Texas Munster family; I stood baptized by my visit to the Violet south.

My words were simple as she sat on the ugly dog-hair covered, cat-puke laden, stinking brown and tan-patterned plaid couch in our cluttered living room, recounting the now rote and memorized drama and cursing of her mother's latest checked-out responses.

She spoke of her father's cheap shots, of her mother's racism and surrealism, of her sister's alcoholic acting husband and cult-like engagements, of her brother's millions, his Barbie workout wife's perfection, other empty things.

She began crying and was allegedly in great pain from this sad and pathetic family movie, but I had seen this all before; to me, it was simply a rerun. Her pain was deeper than them or me, and I was not the cure.

"I can't do this any more," I said, without feeling. "We're finished."

She was stunned, and somehow still needed me to embrace this, the latest memorized conflict with her sick family, but I had nothing to give and could not wait for the right moment to be kinder in parting.

"It's over. I will not do this any more. I'm leaving," I echoed firmly for her absorption.

Somehow I knew that in a Judas-like manner, I had delivered the predestined blow of absolute brokenness and shared the gift that my brother had given me—a gift that would move her into self-healing and ultimately into what I had learned about the paradox of humble and free. She deserved this painful gift.

A year or two of pain and she would be free like never before, grateful for the once perceived best friend who could look her in the eye at a most vulnerable and trusting moment and free her from their decaying orbit.

Like a light switch, it was turned off; it was over, and she was left alone to deal with her dead marriage and seemingly long-dying family. I knew that her kids would be there for her, no matter what. They, like her, were so beautiful, and so strong.

"But, you're my best friend," she gulped, tearful and unbelieving.

"You're not mine," I said coldly, while adding a surprising shot of cynical anger. "Pay more attention and raise your standards."

I suddenly felt teetered on the edge of evil, as though someone else were speaking through me; but I knew my cruel resolve.

I slept on the couch for a few days and then moved into an efficiency apartment. There was, of course, the first in my life moment of absolute truth about "another woman" and the understandable public beatings as Leslie shared my scarlet letter with her friends, my workplace, my boss, and our shared community.

I understood and felt compassion; but, then, being duplicitous, I didn't understand and felt anger. Nonetheless, I deserved it and it was true. Ultimately, I used the prying and tearing energy to focus on moving south.

In the same hour, without consultation or coaching, without previous discussion, or even the realization that it could happen, Violet looked her husband of 20 years in the eye and said, "I'm leaving you. I can't do this any more."

Violet's husband now paid for his past sins.

He had moved upstairs and did not touch her for a year after their fifth year of marriage; she had moved out for a year at 10 years of marriage, and returned only for the promise of change and for the love of their two young boys.

He didn't change. Despite her beauty and encouragement from friends, she never cheated on him and was a faithful wife, until our time together.

We each felt no further need to justify past love or mere existence. After our decisions, Violet existed as an abused shadow in the corners of their home for about 60 days and then moved into an apartment in Baton Rouge. We each agreed that even if we could never be together, we could not continue in the lives we had once promised.

We interrupted growing passion and shared a strange form of grieving and pain via our next months of telephone dating. We slowly moved from what was to what could be.

The next year was filled with resume refinements, trips to New Orleans, near-hit interviews, deep love, and 12,000 minutes per month of cellular conversation.

We read Faulkner, shopped, watched BAMA games and movies, and shared a friendship that likely only God could have allowed. He likely had authored only the friendship, yet we were intense and passionate in our love. As we grew, our one-time spouses grew sicker and then started healing, and this chapter of our collective lives wrote itself to an end.

I gave necklace trinkets to my friends John A and Ryan H as I pondered the way that God might bring us together, and somehow knew that this gift was speaking to me: "EWOP" it said...*Everything Works Out Perfectly.* All I finally had to do was shut up, suit up, show up, and leave it alone...*EWOP.* My wife had tried to explain that, but I could not understand her teaching.

I began to put success, paychecks, and time into perspective and, amazingly, felt the love of God like never before. I slept like a baby while time passed both slowly and as a blurring snapshot. I became absolutely aware of my brief mortality and of the precious gift of human existence.

I awoke each day thanking God for my life, for my health, for my sobriety, and for this day. On gray days, I thanked Him for this "*beautiful* day." I prayed *only for knowledge of his will for us, and the power to carry that out. "Let Patience have her perfect work that you may be entire, wanting nothing,"* I thought. *"...wanting nothing."*

Suddenly, on a Friday evening as I played with the Internet and filled-out an electronic application, just to see how it worked, I snagged a great job, custom fit for my twisted work style.

It required a significant cut in pay, yet was with a damaged and beautiful organization that needed some nurturing, and I fit their menu of style, experience, skills, and abilities perfectly.

In filling out the application, to the question, *"What traits and abilities do you think the Director of Human Resources for our organization should have?"* I responded, *"Mine."* I had never been so flip or arrogant, and really didn't intend to be this time, but felt so beaten by runner-up placement that I no longer had the energy to *sell* myself.

Three interviews, a visit, and a fancy dinner at New Orleans' restaurant *AUGUST* later, it was locked. Dinner was with the headhunter, two leaders of the organization, and my sweet Violet— POOF...I was headed to Louisiana.

They never even wanted to look at my now well-refined resume and, after meeting Violet, asked me one simple question: "Now, WHY were we recruiting you and not *her?*"

We all smiled in agreement and I was off to start what I believed would be the final perfect chapter of my now happy life.

I would commute 162 miles a day from Baton Rouge to New Orleans East as we planned our little *shotgun* house life "forever." This "forever" would occur when Violet could retire and we could move to *New Orleans* for good. That would take two years. Nothing could stop us now.

It was magic—and I knew that she deserved magic—as I gutted-out the grueling miles, cranking-up CDs and, for some reason, embracing a new driving mania for House Music and Trance.

Being bipolar, I underestimated demons and exhaustion.

They drove with me every day, as evil car-poolers, riding along, me driving, and them driving me mad.

I skipped AA meetings because I was always on the road...leaving at 5:55 a.m., arriving back after 7:00, or later, most nights.

"She's too good for you, too beautiful, too cultured," they probed, at first quietly. "Maybe you were only her manic excuse for leaving a bad marriage, and she's thinking clearer now. She is stable and getting ready to retire after a 30-year career; you fucked-up your career like a goddamn leap-frog, ya alcoholic bastard."

"By the way, your car is going to break down soon and you won't have the money to fix it. If this Mayor isn't reelected, you'll be fired by the new régime, ya know; even the head of the union told you that, and then what'll she think of you, Mr. unemployed *Yankee*?"

"Your credit cards are tapped, and Christmas is coming. Maybe you can get another credit card *with your $21,000 pay cut* and all? You're still on the tax bill with your ex-wife, so you'd better pray she keeps paying Uncle Sam. Good thing *SHE* has integrity."

"Did you notice that your shoes need replacing and your pants leg is frayed; what an image for Saks lady to walk around with. Grab the credit card. Hum? Speaking of hum...Listen to the hums...Sounds like you need tires. Notice how they slid when you tried to stop on I-10 in that rainstorm the other day? You about pissed your pants! That was funny."

"Hey, don't you think she's looking at you a little more distantly lately...and maybe even less? Doesn't she seem more irritable now, like she doesn't respect you as much? Feels familiar, doesn't it? And, what was that look the other day when you met her boss at the market? Did you see the secret gaze? Their eyes kind of locked and he blushed when his wife noticed that the stare lasted too long. Are *they* starting an affair? Probably just a look of respect; though, you know, the look she used to give *you*...when you were new and all. What goes around comes around. You're not magic after awhile, ya know? Never were."

"Oh, hey, did you hear her play the piano, by the way? She's like fuckin' Chopin and you've been playing your guitar for her, to what...*impress* her? Shit. You should be embarrassed. You fucking stupid *dolt*. Jesus, what were you thinking when you moved here? Go home, *Yankee*! Hide on the little rural pancake. You ain't welcome here."

"Let's be straight. You ain't southern culture. You just figurin' out that y'all killed piles of us...said you won the war...but you didn't even know who you were...still don't? Thanks for savin' us. Let's see, are you a Yankee here, or a Cracker Mother Fucker? Be invisible and die of our shared unspoken hate. Learn the accent, but always know that you're a fake southerner. How's your *mask* working now, ole son? Ya know, you *do* sound funny. How's your little *blending countenance* working now?!?"

Dark thoughts pounded like Huns at the mind's door, rhythmically thudding their angry log to the drum of thumping asphalt as the car screamed along, day and night...night and day...

"Sounds like a bad tire...maybe even front-end damage. Boy, that's gonna be expensive. Stay and pay. Isolate. Stay and pay. Isolate. She's too good for you. Fake southerner. She was a cheerleader, for Christ's sake."

"Your shoes need replacing and your pants leg is frayed...looking at you less and with less respect...what *was* that at the market? You sound funny. Fake it 'till you make it! *Happy* faces now, don't let her see how sick you're becoming. Ohhh, puttin' on the mask again, are we? Well you better, Yankee Boy. No, you better not. Have to. Can't. Do it! Don't."

"Ok, try this, Yankee: Hide if you must to save this thing. You'll *probably* get better later. The mask probably won't grow *into you* this time. Just take it as a Band-Aid...a temporary fix, just for a little while...'till you *blend* better. You can trust us; after all, who knows you like we do?" I knew these voices from before. Now they were claiming to be southerners. They even had the accent.

Paranoia and bewitchment satiated me. My soul burned now, far beyond ache. I ached fully with fear and familiar depressed isolation.

My new advisors chanted like a children's choir singing only minor chords. They were now sly southern demons in a frightened northerner's head. It was an ironic, familiar taunting by new secret friends to hide me from my love, yet protect her from me. Jesus, oh, God, I knew this pattern too well.

After nine months, with growing agitation, I moved to New Orleans and lived alone, having weekend visits to and from my Violet, but demanding isolation. She didn't change, but I did. I was bipolar battered.

The added time for meetings and solace did not solace me, it simply moved the demons into an efficiency apartment where they became more efficient and there taunted me effectively.

I had seen a therapist for five years...I knew better and I knew what I was seeing, but I couldn't find the strength to stop it or to cry for help. I allowed the mask's reanimation.

First I moved to the St. Charles Regency, but it soon sold as condos. So, I was forced to move again nine months later to the Esplanade at City Park where, if it were possible, I moved into an even deeper paranoid fear.

No matter how New Orleans people treated me—and they treated me *wonderfully*—I felt more and more alone, and more and more like an AWOL union soldier surrounded by starved and tattered confederate troops, I, and they, each displaced by an instantaneous void century and a half, all dead, communing ghosts in a neutral ground of the New Orleans night.

Chapter 12
bipolar hell

My *re*appearance from masked hiding was a tsunami of cold and sweat-filled personal horror. I felt tremors in the distance, which caused intensifying fights and periods of isolation, but ignored them until it hit me fully that I had destroyed this, the hope of my dreams.

The New Orleans night no longer whispered to me; only a grating feeling of anxious loneliness and jealous economic and emotional fear called my name.

Complete isolation was absorbing me again, and this time with louder silence and darker light than ever before. The *undiscovered me* had slithered through my mind and found me again, even here in the midst of a trusted, reliable, and faithful love from my Violet one. The *sober* doom of knowing it, and the distant thundering of the four horsemen, was absolutely unbearable.

I stood as an on-looking child, with my arms at my side, as I knowingly murdered this incredible love, and I knew that somehow—amazingly even *more* unrefined than the old me—I was again the same raging script; the *me* I feared had reappeared to steal my life and destroy its fragile hopes.

I had never felt so powerless. This now stirred a bitter cake-batter of actions, senses, imaginations, dreams, thoughts, fears, and defects of character. I was hopeless, isolated, alone and perfectly cooked under the pressure of a few hundred hot and humid sleepless nights. It made drinking small and death a hopeful friend, so I vowed not to drink or kill myself...just for today.

I had embraced a growing travail for nearly 11 months, but ignored it as a painful spiritual awakening, memory echoes, transition, speed bumps, flaking lumps of character defect, or residual thought.

I kept believing that I was *not* the same, believing that I was healthier; thinking that not drinking, attending meetings, sponsoring people, praying, faithfully taking anti-depressants, and working steps had removed my largest shortcomings—thinking that these paralyzing little quakes would pass. They did not.

In the dawn of winter, it snapped and unraveled into a blizzard of dark and blinding energy.

On that day, I emotionally beat her out of my life with an anger and wrath that even God could not cover or tame. This time it was over. For the first time in my life, I did not need the reflection of another woman to woo me away. I needed only *Terror, Bewilderment, Frustration and Despair* to join and surround me and end this whispering season of peaceful grace and loving goodness.

I reflected, without protection now, upon the underlying shattered pieces that energized and drove this fierce madness.

Somehow, the more I loved, the more violently I ended love and the more power I had to be cruel. This time was catastrophic and nuclear by any historic measure. The cruel, unkind, uncaring, secretly selfish, protecting—yet bloody—spiritual violence of this ending left me gutted, breathless and trembling with fear.

Over a period of months, without provocation or apparent cause, and filled with growing remorse, I destroyed her, one conversation, one word, one abandonment, and one look at a time.

I did not understand why, but knew this to be a violent eruption of a well-set pattern.

I cannot describe the pain of watching this angry man form from the little choir of demons and emerge from my mouth, soul, and body to drive away the dearest light of my life. I cried alone for what he had done.

I knew that I was powerless over this evil *thing*, and felt small and helpless as he peeked his head around and through my reason and then slowly slithered through, and poisoned it, with cynicism, jealousy, and fear.

He sometimes changed my eyes from blue to raging green. The beast injected emotional Novocain to keep me at bay, but even that was not necessary. Despite years of counseling, meds, AA sober time, prayer, and pleading hope, just *for* some hope, I knew that he was stronger than I. I was a helpless child.

I did not know when he would bubble forth or the end of his vengeance. When he slept sometimes and Violet looked at me, I could see that she wondered who she was looking at. She looked now with a spirit of guarded trust and hesitation. I knew that the yellowed script and its angry worker had beaten us beyond repair as the smudged, mean, and sweaty blacksmith had done in prior plays. His fire burned and his scorched hammer pounded without mercy.

I loved this woman more than I had ever loved anyone except my brother. But, when we stood facing one another and she asked if I wanted her to stay or go, I said, "I don't care." When she asked if I loved her, I said, "It doesn't really matter," and when she asked if she might keep the cell phone that had connected us for so long, I said, "If a phone rings in the forest and no one answers, did it ring?"

I watched her flush, fight tears, pick-up her pride and her bags, and walk out of my apartment with a gliding mix of stylish dignity and slumped brokenness. The phone stopped ringing, the emails stopped coming, and a deathlike silence filled my now fully empty nights.

I somehow hurt for Violet as I had hurt for my brother, yet I could not love back enough to protect her. I was tired of hurting her and was too afraid of the angry man within to reach out this time. I loved her deeply, but couldn't control the beast within.

Now the Violet light that filtered itself and rippled tranquilly off the late night waters of St. John Bayou onto the ceiling of my Esplanade at City Park apartment whispered to me again: "It is over."

I lay sleepless on my interlocked fingers, staring at the silent rippling ceiling and listening to these new voices of the New Orleans night. I ached and ached and ached alone and ached and ached alone.

The Bayou's violet ripples faded to sunlight while my heart grew amazingly even darker from staring hopelessness, the demons' frog-like singing, fading *Boudoir, Thymes Goldleaf,* and a burning lack of sleep. I was dark enough to reflect back at the Bayou.

Through my life's experience and choices, I had not become a serial killer, only a possessed, self-effacing, random sociopath who had no real use for other human beings, yet cried deeply to touch them.

When the loving couple walked unawares to the end of my secret and memorized pretensions, my relationship landmine exploded without warning and the couple was gone. With Violet, this guilt-triggered metaphor was far deeper and surgically painful.

It was as though we were strolling hand-in-hand through a singing bird and purple flower-filled meadow with the warm sun shining and violet fragrances wafting across a gentle breeze. We were floating into the harmonic, peaceful, and echoing sound of waterfalls, orange and blue butterflies, and chirping crickets.

At that moment, I suddenly screamed with violent cursing rage, tore my clothes, changed the scene into a two-dimensional cardboard backdrop and ripped it to pieces, destroying not only the scene, but its beholders. It now sits smoldering in a rusted garbage can, in a weed-covered lot, in an imaginary Parish, with no known address.

The demons were lightweights now.

A thousand small angers and resentments had become a low-level roaring and a dark fire of evil in my soul's yellow-flickering abyss. I burned even more at the logic that I was in control of my choices and that, even in the absence of that, I had asked God to cover and remove my defects of character, yet here they were-- visible.

I had not *humbly* asked God to remove my shortcomings, but I was humbled now. Even unbroken fragments of my brother's passing were now completely shattered. I was *fully* broken.

Perhaps this base shortcoming had to become such a powerful entity to get my attention. Perhaps Violet was the ultimate price of desperate seeing.

I replayed years of what I believed was honest step work and counseling and felt ashamed and cheated by my lying heart and soul for their conspiracy in hiding an evil-hearted, rentless tenant. I could not continue knowing what I now knew about myself and want to live. Yet this was as darkly freeing as when the ole man died. He simply needed to die again.

"Useless 'till broken," I reflected, thinking back on a powerful sermon I had heard. "I am now broken indeed, tired of hurting my fellow man, tired of destroying good women...simply, tired."

But, I knew myself well enough now to know that this was disguised and subtle bullshit hiding the true sociopath. In fact, I could easily use compartmentalization and a new relationship to kill pain, enhance euphoria, and do it all again, and again, and again, and again.

For some reason, I now wanted to take a stand on this battleground. I had to face the hidden beast and taunt it into the light to beat it and its Godless dominion. I was Legion.

I consciously did not wish to do this to another love and stung with remorse that I had done it to three
good women and now my grand Violet.

Fear welled inside me as I recounted the unnamed four horsemen thundering across the Kansas plains to destroy me in drunken years gone by.

I thought about their guiding spirit, the *"chilling vapor of loneliness"* and, for the first time, I understood the deep personal nature, and even the deliberate order, of their names: *Terror, Bewilderment, Frustration and Despair.*

Again they galloped, their sixteen hooves echoing with ricochets of gunshot-like sound among the long tenured live oaks of City Park.

There, they paused in brief strategic fellowship with the cold sculpture of their General Beauregard, reliving the necessary horror of victory and old killings, and allowing their horses to snort and gasp heavy air in the New Orleans night. They laughingly mocked as they fellowshipped, planned other deaths along the way, and taunted me—a pathetic little afterthought prey.

My Brendanized flirtations with suicide made me careless enough now to dive into this obscuring blackness.

I could see that the monster transcended all ideas I had of time, space, matter, reason, or even existence. It was a timeless vacuum, dark and horrible beyond my imaginations, yet it somehow intrigued me as perhaps the only logical embrace of this now bitter life.

I laughed aloud at how my best-reasoned words could become a stick-man in the hands of a formless ghost to beat me senseless and stupid on Earth's interior battleground.

I flashed now to a time when a psychologist listened patiently to one of my contorted "if-then, if-then" conclusions and then looked horrified as I said, "That's logical, *right?*"

His response was bewildered, yet simple, "No. That's *ILL*ogical." He used his finger to accentuate and underline the word *"ill"* in the air. It had seemed *so* logical to me, not sick. Logical, or illogical, I now knew that the monster infused me.

"I don't need to do anything to *see* the beast," I concluded. "Dive *into* it." It was cornered within.

"Compared to managing life and its loves, you cannot fail in this unmapped journey or its enjoined destination, and you are not now vulnerable or able to be taken hostage by fear, or by horsemen, because you are willing to go mad or die. Death is ok; life is ok; elusion and delusion are not a fleeing or a shield."

I lay for battle. *"Dive* in, or perhaps, for visual aid, take a child's toy to the gates of your little hell...Perhaps...Ah, yes...a *sled* that you remember! That's tactile and innocent in your memories if you need such assurance. You've learned one thing for certain: It's all learned anyway."

I thereby concluded and decided to plummet down hell's damned corridors into my deepest soul on *a sled*. I would put off suicide to see how dark darkness could become. I resolved to put on the "mask" of a *HAPPY me* to avoid being discovered by coworkers and surface-feeding friends in the days to come, and knew not how long the ride might last.

I chose any starting point, taunted the horsemen over my shoulder, and grabbed a rusty smelling antique wooden sled from the milk-stained barn wall of my mind to ride into jagged unknowns.

"Follow me, you bastards. Let's ride together. Bring the General and his now dead heart and pistols if you choose. Perhaps I am the tiny prey, but perhaps it is *you* who will see your vain conquests. Perhaps we'll see together. Our flirtations will soon be over."

The *"chilling vapor of loneliness"* became a tingling sensation cloaked in a confused mixture of cold chills and warm sweats...I felt a fearless sexual carelessness as I sat on the sled and accepted its predestined theater—intertwined with my flesh—of the living and the dead.

Someone female, wise, eternal, and unseen, explained to me that the ride was free, yet demanded complete surrender and acceptance of visions without judgment or immediate corrective action. I was along for the ride as long as I obeyed these rules. *"If your life is definable, you are not being...only pretending."* I recalled from poems past.

I could feel the runners moving slowly from a small piece of rich-smelling black dirt in a fertile hayfield of my youth, through falling snow, across the orange maize fields where I killed pheasants each winter and along a track of endless farming circles, dust devils and bloody beatings. A mix of this dirt and my father's anger had created the horseman, *Terror,* one fist and one word at a time, and I knew for certain now that he was the first horseman.

"Come on, you mother fucker," I taunted as I gripped the sides of the sled with both hands. "You can't hurt me now, 'cause I don't care; remember killing Violet?!"

I looked into the bottomless spiral of my formless hate—only hate. "You can kill me; I may even do it *for* you, but you won't beat me today." As with all resentments, this focus became distant crosshairs and guided my sled to its first destination.

The un-oiled screeching of old machinery could be heard in the distance as the sled moved along its uncharted and uncharitable path.

Perhaps, if I had a guide, it was demonic and it was the demon's plan to trigger my fears with visions of my life. Perhaps, as agreed to, there was no good or bad, no right or wrong...no anything...only life's events as they were stored and filtered. I didn't see. I didn't know. I didn't care. I needed to listen and observe; that's all.

Accommodating, the sled stopped and I watched as a skinny, trembling, snot-sucking, burr-scalped, poorly dressed, cow shit-covered, ugly boy emerged from beneath farm equipment with its wide dirt-polished, six-foot steel "Vs" which indiscriminately swept and cut beneath the weeded earth.

He ran pigeon-toed, freezing, and nervously pissing his shit-smelling pants, into the white box-shaped, ghost-filled opaquely shadowed garage.

The garage was filled with nameless chrome, random, rusty, unreadable numbered tools, oil cans, shovels, and wrenches. All were scattered across the grease-stained and dirty floor. An unseen clock timed and ticked his *predictable* failure. The ole man plotted and conjured how best to repay from his learned and stored reservoir of daily violent needs.

I shamed to know that the boy was I and I would know the demon's friend anywhere.

He was a man who seemed bigger than his 5' 10" perfectly-muscled frame. This was because of his aggressive forward leaning, *always* angry walk, sun-baked, cracked, and leathery balding head, clenched jaws, dirty jeans, and blue denim shirt (with its sleeves rolled-up to the elbow), powerful scarred hands, scuffed boots, booming voice, and fire-filled, piercing green eyes.

He was fueled with a rage that had been shared for generations by father and mother, husband, wife and children alike, and he could strike without warning to burn any part of a child with a stick, a wrench, a boot, a look, or a back-handed slap.

Nothing hit harder than his words, and if he loved, it was only stated in the form of providing for his family. Work was his existence and acquisition of more land to farm was the measure of his success. More land, more work. More work, more value.

I knew that I was lucky to be raised by a man with this drive and discipline, and I knew that if he could overcome the remorse of beating me by simply dying, I could overcome the remorse of beating my own children in a head-on way. Beating the emotional beatings I could give a true love was more elusive.

The man had no profession of God, and thought church an excuse for getting out of one's chores, but he had an honest heart and integrity in every way of running his business.

He was known for straight furrows, straight answers, prudence, and quality farming. Given this impression on the neighbors, one learned to be still and laugh with him when he laughed and joked with the neighbors and their kids.

No one needed to know that he could never treat his own child, or more aptly stated...his *step*children, with humor or affection, lest he violate the blood covenant of his childhood teachings. Even now, it seemed aloof, and shamefully arrogant to interrupt this scene with a grown-up's mind, so I allowed myself to become a blended child again, fading to simple observation.

"The nine-sixteenths, Goddamn it!" He roared as I stood shaking and looking for something that fit the bolt that only he could see.

"Not that one, you stupid dolt," he would flash as he landed the backside of his greasy, cracked and callused hand across my lips and I tasted blood. "The BOX-ended one...and bring me the small vice grips and a cotter pin too! Not the big ones, and not the little rusty ones...the *small* ones! NOW, Goddamn it, you stupid fucking dolt! When I yell 'shit' you come slidin' on a shovel!!! You stupid little fucker! I gave you life, and I can take it away! (This baffled me by the way...but there it was again. I *thought* I remembered that!) Quit fuckin' around and bring me that Goddamn wrench NOW...That's not it, Goddamn it! And where's the fuckin' vice grips?!! This is a *medium* cotter pin! You can sing Goddamn toothpaste commercials and can't even remember to bring me one fucking, simple little pair of vice grips and a little fucking cotter pin! "

Suddenly I recalled how I hate to read and how I always feel pressure and fear when someone asks me to find or hand them anything.

I always froze on GRE's, SATs, LSAT's, and every other test that would measure my intelligence or my *value* as a human. I always just thought I was stupid, but perhaps I was just afraid of making mistakes. It was the same feeling in the test that it was under the machinery. Stupid was simple.

Even though I had learned to study and pre-think quick and funny answers, and I knew that under that I was shallow, afraid and unlearned, I forgave myself just a little during this stop of the journey for being lifetime-stupid and believed that perhaps I was only learning-ignorant.

Gradually, I realized that the sled had gone a few miles down the road and, from it, I could see, feel and hear fat moss-colored farm toads with cold white bellies croaking, pissing, and wiggling in my hand as I eased them into a wedge-shaped gap within the spinning, unprotected rubber V-belt of Grandma's water well and then let them go to watch their guts squirt all over my shirt and to watch the belt throw the gutted carcass around its circle a couple of times before the larger pulley cut the toad in half and threw its body two directions away from the pump—or simply flung it. I was always very careful not to catch my shirtsleeve or fingers in the pulley. If only I had known then that, eventually, it would have hurt me less.

Sometimes the toad would get off-center and its flattened carcass would fly away intact. Sometimes it went around once, sometimes twice, rarely more. The physics of this interested me.

It felt good to hurt something and to do it with detached feelings as curious child's play. Acting-out and building the *"sins of my youth"* would allow me to later steal *"remember not the sins of my youth"* from David's Psalm and to beg God's forgiveness for these cruel and heartless days.

I recalled watching the ole man chill a hot Coors beer on a burning Kansas day using a vaporizing white blast from the propane hose as he was fueling the tractor. I wondered later, as I watched a toad hop along, what would happen if I froze it like the beer. So, I tried it.

The toad turned white with ice as the propane cloud immersed it, just as the beer had done. But then, the toad simply thawed and hopped away. This fascinated me and I wondered if the freezing sensation "burned" the toad as cold propane had done to my fingers when they were exposed to it, or if it felt nothing, or, being cold blooded, simply felt cold. The memory of a white frozen toad reminded me of my snowy journey and returned me to the passing sled.

It frightened me to reflect now from the sled and know that serial killers begin this way. I wondered why I had been delivered from their soulless destiny. I felt deep shame mixed with reflexive humility, grace, and gratitude, and prayed for the children who do not find the unreachable exodus of grace.

I knew that the horseman *Bewilderment* had first taken shape for me from the guts of countless toads and that he rode with *Terror* and tracked me by smelling my fear.

Was this what I now built relationships on: A doubt that forgiveness had occurred, or fear that I was still that sick, inept, dirty, snot-and-shit-covered, ugly, and angry child, despite my deep remorse and its best adult laminations?

Mainly, the ineptness left impossibilities because it was a human weakness designed-in by the Maker, and could only be crutched by the intervening graces of God. Yet, obviously even residual ineptness, caused by memory, left a gap of doubt too big to build confident, healthy relationships on, so I knew that there was a sand-filled hole in my foundation.

I could never let them see my ineptness, fear, or lack of character. I would attack before they could see it or when I began to see in their eyes that they were now examining me more closely. If I waited until later in the relationship to *react*, this examination appeared to turn into disrespect for me, and that sent me running.

In every romantic relationship, I was torn by the desire to challenge their every comment and defend myself as having redeeming value, which led to escalating conflict and rage, *or* the deep-down desire to simply run, knowing secretly that they were right. My history was this pattern.

I suddenly felt naked so I trembled and flushed with shame. As agreed, the sled left no time to think, judge, ponder, or correct; it moved on.

I rode past hanging electrocuted birds. There was a dead kitten who, after being thrown enough, or rather, finally spun in circles and then thrown, somehow failed to land on his feet, as I had been told cats *must*.

I rode past hidden masturbation as pre-alcoholic euphoria, and as a release from pain, in every dark corner of the farm's outlands and crannies.

I rode past early "teachings" from cousins and the shameful one-time event of botched experimental sex with another 11-year old. For an instant, disregarding the shame, I was able to step away from it and ask how one knows such things as "sexual preference?" For me, though, there was an instant realization that *whatever* sex was, this was not it for me.

I spent years of begging prayers that no one would ever find out about my sick abuses or the *homosexual day*. I wondered how many children are never relieved of this horrible whipping master and its black granite weights.

I rode past, and glimpsed at, the realization that all of that youthful sexual energy was hidden even from early girlfriends because I was too nice, already too phony, too embarrassed, and too shy and afraid to expose my honest feelings.

I somehow never outgrew the child*ish* simplicity that sexual orgasm was a release from pain, not intimate bonding. Perhaps, seeing, I would outgrow it now.

I recalled the pretty girls that my high school buddies said they had fucked, and that they had even described in clear-colored roadmap detail what they rubbed that turned the girl on. But, then I remembered my being with this same girl later, passionately kissing, ejaculating in my pants, and then being called, "the nicest guy they'd ever been on a date with." I couldn't rub that place; I was afraid. I knew that their complement only affirmed my intimate phoniness and further nurtured a self-resentment towards the weaknesses in my already mask-covered emerging manhood.

Realizing that these things became an entangled part of my empty abyss, and now knowing that my fear of them was a form of taxidermist glue, did not slow the sled's journey; it moved on and I scolded myself by saying, "Stupid dolt, you've had years to solve this riddle and you've failed at it...you are still a fake; knowledge is not freedom; you'll always fail."

Terror and *Bewilderment* joined at this intersection of the journey with their inevitable companion, created from my powerlessness over inept seeing and impotent choice, *Frustration.* The three of them watched as silent hunters from the shadows, unwilling to attack a muttering, weaponless man on a child's sled.

I felt the price of admission fading, and death hurting in my chest, so I rebuked fear, judgment, and analysis in favor of continuing the now exhausting and grim ride.

I reaffirmed that this day I could not care about solving the riddle or finding truth; I just wanted to ride into the beast's heart and know its evil power.

I didn't even care that down deep I knew that knowledge of it would not bring healing, but might instead become some improved mask of psycho-babble bullshit for me to put on and justify my next woman-seeking persona as it failed the time trials. Out of respect for the ticket, I accepted all of these conditions and so the sled moved on.

Suddenly it was Christmas and I was looking at the warm multi-colored bubble lights on our prickly-needled green tree. I wondered what Santa would bring me.

I could smell the pine, feel the warmth of our floor heater, and see the red and golden glitter of wrapped packages.

I knew that Christmas was a magic time and had no way of knowing that it would become a time of angry rage and hypocritical flashback in all my years to come. Perhaps the sled grabbed this memory only so it could gain some speed on snow before it came to the snow-covered, jagged rock canyons of other memories.

"God love Christ, but fuck Christmas," I thought cynically. The sled glided on.

My feet were intuitively trying to guide the runners by pushing right and left, but I continued to hang on with white-knuckle pressure as we made the next turns.

I suddenly became aware of a falling sensation and jumped, as when one kicks a leg at night, because of impending dreams, no reference points, or perhaps a dreamer's fear of heights.

I was plummeting down a snowy gray granite canyon wall and my last lighted glimpse was the concave shape of General Beauregard's missing metallic rock.

He had been carved from this even before he was born and before his proud likeness, pistols, stirrups, and spurs were shaped in metals, medals, fire, and bronze. It was before the sediments surrounding him were formed from the guts and flesh of, not toads, but hopeful or hopeless men who fought or cowered in the face of their given life and its brief destined battles—each of which now slept and became the disimpassioned earth that once bore them.

The sled passed, or my mind flashed to, a windy day when it was 20-below zero and the ole man backhanded me from atop an ice-covered windmill. I tasted warm blood as I almost fell 30 feet, but caught myself on the catwalk. He didn't notice.

I wondered for an instant if this caused my fear of heights, or if perhaps his not noticing caused it. I instantly knew, though, that acrophobia dealt more with my character and overall fear, then with any single event. I knew that this was an example of my using words, self-pity, and "ill" logic to cleverly explain something that I really did not understand.

Oh, if only I could blame my every weakness on daddy's passed-on abuse and hand that great power to a dead farmer. Perhaps, then, my children could use this escape from me and be more hopeful as they found themselves destroying relationships, hurting their families, and justifying anger with *logical* lies.

I saw an early, non-drinking, resentment of my daddy's mother, Dot, as she offended me one day and I resolved to *never* visit her again.

I saw that I honored this decision and never saw her again until she was frightened, dying alone, mindless, and old in an understaffed hospital ward for the senile. At that moment I viewed her with detachment, as though she were a wrinkled, shaking, crying, soon-to-be-gutted toad.

Proud defiance blocked my childlike shame even now, but from the nearly stopped sled I was forced, uncomfortably, to ponder more.

I saw memories of Grandma Dot's beautiful five-foot-long, perfectly white, hair falling gently from a tight bun on top of her proud head, as she released it, and I saw memories of white flowers turning green, red, purple, or blue tomorrow as she snipped their long stems, smiled sweetly at me, and placed them in thus-colored waters today.

Snipping roots, immersing in dye, and exposure-time could actually change something's color. The flower only had to be broken.

I was flooded with memories of working with her in the garden, of walking hand in hand to her gothic red-and-stone piled barn, and of looking at old brown-tinted family pictures through her antique oak-framed, mask-shaped magnifying goggles.

I could recall smells as I remembered her apple, raisin, mincemeat, and rhubarb pies with their carefully weaved top-crust or a sugar-covered, golden solid top-crust carefully sculpted with holes painting cleaver baked pictures of flowers from Grandma's keen mind.

I remembered the story of when she was young and eating dessert. They apparently brought a cousin into the house and near the family's table. He was covered with a blood-soaking sheet, blasted to death in a hunting accident.

I remembered that she had graduated from KU in only three years with a degree in journalism when women didn't go to college.

I remembered stories—true or not—of how she put the farm and all its possessions in her name, struck his name from everything, spread the story, and fiscally neutered her husband, Everett, because he was an alcoholic with a gambling habit.

I remembered that she allegedly beat him within an inch of his life one night when he became a mean drunk, and I remembered that her own father had been killed by jumping from the top of a grain bin and landing on a pitchfork that went into his groin and perforated his lower bowels causing a painful, traumatic, and uninsured death.

I remembered the missing part of her upper right ear and her telling me, with a wink, that Grandpa had bit it off.

I recalled shitting in her outside toilet, reading the Sears catalogue, and dreaming of a guitar or telescope that I might someday own.

I remembered gathering eggs and her grabbing and tossing a 4' long bull snake out of the chicken coups without flinching.

I recalled these things, but ignored the recollections. Rather, I glimpsed at my early ability to "compartmentalize" even her, my wonderful Grandma Dot. Other women were easy compared to that.

I wondered what happened to Grandma's husband, my granddad Everett, who had worn my brother's middle name.

I recalled him driving around in a fancy red Buick, frail and smiling sheepishly, hiding packs of cigarettes under the seat, and cleverly hiding from his wife of many years.

Grandma didn't drive and he was like a pale vampire who moved about by day. I could not recall ever seeing him at night. Hum? I wondered when they buried him, or when he passed. He just sort of vanished, like vapor, and I did not notice it until this journey. My powerful dad looked exactly like his father in the coffin: A small, frail vampire, not a red-faced, roaring beast called "*Goddamn It.*"

The sled's passing blended with memory, and I was no longer sure of what I was seeing versus what I recalled.

I seemed to have no time pressure and nothing felt like a test that I would later have to pass. I relaxed and reflected in this frozen state of warm passage.

I vividly recalled my daddy's brother, Luke, sitting down at the age of 38 or 40 in a chair at Grandma's house, breathing heavily and dying that moment of alcoholism and unfiltered Lucky Strikes. I don't recall the funeral. I must not have been invited.

He died in the same old chair where I looked at brown-toned family pictures. It was as though he were always in that chair with me, as though he never left it as a child.

I clearly recalled my daddy looking afraid for the first time ever as the ambulance passed, lights flashing but soundless, with his youngest brother dead in its cargo hold.

I remembered Uncle Luke looking purple and sheepish once as he peeked from behind a tree after running his truck into a bridge railing...and I remembered my family's discussion of whether he was drunk or had experienced a heart attack, given his purple and pale colors that day.

I remembered yanking Uncle Luke's "throttle" handle out of the dashboard and nearly running over a herd of cattle once while riding behind them in his ole green Chevy truck.

After watching him flush with fear and bobble with both hands at the rusty throttle unit for what seemed an eternity (as we *roared* towards the cattle), I recall his toothless, gut-laughing response to my stupidity when he finally pushed the thing back into the dash. I remember now comparing it mentally to the harsh hand that his brother would have delivered for this same lesson.

"Well, hell, that was scary! Don't do that again, ok?" Uncle Luke chuckled, pulling a flat pint bottle from his coat pocket.

I remembered that I loved Uncle Luke's childlike manner, and that he was apparently always a drunk, but everyone loved him. I remember that my brother became just like him, lived like him, was loved like him, and died in a chair, just like him...but sober.

Daddy's sister Donna popped into my head long enough to remind me that she would live forever. I realized that she had the genetic grit of my baby sister, Mary Ellen, but was more intemperate, more defiant, and deliberately unrefined. She was fun and loving.

I also recalled that daddy's brother Francis died as he had lived, without notice, sometime during my college life or thereafter.

I loved Aunt Donna's kids and I loved cousin Red, the oldest son of Francis. Red had been born 100 years too late.

He restored and drove a Model-A truck to high school and never changed his watch to align with daylight savings time—never. I cut off his younger brother Joe's right little toe with the iron hitch of a hay wagon when we were kids. It had to hurt like hell, and it squirted like a geyser, but he seemed to forgive me, as he became much bigger than I. That was an odd and frightening day.

The sled seemed to sense my calmness and gratitude and, thus, jumped over time and events, a quarter century, to Wichita.

There, I saw nine-years in the airplane business and recalled that it was all a falling sensation and my then-definition of hell on Earth.

It was like having a thousand Godless ole men asking you for things in words you did not understand or care about, and calling you names in acronyms without the dignity of direct eye contact, blade-up "wet work," or even a face-to-face slapping embrace.

I only reflected that I had no trust of people after this season. I had a resentful anger that dwarfed all childhood battery, and lingered still.

I was afraid to see a man in a suit for two years after this *career*. I reasoned that this phobia, like acrophobia, had a name like suitaphobia or ropaphobia, or something obtuse for people with my anemic logic to explain things that they did not understand to cleaver people who eagerly seemed to understand and didn't really care.

I gratefully retained the Bomber Plant's gifts of "process thinking," but was as drunken and soulless as I had ever been when I left this *career* path, and as I desperately prayed that God would give me back *any* form of sanity or peace.

The sled, thank God, ran along my next jobs and I saw that they were visible as an answered prayer.

Perhaps this was all I needed, for now, assurance that God had worked in my life *ever*...then I could rest assured, and perhaps even be released by grace, from the *sins of my youth* and from my inability to have and keep relationships.

"Oh, he was such a good, yet tortured man," they would quietly lament in food-filled gatherings around my passing. I fantasized…but then again, I knew that most of them—thanks to my phoniness—really wouldn't know me at all. It was not their fault. I knew that I would be cremated to save money and pomp.

Each person's eulogy was at best an illusion, a check-marked list of human approvals to most people, and a mirror of illusive sharing for judgmental comparison by people who compared their own illusions to those of the deceased.

The sled had almost stopped, so I leaned forward and pushed with both feet to get it moving. I somehow fully relaxed in fantasizing myself dead, quiet, and without hatred, hope, or defenses. I liked being with my brother, his son, and Uncle Luke.

Ah, so this is why I am etherized! Here we were at the deep and dreadful heart of the beast.

It is a place where the very life of the rider is sucked into the color of darkness and the pupil becomes the dream.

The sled, the darkness, and the rider are one. The feeling of being absorbed is so total that one cannot even recall his Christian name. Exhaustion fills one's senses and horrible desperation grips one into crying, "Who *ARE* you?! Remember your name or you will not return to your body and will recall yourself no more."

Death is your nearest realm, closer than life or memory's dying battery. This point is both the highest and lowest in the universe of thought and not measurable by any calculator, judgment, or instrument of man. It is the purpose of the ride and so far beyond reason that to assign it a purpose is vain deception. Not illusion, not delusion—endless nothingness where you can be absorbed and given proper context because you have no context at all.

I had seen this place's twin once before in a dream.

There was an old wooden mansion standing on a knob-shaped hill, surrounded by wind-blown, chest high grasses, and dimly filled with flickering and age-yellowed candlelight, stale water, dead people in séance, dancing vapors, and the dry ice-like misty stirring of an aurora of every imaginable light.

In that dream, I spoke with the dead, verified the age of things as being 175 years, and then stood on the wood-rotted back step, looked into the infinite eternal distance, became drawn as one into the dancing soft prismistically-refracted spectrum of misty lights, felt a gently cooled moist breeze hit my face, and dove uncaring into it all.

I was nearly absorbed into the eternal before I *shouted* my name as a baffled, suffocating man and awoke from the energy drain of it.

My mind was spread across the 40' x 20' room and pressed against the windows like a flat piece of living transparent glass, and I knew in waking that had a window been open, I would have been no more. I recall that in those days, I had only begun to drink and had done no drugs. This is darkness; that place was light, but they are the same place, and they are real.

This is a sober vision; that was a young man's sober dream. Somehow, they are different doors to the same universe.

This time I will not respond with a dying man's reflex by trying to recall my name or scratch at the mountainside to return to my fading earthly body...it is this, after all, that I entered the ride to discover and transcend. Why, then, would I end it by fleeing or awakening to just another masked illusion coincidentally named after me?

I hadn't quite immersed in it. "Go, Sled." I thought. "Reveal the conscience within the illusion."

This time, dark lights have replaced the misty siren's beauty, but the invisible shape of it is the same: Shapeless. And the vast power of it is the same: Omnipotent. In reference to me it is eternal. What is not me is all else, and the color of its cloak matters not.

I now began to fade back into the dull sensation of reality and knew that my answer was not in words or feelings and, while planted and growing, would not be illuminated today.

The ride was over for now. I knew this, and regained the breathing and awareness of sitting alone in New Orleans with its police and ambulance sirens, gothic cemeteries, and 300 years of unseen personal destinies.

I had seen much and discovered nothing. I felt no renaissance or awakening. I had been a child staring at a gravestone to ponder its meaning and a man in his grave staring at himself as a child, yet I had discovered nothing tangible to change me.

I sat feeling beaten and hopeless. *Despair* appeared to join his ever-present mounted brothers and they rode away conversing of castrated and irrelevant prey. I was not worth the kill today and had drained even them of violence and anger.

I felt desperate and empty from the drugless journey, and ached to know that I was still pretending my life to avoid living it. I knew that I had gained no wisdom, had proven no principles, and had returned to a place where I had run Violet cruelly from my life.

I could not blame my stepfather or our abusive family relay. I could not blame alcoholism or upbringing. I could not blame learned phoniness or childhood sins. I had no wisdom and saw only in the empty dark remnant that I was trapped by a lack of knowing why I would treat a woman and a best friend in this cruel and empty manner.

As a coward, I did not die today.

I would miss Violet while I likely lived unchanged and while I invented and projected a new me. However, I would always know that, short of a spiritual awakening beyond the wisdoms within, I would remain trapped in the rehearsal of another act leading only to the hopeless 8-shaped scenes of the acts I had already played.

I still knew that this limited player could not sustain an intimate knowing of another human being or treat them with the dignity and kindness that any audience would regard as reasonable for another run of the performance.

Chapter 13
Good days and Violet

Beautiful things are often simple and the simple matter is this: It began, it was, and it ended. Violet was a creation of reflection, invention, and experience.

I had set my phone's LED-call light to violet when her calls rang, and thus she became my "Violet." This gave her some emotional special place in me. All other callers were blue.

It created and took more energy, faith, and passion to build this love than any before and, thus, like the farm of my youth, it seemed blessed, indestructible, and forever; but it was not.

I reflect now that the nature of love is eternal, and that *love* is a gift of God shared with mortals, yet somehow weakened by the mortal will.

I esteem love to be something which floats about like a wafting translucent blanket, landing unnoticeably where it will, and silently bonding those on whom it lands, until it must leave or the players corrupt it.

I visualized that Violet and I shared a love that had once landed on old ones as they sat on a porch swing, smelling freshly cut alfalfa, and listening to the balmy sounds of purest night.

They had lived in a time when there was no machine, no electricity, and no man-made invention to make noises in the chirping starlight.

They had shared the blanket of purest love in a simple time, and thus found the purest life that could be granted, until they both died and freed the blanket to rise again, like a night mist into a timeless sky, seeking its new landing place and its new inhabitants.

Violet and I were those people for a season, but our mixed character and this floating love were not strong enough to stay the distance in a complex, noisy, machine-filled, depressed, obsessive, electronic, jet-driven, emotional Stone Age.

We did not sit on the porch and listen to the quiet chirping of Louisiana or Kansas nights.

We drove, shopped, ate, and were consumed by carnivorous consumerism in the form of food, cars, CDs, movies, fantasy, perfume, visitation, and clothes.

A fixation with hairstyles, success, commuting, work, color, image, and nails tore at our blanket, and pried and ripped between a city girl's dreams and a farmer's simple way. Add the hybrid demons of fear and insecurity into this chaos and chaos was its faster-growing harvest.

There are not enough words or modern moments to patch a tear in Love's eternal blanket and, when it is damaged enough, it moves on seeking the refuse and repair of two who will fit neatly into its newly torn, yet ancient healing, fabric. Its tearing and healing will often fit with theirs.

As I saw Violet in Saks with her new love, I reflected that what we had was beautiful, even bonded by truest love for a season, but inevitable in its ending.

When I saw her eating with her new love at the Royal Blend, I knew that their recent marriage had reawakened her youth and replaced our once-shared old age dreams. Our "forever" was now for never.

Could an identical backdrop with a new love be anything but another actor playing an identical role in a scene once shared so intimately?

There was she and her new love at Saks, shopping. She and her new love at Petunia's, surrounded by brightly animated gay men, eating. She and her new love at Houston's, sitting at the bar, eating a traditional salad with chicken, drinking iced tea, with two pinks and a blue, laughing. She and her new love in the French Quarter...stopping at Café du Monde...walking. She and her new love ...

I asked her once if it bothered her to use the same pet names on her new love and she said "No." Likely, as always, I misunderstood her, but something died in me that day, or realized that it was already dead flesh.

How could the same words pass through her lips, and even her heart, to another and not feel cheapened by prior wear?

Yet, 12,000 minutes of conversation per month may have been filled only with future echo of words said to a love that was simply not *yet*. Perhaps I was hearing her words to him while *their* blanket of love was searching to find them and our blanket was passing through and merely resting on its eternal way. Likely, we were the accidentally cheapened, and he the destiny.

Why would another not merit new words to describe their unique love? But, perhaps we were not that unique, he and I. Perhaps we were just blow-up or comic book characters in a fantasy world sculpted by advertising and materialism—just another shape, touch, and color in the pretending scheme of it all.

Most likely, perhaps, as she said, I had not known her at all, or perhaps, she was simply a manic actress and I another tryout actor in her unfolding play. He would replace other fallen actors now and play her final scenes.

I surmised that it would *perhaps* take three years and nine months, or roughly 1,367 days, to discover the emptiness of a new actor in an identical backdrop, with identical time—and identical words—but I knew that this was for her to discover and then reflect on, not for me to cynically script.

Her *agreement* was, for once, intense..."That's *NOT* your business," she snarled with a detached greenish-blue stare that made me see her despising me and laughing with him in every backdrop that was once only ours—and others that I could never afford. It was a look of defiance and anger, which hit like a car wreck with its intensity and conveyances. I was the stranger. If it were that I had not known her at all...irrelevant. I did not know her now.

Sour grapes made poor wine for a sober playwright, and she was no longer willing to drink it alone.

The option to this all, and the likeliest truth, was that when removed from being alone with a phone in violet-lighted darkness, and when placed in her personal space, I had failed to answer the call.

I felt the jealous and angry tearing of this dull explosion and finally wished her well, based on faith in her new hopes, and not based on what I knew or saw.

She was not as healthy as she believed, nor I as sick, and all degrees of truth in the middle and beyond. Violet was becoming a sweet and angry memory and not a color or a touch. She now compartmentalized as unbearable pain, which I turned slowly into a fading blue.

How could I process this loss? How could I explain it to my reason or my understanding? Two of four beings in my head helped me.

The analytical numbed and *the poet* awakened to guide me in this wisdom.

The blanket had fled. If it landed on her and her new love, or on lovers a thousand years hence, was not mine to know; it was no longer ours and it was most surely gone from our presence. Her cold stare and recycling of words to another told me this.

With the poet's help, my mind went, out of desperation, from words to sound and vision.

We were as two children playing on flatbed rail cars, jumping and laughing between three parallel trains, and so, we failed to see the movement as they departed while we jumped from train to train to train.

Suddenly, when it was too late, we noticed that we were trapped on separate outer trains and that the tracks had branched—like a cold iron *fleur de le*. We didn't see that the trains were moving quickly now, and that only the illusion of a still-shot had been created for a time as the trains simultaneously gained momentum and moved parallel at identical speeds.

As we helplessly called to one another in our parting, we knew that the illusion had always been a reality...we were always moving into the future at a faster and faster pace believing we were safely together when we were not.

Trains and their cars moving at identical speed gave the illusion of stability and unmoving unity, but when the tracks branched, she was on the car branching right, I was branching left, and our middle car was hurling straight into the unknown.

We called to one another, and then phoned, but, with the growing sound of wind, speed, rail, clanking machinery, and ultimately distance, our calls became faint...then silent. We were no more and our destinations were no longer known to one another or even to ourselves.

If my phone rang violet now, neither of us could say where we were, but we knew that we were not together.

If our trains would ever meet again was unknown and if they were to meet, the prospect of our cars aligning was infinitesimal.

"Fare thee well, sweet Violet," I prayed sadly and softly as the cold and rhythmic sound of real clanking wheels and passing train whistles filled the New Orleans night.

I thanked the poet as we bitterly wept.

Chapter 14
as in water face answers to face, so the heart of man to man

I used to think this proverb meant that one found the truth in another's wise counsel. It doesn't. That is found in other places like, *"In the counsel of many make thy war."*

I see now that the band created music, but indeed, music created the band.

Music, like wisdom, patience, and understanding, has a female persona of its own and we are but beings with butterfly nets to chase and catch its elusive, charming, eternal, and fleeting beauty. To proclaim *the writing* of a great song is as vain as believing one created a child.

You cannot WILL yourself to find them, and I see now, through the eyes of music, that a soul mate can only be seen when you see *his* or *her* countenance as you look in a mirror. One's heart sees its own reflection.

When spirit-filled hearts reflect, you *may* win. When wanting hearts reflect, you will lose. That's what this scripture meant. I saw it in a hotel room window one night when I was lonely, drunk, tired, far from home, looking at myself in the dark window's reflection, and wanting in heart.

I was always looking for something in the eyes of another, for some life-altering direction, simple approval, or respect that I *thought* I needed or deserved. I was always writing poems only to find that they were blind prophecies or music only to find that it had simply re-bent a poem.

I could not find the truth, but by reflection, and that truth came with a time-released remorse and pain that was not what I had envisioned, but rather became a truth that was deceptive "fact-truth," as when someone tells you that you are fat, that you are stupid, or that you are ugly, arrogantly proclaiming it as *"truth."* Whispered in one's own voice it becomes so believable.

Past loves seduce this truth, looking better or worse with reflection. This truth is but a Chinese finger cuff.

Truth, I now see, is God's business. He hides it where He hides music, children, love, and vision.

I looked only for myself in others and found only chasms of loneliness and personal distortions in my desire to then bend myself and love them. Time unfolded a puzzle that was not my vision, yet proved to be so much more in its revealing of other people as angels in watery mirrors.

Each piece of the puzzle interplays, it seems, with other unseen pieces to intersect lives, to *blend* what would have been an individual's time and space and, thereby, to spontaneously begin and end journeys shared by this hidden mixing—no matter what our plan.

Only an unseen Power knew the unfolding of it as we wrung our hands and played our hopeful roles.

What was seemingly cruel was sometimes ultimately healing and what felt like healing was sometimes healing, but was sometimes only a restful pause caused by human exhaustion—God's favorite meeting place.

Character and its defects are perhaps one and the same, like a crowbar that is used for prying—and prying used for good or evil—yet the tugging itself is un-chartable energy for propelling life forward.

Pain often seems unbearable, purposeless, and endless, but it pries unyielding until the being within releases those hostage captives that were held so crowded, and once, so well meaning dear.

How the stirring human batter of past loves became so collectively over-leaven and galumph eludes our best thought, knowing, and prayer. When one is stilled, fresh eyes are offered vision—yet again.

No relationship was wasted. Soul mates do exist. They exist perfectly *ONCE* in the delicate balance of flesh and spirit, good and evil, right and wrong, hope and hopelessness, shared values, principles, differences, similarities, debris, pause, and the simplest actions *or inactions*. They are neither created nor discovered; they are both, formed in finite and infinite brokenness.

We ultimately see one day as we stare into someone's eyes, reflections from a pool of tear-laden spirit, and want only to drink of them, but would die of thirst if the other thirsted less or more.

The mirror of living water tells us that we do not know, that we never knew, and that it did not, and will not, matter.

We only know fully now that we are not alone and that we are reflecting, for the first and final time, the image of a caring God who pressed us sore with his guiding hand and then patiently waited.

She sat...beautiful, small, and silent in the dimly lit meeting hall.

She always arrived late and left early.

Her hands were clasped in her lap and, though she tried to sit deceptively and proudly erect, her head tilted slightly downward, conveying brokenness. She was sad and angry, hurt and in pain—that was clear from her countenance and from a deliberate lack of human contact. She interacted with no one, looked at no one, listened with random teary eyes and detached sadness, and then abruptly left.

She had long light-brown-to-blond hair with innumerable waves and curls that refracted what little light was in the room, as sunlight dancing on a stilling-evening pond. She had a smooth, sad, and angelic face that made her seem somewhere between 32 and 35 years old.

She finally opened her mouth one night and (I thought) said that she was, "Lisa, alcoholic," had, "a couple of 24s," and was, "going through some relationship and job problems right now."

She quickly said nearly everything and nothing in about as few words as I have ever not heard. I was amazed at her minimalist painting with the unspoken.

I wondered who she was and I couldn't stop thinking about her.

My relationship with Violet was over and, for once, I was serene just to be angry and bitter, alone, chain-smoking, and needing nothing today to fill me up. I had taken the sled ride to hell without apparent answer, yet it settled inexplicably in my soul now as calmness.

I surmised that this woman was an aerobics instructor or an avid swimmer because she arrived each night in pink or salmon colored sweat pants with wet hair or hair in a ponytail clipped to the top of her head.

She had the most perfect body I had ever seen: Size 2, perhaps 2-petit, but strangely, I was not attracted to her beauty, but to her presence. Surprisingly, I didn't want to fuck her, I simply wanted to *speak* with her.

I know now that no words can describe a soul mate and that accidentally finding a flawless diamond covered with garbled flakes of coal dust is likely akin to one's first sighting of that person. I know now that one's soul mate may be described by another friend as a person "with a lot of problems."

And yet, honesty, brokenness, and God's perfectly timed grace becomes the dirt-and-pressure-based, dried, molten crushing that makes that person's character, pain, and problems fit perfectly with another's character *defects* and with an accidentally shared repentant readiness caused by the crowbar of life's separate and rutted prying and scraping of spiritual rivers—bending and twisting until they meet and share their ruptured banks, in a debris-filled, muddy birth, and *then* are slowly blended into calm sunshine and sparkling diamond waters.

Two souls could not fit until they were thus hurled, swollen, twisted pure, and basted by life's painful destinies.

The absence of torrential tearing by this unseen *nature* would leave only riverbeds of polished stones and mountains of un-pressed coal—not living water, not diamonds, not eternally mated souls.

Two young and undefiled souls cannot mate until they have endured the seeming earthly hell of a Refiner's fire, and any Godly preacher will affirm that the refiner's gold is not pure until it has been fired and strained, melted and refined, removed of impurity, finally reflecting its beholder. THAT is the reflection one truly seeks. Young souls may be destined to meet, but they will endure the fire to mate.

I watched her come and go in meetings for a couple of months and then, one night, as she sat behind me, I asked to borrow her pen.

She looked at me the way professor Youngman had when I was accused of subversion and then, with a karate-like jerk, handed me a green-inked pen. I pulled out one of my business cards and wrote this note on the back:

"...I don't know if you are in a relationship, or interested, but I keep thinking about you and would like to take you to dinner, AYC? (Sorry for the timing)"

I had never felt more self-centeredly paranoid or obvious in an AA room. I felt as though the entire room was aware of, and misjudging, my honorable, clandestine advances.

The room seemed unusually well lit tonight, like the sun was shining from a ceiling fan.

I sweated as I shook and wrote the note with the card wobbling on my right knee. I didn't want to be conspicuous so I sat nodding and *apparently* obviously listening to people share, with my completed "appeal" in green on the back of my card and the card now slid under her ink pen's silver pocket clip, waiting for delivery.

I sat, tapped the pen, and sweated...tapped and sweated.

I debated giving only her pen back; she would be none the wiser and I would not be vulnerable but, instead, I suffered and thought more.

No, I would give it to her, note and all! But, nonetheless, I would wait until the entire room was not watching ME, as I knew they certainly were.

Suddenly she tapped me on the shoulder and said with piercing eyes, a disdain for my existence, and the unspoken word "NOW"..."Can I have my pen back, *please*?"

I turned super-mechanically RED, and handed it to her...pen, card, and shaky green appeal...sub*lime*ly and with casual movement so that none would suspect my subtle affront. I waited sweating and feeling stupid forever, and for ever trying to know her.

"What an idiot. Jesus, what were you thinking?! Stupid fucking dolt!"

Then I thought better, "No, you're not a stupid fucking dolt...that took courage."

I sought God, quieted daddy, and calmed some, reverting to wet-light red, then a drier pink, then pink, and slowly back to flesh colored again. I did not turn around to look at her. My heart thumped noticeably; I feared that she and others could hear it like Poe's Tell Tale Heart.

She always left early, but not tonight. She stayed and held my hand as we closed with the AA circle Lord's Prayer. Then she turned and faced me, smiled—the first time I had seen that—and said, "I'm truly flattered. Thank you. But, I am trying to work out a relationship right now, so I'm not available."

"If you find later that something has changed, please feel free to call me," I responded unconfidently, and completely surprised by the words.

"Thank you, again," she said. She then hugged me, and I felt clumsy, but absolved of fear, as she walked away.

I knew that I had done the right thing for some reason, perhaps only to let her know that I found her desirable in this, her time of struggle and pain, perhaps only for me.

I had faced my fear, and that was what really mattered right now. For me, a few green words and a borrowed pen were akin to scaling a mountain, fighting a battle, or standing up tall to the ole man tonight. I thanked God for giving me the courage to act *at all* and hoped that it wasn't over, but knew logically, that it was. I felt good for trying.

I didn't see her again in a meeting for awhile, and concluded that, on reflection, I had made her uneasy with my inappropriately timed appeal, and had thereby driven her off to another meeting hall where she could be wounded, heal, and be left alone. I again felt stupid.

It was nearing Easter weekend when my phone rang one night as I drove to a meeting. I did not recognize the number, or frankly, want to put energy into *any* conversation; I let it go to voice mail. When I returned, I was instantly filled with a fluttering stomach to hear this message:

"Hi...umm...this is Lisette, from the Solutions Club...and, umm...if you're still interested in taking me to dinner, or a movie, or something, umm...I'm available, so...Ok, feel free to give me a call."

I was shocked and blown-away. I replayed the voice mail several dozen times listening carefully for spoken and unspoken meanings.

People who lived in the mental high-rise of my brain began to look out windows and lean over railings as I...umm, WE...listened to the message again and again and again, dissecting, dissecting: 37 words, pauses, inflections, punctuation.

First, her name was Lisette, not Lisa...What a beautiful name...no doubt French to go with her petite and soft appearance.

"Second, weeks later she is calling *US*! Yessss," Jumped in the poet!

"Me," I corrected.

My heart leapt for joy, but then calmed itself, shut up the poet, awakened the analytical for cooler counsel, and we all listened together for the meaning of each sound and word.

Mental neighbors listened-in too...nibby bastards, but they also lived between my ears, so no hiding most things from them. It was times like this when I wondered if my program was working. It still seemed that too many people communed in my head.

"Oh, well, it may take us all and we seem to be getting along tonight so, let's analyze," I thought.

The "umm" word several times told us that she was not comfortable calling and that likely this was not normal behavior for her. The words, "dinner or a movie or something," said that she liked movies and might not like dinner because my card had only mentioned dinner, not "dinner *or a movie or something.*"

The poet in me jumped around like a waiter at Petunias and said, "I wonder what *'or something'* means. I wonder if she likes things that *I* like? Maybe she likes just watching movies at home or vegging. Maybe she likes...Oh, GOD, but what if she likes daaancing!!? Oh, NOooo!"

The analytical quickly shut the poet up and commanded, "Listen carefully; let's play it again; don't assume or surmise. This is a critical point in a relationship, being sensitive to her needs and wants when you call her back. Let's learn all that we can now."

Another voice added, "Don't sell God's role short by trying to figure everything out." It was the chain-smoking little sponsor.

Yet another said, "Random inertia...there *is* no relationship yet and may not be. Random events. She's just fishing you as one option, that's all; you're just one option for a good time since her relationship ended." The sociopath.

Another said, "Why are you so worried about figuring her out, about wanting to know what she likes and dislikes? Wanting to put on a mask and act yourself into another three-year slow-death lie, are you?" I didn't recognize this voice, and it rang true.

Sociopath concluded, "Hey, asshole, she may be using you to make her boyfriend jealous as a ploy to fix the relationship...you may not even be relevant." That stung.

"Oh, yeah," I retorted, embarrassed, "Then why would she say, 'Feel free to give me a call'?!"

"Because when the phone rings and it's you, she *wants* her boyfriend to hear the conversation, to make him jealous, Asshole. That's the point. Damn, you're thick sometimes."

Sociopath, A-student prick. God, I hate that guy, what a fucking know-it-all, and he just loves embarrassing me.

"Stop! Jesus, call the woman back," said the little sponsor, puffing on a filterless cigarette. "You are not a healthy group of people to be solving this, number one. Number two, you're second-guessing life, and three, you're second-guessing God. All that comes from this bullshit is fear of the unknown and *action* is the only way to address it. You may all be right, who knows. Let's call her and see what unfolds. Let life be what it is sometimes, ok?"

I dialed the phone.

"Hello," said Lisette too quickly for me to concoct a debonair speech or even breathe.

"Shit!" I thought. "Why can't I draw on the smoothest talkers in my head when I need them? The fuckers are always there giving me advice, but never there when the pressure's on."

Now it gets foggy, but I basically said something about, "Thanks for calling me back, and I was calling you back to see if you were still interested in going to dinner or a movie or something..." or something like that.

"Well, I'm on my way as we speak to an Al-Anon convention in Houma this weekend," she said confidently, "But let me call you when I get back to town and we'll hook-up, ok?"

This was not the voice of the broken woman I had watched weeks earlier. This was a self-aware woman with boundaries, confidence, and clarity of thought.

I felt both relieved and rejected by life's events. I wanted her tone to say that now was the moment she had waited for all her life, and how about tonight or tomorrow for dinner and a movie? Let's get together as soon and as often as we can and live happily ever after—both AA people, healed, whole, delivered from lies, and now fulfilled by fate's wonderful prying and turning of our lives together.

I heard some disharmonious mix of *As the World Turns, Taps,* and the *Jeopardy theme* playing in my head. I could hear the submarine commander in me honking the piercing horn and yelling, *"Dive! Dive!"* I could hear Ice Man shouting *"Engage, Mav, Engage!"* Fear and anxiety gripped me. I began sweating profusely. Hopefully she couldn't sense it.

"Ok," I finally responded. "Nice talking with you. Catch you later."

"Ok, bye," she said, quicker than a gunslinger, and hung up. Gone. Just like that. Gees.

The group of neighbors in my head stood stunned. Dead silence. None were so sure or wise now; even the sociopath was derailed. *"Ok, bye, click."* Hardly room for a comma.

"Autopsy, anyone?" I appealed.

"Well," said Grandma Rua, "You're still in the game. She said she'd call and 'we'll hook-up', right?"

"You're fucked," retorted the sociopath. "She's just being nice." Others began to murmur their thoughts and feelings. I was tired...Hungry, lonely and tired.

"Eat and go to bed," said the little sponsor.

And so I did. I did not know what this event would lead to. Hope sank. I had never called anything correctly yet, despite my best wishes and plans. Besides, I had told Violet that I would never love anyone more, only *better*. What I meant was determined to both protect a new love and to honor love now gone.

I would not allow myself to fall in love as deeply again and would thereby control my passions and emotions to treat any future lover with a more deliberate and detached kindness. It made so much sense to me that I actually believed it.

"We'll hook-up," I heard in my head as I drifted-off to sleep. "We'll hook-up...I'll love better, not more...We'll hook-up...Better, not more...*If a phone rings in the forest and no one answers, did it ring?* We'll hook-up...Better not..."

I could hear water softly and rhythmically dripping into a pan in my sink as I floated..."dripping, ring, hook-up...dripping, ring, hook-up...dripping...ripples...a violet stone...water rings...a-long-and-three-shorts...water rings...a stony well...ripples...*her* face...*heart of man to man.*"

Chapter 15
not a very big talker

Our first date was Easter weekend. We met at a noon AA meeting and then agreed to go to lunch.

One could feel the eyes of the others in the AA group wondering if we were "together" or what was up. I could see that she did not like this at all. I had never dated a woman "in the program" so hadn't even thought about "AA gossip." I had only heard about it. I wasn't one to think of it much now.

I exuded external defiance, far offsetting any internal sensitivity that my mental neighbors and I could muster.

"Fuck 'em," I thought. She, though, was far more experienced with AA circles than I, and not everyone in the circle was healthy enough to wish you well—especially perhaps ex-husbands and ex-boyfriends who were in the program. She was wiser than I.

We drove separate vehicles to a restaurant on West Metairie and sat at a tall table for two with that strained emptiness that forms the vacuum of sound in each new universe.

"So," I asked completely inappropriately, "How old are you, anyhow?" She looked floored and amazed.

My mouth knew better. Any *dating* or *woman 101* told one NEVER to ask *that* question: But, certainly, *never* as a first question at an opening meal of a first date. Whaaaaa?

"I'm 45," she answered calmly, but with a clear question in her eyes as to why any man would *ever* open with that relationship-killing question.

"Oh, good," I said. "I was afraid you were 32 or something, and I didn't want to waste your time if you were near my daughter's age." She smiled forgivingly and I saw clarity in her that attracted me.

"They have good salads here," she injected, looking down and opening the menu.

We talked comfortably and I discovered that she was from deep generations of French blood in the New Orleans area, that she had a HUGE family with scores of cousins and three HUGE brothers. She was 5'4", they were 6'4"...she was *maybe* 110 (and I doubted that), they were 240 and up. I remembered attack chicken and "don't fuck with the ole man" for some reason when she said "...and my brothers take good care of their little sister."

We conversed easily. Nothing felt pressured or forced. That surprised me greatly. I learned that she was spontaneous when we left and I asked if she would like to go to a movie...like, now...and she said *yes*. That surprised me also.

We dropped by her house before the movie, whereupon I met her best and most trusted friend, a "dog," if one could call her that, *Ladybug*. She was a native Louisianan, a Catahoula, and no doubt the most beautifully colored and brightly-spirited animal I had ever seen, of all animals: Like Mommy, like doggie.

Ladybug had short, stout gray and white legs, a powerful looking body and probably weighed 60 pounds.

She was falsely large looking because of flowing hair which parted perfectly down her entire back and which had a predominantly gray and silver impression with light mixes of perhaps a half dozen other colors, including faintly visible black spots, like a Dalmatian. She had white boots that ran ¾ up the front legs from her giant white webbed feet and had white booties on her powerful webbed back feet.

She had a glassy-looking bluish right eye, which contained a perfect dime-sized brown comma. Her left eye was brown and almost glowed red. It was unusual for me, but I took the time to look into her eyes, and felt a sudden sense of creation's wonderment.

Ladybug moved gracefully and, like her Mommy, seemed coy and detached, yet friendly. She allowed me to pet her, but I had the sense that she could engage her wolf-looking facial countenance and teeth to tear someone to pieces if they messed with Lisette. They were connected like sisters.

Watching Ladybug move slowly and invisibly in the yard to catch a wall-perched chameleon affirmed stories I had heard about the Catahoula being a stealthy hunter. Feeling the balance of love, obedience, and subdued fierceness in Ladybug made me now believe buddies who told me that their "State Dog" was a culturally appropriate 600-year old melting-pot mix of the Catahoula Lake Indians' pet and Spaniard war dogs.

Ladybug seemed like a human trapped comfortably in a dog's body, and had the same spirit and personality as Lisette, who now seemed somewhat like a Catahoula trapped in human form.

She instantly liked me, and I her, which was unusual for the farmer in me who had a history of naming, feeding, and eating animal friends—perhaps luckily—excluding Dollar the dog. Mommy accidentally ran over him one day in a dirt-field.

The analytical and the poet agreed for once that this multi-generation French Louisiana lady had selected her dog carefully to reflect her native roots and to affirm her family's connection to New Orleans and Louisiana. Even the sociopath agreed unusually with this dog-selection logic. This was a VERY rare agreement. We were all childishly mesmerized by the two beautiful women. The little sponsor chuckled with childlike joy.

When Lisette told me that Ladybug liked me, I felt honored. Even the sociopath blushed. But, when I thought about the fact that she trusted bringing me to her house on our first date to meet her baby, the sociopath said cynically that it was because I seemed harmless and trustworthy, not because she felt any particular "trust" or attraction to me. Sadly we all agreed with his assessment—a harmless old man with a dog that could tear him to shreds.

Just for closure to the team, I asked Lisette if she had picked her dog because of its strong tradition as the Louisiana State Dog, and because of the Catahoula's reflection of her family's roots and culture in the New Orleans area?

"No," she exhaled, with the look of someone responding to a fool. "I picked her because she has short legs and won't jump over the fence."

Hum? I thought of Yogi Berra's saying *"If ya don't think too good, don't think too much."* What an idiot.

Everybody in my mind's high-rise strolled off embarrassed for my much thinking; even the sociopath seemed to feel sorry for me at that moment.

"Oh," I responded.

We agreed to meet again on Sunday to do something, inasmuch as the *movie and a salad* "date" felt very relaxed.

I had a couple of friends in from San Francisco on Monday and so I called to see if she wished to join us for dinner Monday evening.

She quickly responded, "No. I'm sorry, but I have other plans."

I went to dinner with my friends and then began to leave her messages telling her how much I enjoyed her company and sharing that I hoped she felt likewise.

One day, two days, three days. My messages went unreturned and my spirit began to sink. I thought that we had some connection, but then I began to listen to my mental neighbors reminding me that perhaps I was reading my own wanton reflection in her actions. Perhaps I had not listened or seen at all. Perhaps she did not feel this consecration.

She had told me that she was coming out of a 3-½ year relationship with a man in the program and that she had been badly hurt in the process. This was the man whom she was trying to work out her relationship with when I first handed her my business card.

I failed to ponder that a healthy and rational woman might not heal so quickly or use me to anesthetize her pain. I had not been exposed to many such women in the past few years.

She told me that she had been married to a man in the program for several years and that this had also ended sadly.

I had never dated anyone in the program; she had rarely dated outside of it. She realized how sick AA men could be, likely me included.

My self-esteem *erected* to be recognized and demanded justice. I was not these men! Didn't she know who I was?! I would take one last run at convincing her, and so I called again on day four.

"Lisette," I said when she answered this time, "I've left you some messages, but I decided to try you again. You apparently haven't called back." The air was empty.

"No," she flinched, "I haven't called you back. You are moving a little too fast for me. I told you that I'm just coming out of a relationship. I have a lot of things to work through. I'm in the middle of a fourth step, seeing a counselor, and some things. I'm really not in to jumping into another relationship right away."

I was crushed. It was like having a stone dropped on me. I had never been this wrong with my instincts before. I couldn't believe it.

The sociopath in my head danced around and taunted me like a 5-year old... "Nah nah nah nah nah naaah!"

God I hate it when that arrogant prick is right! I should have listened to him. The poet sat sobbing with rejection. The analytical looked stumped.

The sociopath was right! "Fuck! Fuck! Fuck! When I listen to him, I don't get hurt. I compartmentalize and I isolate and I hurt, but no one knows and so I win. Well...fuck her!" I was angered with embarrassment and my poet was crying like a big baby. I burned with rejection.

"Well, maybe *you* have picked poorly in the past, but maybe now I'm being held accountable for *their* sins. I've been honest and nice to you. Maybe I'm different than them. Maybe I'm better."

It sounded like I was not pleading my case, but simply pleading. Where was my shame?! And, Jesus, I didn't know her well enough to be saying these things.

I felt like a stupid, begging child and couldn't believe trite words like this were coming out of my mouth. I also quickly reasoned that she could hear my anger and might therefore easily conclude that I was a rage freak under my hurt, just like one of the others. I shamed to know that I once was, for a long time.

It all felt clumsy, hurtful, powerless, hopeless, surprising, and ironic. I just wanted to hang up and run, but NO...I had just pled and led with my chin before I thought about how stupid it all sounded, so I had to be man enough now to take the full measure of rejection. So, here it came...

"I know you're a nice guy and all and I've had fun, but I just want to have some fun right now and give myself time to work through some things. You're just moving too fast and that's not what I need right now." There was silence on the phone.

"Shit! Fuck! Fuck! Fuck!" She nailed me and I deserved it. "Fuck!"

"Ok," I retreated meekly, "Well, take care. I'll probably see ya around." I hung up.

The *compartmentalizer* in my head prepared like a seasoned guillotine to do its trusted work and end her once and for all. This chamber of my heart and mind worked even beyond the sociopath to save me from pain and trauma. I suddenly recalled old and repeated uses of this instrument and its chamber of horrors to "protect me." For once, I remembered the price.

First there was Grandma Dot—the prototype. She hurt my feelings and I never went to see her again until she was babbling with dementia. Fuck her. It took awhile, but I won. Compartmentalized.

Then there was Jan, my first college "true" love, and the reaper of my virginity—production unit one.

I trusted her completely and didn't think that my immaturity, occasional blackout drinking, or fits of rage would cause any real relationship damage. But, it may have.

For whatever reason, she fucked around on me about a year into our love, broke my heart to pieces...and broke it for the first time. She fucked a guy from her hometown while I was working on a bridge crew in northwestern Kansas and while she was home for the summer.

I was devastated. I didn't know what to do, so I dated her long enough to study her, analyze her, seemingly "forgive" her, plot, use, and finally reject her when she came to visit me in St. Louis two summers later.

I broke up with her as though she meant nothing and as though I felt nothing.

I almost believed it from my tone and delivery. I did the job *so* well that it impressed even me as being sincere: Draw her near, gain her trust, and destroy her without mercy. Process: Name it, feed it and, then, kill the fatted cow. She deserved it; I was sure of that. I enjoyed the simmered blood of this revenge-filled meal, and then raised my glass to toast her pain.

I visualized shrinking her down to a tiny person who would fit easily into a pint Mason jar.

I shrunk her, poked holes into the lid, lowered her into the jar and screwed on the lid. I carried the jar down the psychic steps of a musty, dark, damp, cold, yellowed limestone rock cellar and sat her on the shelf with beans, corn, onions, crickets, spiders, and beets. There she remained as I exited the cellar, and I felt nothing for her again. She was shut off like a light switch and I felt nothing. Compartmentalized: The process was now cleared for full production use. Out of charity, I left a candle burning in the cellar.

There were others. It was casual now. I could almost yawn and do it. The factory ran with little thought or oversight.

I learned that a combination of strong visualizations, time, simmering resentments, drugs, and alcohol could make me strangely self-sufficient. Unfortunately, I didn't think about the collateral damage it might cause to relationships I *cared* about.

I failed to see that, as I got sicker, compartmentalization happened easier, was automatic, and happened only to those I loved the most. I cared about them.

They were the ones that hurt me because I was oversensitive to their accidental disrespect or neglect; I cared about them enough that things hurt so the compartmentalizer automatically engaged to isolate and destroy them—like killing a virus—yet I justified it as saving them from me.

Aerospace managers ran free in my head while wives and children found themselves going to the cellar.

I was becoming compartmentalized. It was as though *I* were in the little jar now. I didn't really care, though, who was in the jar or who ran free. I only cared that I felt no pain in relationships and that no one really got to know me, except for some reason, my brother.

Bill knew me and I loved him so much that he couldn't hurt me. It wasn't possible. That made me wonder for faint instants about the power of *true* love. Perhaps I had never loved anyone except my brother but, if I could love him, I could love. I prayed to God with some Eucharistic humility, *"Teach me how to love."*

Finally, in an accidental epiphany of pain and searching, I unveiled this cruel mechanism and discussed it in an AA meeting one night, using examples and expressing my fear that, "being sober, the jars might begin to leak."

An old-timer sitting beside me on the couch leaned over when I had concluded my grandiose delivery and whispered softly, "Yeah...they gonna leak."

He raised his long-untrimmed scraggly white bristled left eyebrow, winked knowingly, and smiled. He had been there. Jesus, I was not unique in even that much complication and sickness.

In its final hoorah, I described the process with an actual measure of desperate humility to a psychologist that I trusted and stated, "I compartmentalize to deal with things."

She immediately corrected me in the form of a question. "Perhaps, my friend, you compartmentalize to *avoid* dealing with things?" I knew the truth absolutely at that moment and knew that I could use this undertaker's tool no more to deal with the living if I wanted sobriety, peace, love, or even a breath of interconnected human hope. I had to be vulnerable and feel pain. As Solomon said: *"With wisdom comes much pain."*

That night I went down into the psychic cellar, picked-up an arm full of Mason jars, carried them up the musty limestone steps, walked down a beautiful country road in my mind's meadow, and released each person onto the path, starting with Grandma Dot and Jan.

They returned to their full human size as they departed, and each of them smiled, waved, and walked into freedom and the dusty golden sunset of that meadow, ultimately again becoming small as they got far away and finally becoming invisible in the setting sun.

I vowed to compartmentalize no more. I noticed that Grandma turned and walked towards the city in my mind. That surprised me, her being a country girl and all. I decided to leave the cellar's only candle burning.

I did not compartmentalize Violet's loss, so that pain was still quite fresh, deep, and intense. I did not yet know the end of that or how it would ultimately feel.

I did not compartmentalize my 2nd wife when I walked away for Violet...It was harsh, but I did not allow myself to compartmentalize her or to disown my sins in the matter. She thus remained a sweet and trusted friend in my memories, and continued growing as a friend in reality once the anger and tearing of our breakup healed. The true part of that love lasted and taught me that compartmentalization was not an answer—it was a dark catacomb of delusional escape, and had cost me dearly for so long.

So now, Lisette? She had rejected me and hurt my feelings. Compartmentalizing her was no longer in the rulebook; in fact, the rulebook prohibited it. I felt connection, but not deep attraction or "love" so I had some emotional room to run without defense mechanisms. So, what did the program say? Keep it simple. The program always said "KEEP IT SIMPLE."

I pouted for a while, and the little sponsor finally came to me, wobbling and smoking a half-burned filterless cigarette; he made a simple suggestion. "Trust God, and trust her. Believe that she needs time to work through her pain, know that she does not *know* you yet, and know that you have not yet destroyed this frail, yet potential, relationship with pouting and fits. You don't ever have too. Ask her out again, and be willing to be rejected. Grow up. That's the program's simple answer to your *il*logical, overly complex question. Grow and Trust. See if you get a different result."

This seemed too simple to be true, with the only price being pride.

I knew that she was already fed up with my phone calls and bullshit. This would never work; my past told me that. I wrung my hands, waited a couple of days and made what I knew would be the final embarrassing, humiliating, too-near-groveling call.

"Hi, Lisette, it's Doug again. I just thought I'd call and see if there's any chance you'd like to get together this weekend and do something?"

"Sure," she said. "How about Saturday? Maybe we can go to another movie or something. I'm feeling better after some work with my sponsor and my counselor. That could be fun."

I was aghast.

We went to a romantic comedy movie. I ate popcorn; she did not. I drank soda; she did not. I ate candy; she did not. I talked; she did not. She didn't have a sense of humor; I had too much of one. She didn't like gory or violent movies; I did. She didn't understand abstract dialogue and I lived in it. She did not make me guess what she wanted; she told me. She was quiet, cool, sweet, distant, and calm. I was chatty, heated, paranoid, in your face, and twitchy. She was she; I was me.

She continually cried in the movie and so I handed her lots of tissues. I didn't know if she was crying because of the movie, or more likely, because of the pain that it triggered from her past.

A movie on Saturday turned into a Sunday walk in the French Quarter to see the Easter parades. She met me at my apartment and we took the Carrollton streetcar from there. It was fun.

We walked and talked calmly, like friends. I joked a little and she did not understand. She was guarded and friendly, not readable, not careless with words, not flirty or even remotely signaling openness to romance, lust, or a relationship. She said that she was having fun. I could never have known.

As we walked around the Quarter, we talked about common things, AA things, neutral things, family things. She drank water; I drank pop. We finally stopped and ate salads. I liked her, her directness, and her manners. She was a mirror without reflection. I did not know what she thought of me, anything I said, or any action I took, so I decided to simply keep being *me*. This date was already lagniappe. I relaxed. I resolved that we might be just friends, but couldn't help noticing her soft and reserved French beauty. I thirsted to drink more of the clearly honest waters that ran deep inside.

She allowed nothing but holding hands, and even that in *great* moderation.

She spoke nearly nothing of her past marriage or of her recent relationship. She spoke of her family, of her dog, and of her long-time girlfriends and the role they had played in keeping each other sober for over 12 years. She was obviously very loyal to those that she loved and was very focused on living sober. I could tell that she was a good friend to have, or no friend. Complacency did not seem to suit her.

My instincts were as worthless as the concept of north, south, east and west in New Orleans. Worthless. I had no sense of place or direction with this woman, only a concept that I enjoyed her company and felt safe in her presence. I knew that nothing about me would instantly sweep this person off her feet, impress her, or make her succumb to my charm, stories, jokes, or shenanigans.

I had told her one other time that I was unable to pick up a chip for my 8th AA birthday, and I was incredibly honored when she handed me *her* old 8-year chip on this stroll in the Quarter. I decided not to tell her that this meant we were engaged. That was a rare good choice to be humorless. She wouldn't have found it even slightly entertaining.

When I reached to hug and kiss her goodbye as she stood beside her SUV after our day together, she froze like a soft, cotton-stuffed, cloth-wrapped, hard-on-the-inside, totem pole…hands at her side, fists clinched, neck stiff, head tilted back and lips pressed VERY tightly together. It felt like a hug & kiss form of rape—unwelcome and totally without permission on her part. We had existed in the day at hand and only there, and this day was O-V-E-R. There was no warmth and no hint of a future "us" so I resolved friendly complacency, yet mused and reflected warmly. She had so much character.

Our next date was a day at the Audubon Zoo. We enjoyed a quiet and warm day and walked around holding hands and listening to children talking about animals and theories of animals. It was cute and wonderful to eavesdrop on children's wide-eyed and exaggerated fantasies and explanations of beasts, shapes, and colors.

I told Lisette the ole joke about the guy who was desperate for work, and so, took a job with the zoo wearing a monkey suit because their monkey had died.

I watched her face as I described him putting on the monkey suit, sitting, sulking, depressed, yet finally learning to show-off for the kids and, therefore, ultimately learning to enjoy his new job.

I watched her as I described him entertaining the children by doing tricks and cartwheels on the tree limbs, until a limb broke and he accidentally fell into the Lion's cage next door.

She watched my face intently and without emotion as I described the scene, so I continued, "...and as the Lion approached slowly, the man began screaming with terror *'HELP...OH GOD, HELP, HELP'*...until the Lion came close and whispered, 'Quiet, buddy...you'll get us *both* fired.'"

At this point, she looked at me frustrated, possibly even irritated, obviously without grasping this as *humor*, held her arms out in an irritated shrugging motion, shook her head and said, "So, whaaat? The Lion was an actor *too*?" I nodded and smiled with amazement.

I knew that, if God willed, Lisette would be the perfect subject to see if humor is innate or learned, because she had no hint of it nor did she seem to have the innate mental process mechanics to comprehend humor.

I, on the other hand, had a real opportunity to see how much of my humor was the remaining *mask* from my childhood, aimed only at keeping people from getting to know me or looking too deep—a clown's hell and a scientist's dream. What a strange and unreadable spirit I found myself interested in. Me, speechless?

We spent a wonderful afternoon strolling and being largely silent in beautiful moments of zoo land in New Orleans.

I felt strangely serene and peaceful, but wondered if my new friend and I would really ever connect more deeply or communicate comfortably. Perhaps healing peace was the sole content of our being together for a time. I accepted that as possible and good for us both.

Ironically, miscommunication started real connection.

I called and we talked briefly about going to the upcoming French Quarter Festival, the annual big event in the Quarter, so Lisette emailed me some information about it, whereupon I was to communicate back and we would agree on a plan. Easy enough, right?

I hit "reply," sculpted one of the most wonderful, friendly responses possible and waited on her response. It did not come...one day...two days.

Round two of rejection began to hurt, but this did not fit with the character that I had discovered in this woman. Rather, I believed, if she were to reject me outright in this new friendship, she would simply reject me—a call, very few words, bam, rejection—nothing fancy. But, nothing? This didn't make sense.

I waited and finally called her the Thursday before the Festival was to begin. I asked if she had received my email, and she said, "No, I only received *my own* email BACK...exactly as I had sent it to you...a reply with no response, only my email back."

"Oh." I pondered. "I sent you a long, warm, carefully sculpted, and charming response, AND for once, I kept a copy of it. Would you like me to read it to you and then deliver it to you in person so that you can see I actually wrote it? That's weird. Hum? Let me try to send it again, using the same process to see what happens, ok?"

"Follow the EXACT same process or you'll be tampering and vary the result," the analytical said calmly, yet with unstated intensity, his hand on my left shoulder, as though he were steering us in the Queen's Clipper Ship through jagged icebergs in darkness.

The poet gasped with both hands dramatically across his mouth. The sociopath smirked. Others murmured. The little sponsor smoked and winked.

"Ok, I'm hitting reply...I'm pasting the note I wrote...I'm sending...did you get it?"

"Yes," she said. "Hum? But it's only my email to you again; there's no note from you. Maybe you can just forward the one that you saved and we'll see if that goes through." I did. It didn't for some reason, but this told me that she had some sense of analytical thinking and of computers.

I then read her the response I had written and printed it to hand to her when we went to the Quarter Fest.

We laughed and marveled at how the computer's random decision to dump data left us both baffled as to why the other had not responded.

We analyzed the "why" for a minute, but she quickly lost interest, which told me something about both her taste for analysis and her attention span. She had neither. But, a miscommunication computer glitch actually made her laugh. Maybe she was the offspring of a Frenchmen, altered by abduction long ago, or even perhaps a genetic Cyborg caused by alcoholism. I could work with that.

This event's laughter broke through an emotional shell and into a new level of childlike fellowship that made a relaxed and deeper connection. We both began to breathe easier and knew we would have a ball at Sunday's event.

I knew her boundaries now and was beginning to understand small pieces of her personality. I felt calm and a peace in this knowledge and felt a simultaneous loss of anxious expectation. I felt gratitude towards her for straight speaking and clear boundaries. She had handed me no expectations and had dashed my earlier bullshit with honesty—what a gift from an alcoholic friend.

Then she blindsided me at the Festival.

After a couple of hours, as we were strolling along the river listening to bands, running into and chatting with non-mutual friends, and holding hands, she stopped, turned her face upward towards me over her right shoulder and *kissed* me...not a little peck, not a compliant cotton-stuffed, cloth-covered totem pole feeling...a long, deep, wet, warm, trusting kiss. Me, speechless...*again*?

"You look surprised," she smiled playfully, as we walked on.

My head was spinning and recounting the wonderful taste and feel of her lips, wondering how a simple kiss could communicate so many wonderful things about trust, friendship, and connection.

She could do more with no words than I could do with every word ever spoken. I marveled and felt a pilot light of emotion flicker deep inside as a large, rusty blue and white ship passed and a handsome young deckhand smiled, tilted his hat and blew her a kiss from the river.

I knew that no matter what, I did not want to hurt her. She was like a wounded, yet trusting child with her sweet spiritual innocence and playfully open companionship.

On Friday night, she invited me over and we watched movies.

A friend of hers had dropped off their dog for Lisette to watch. We didn't get completely through the entire movie and I ended up spending the night.

Her older brother showed up early in the morning unexpectedly to drop off some items in her garage and, when he walked in, he said to Ladybug, "Oh, I see you both had a friend stay over."

I knew that, smile or not, this was their family's humor, VERY dry and passive aggressive. I smiled and trembled with insecurity. He was a handsome, but giant and initially stone-faced, man.

The next day, we got up and went to the Angola Prison Rodeo. She drove my car.

Several hours up, a couple of hours of vicarious bull-riding and crafts shopping, a small brown and white cloth prison cow souvenir (to be eaten later by Ladybug), a photo of us in jail, three sodas, three bottles of water, one chicken fingers for her and a Jack-In-The-Box burger for me later, she drove us back to New Orleans.

She allowed me to come into her house for a while that evening and we agreed to go to the Algiers Fest "on tomorrow."

At Algiers Point, I actually DANCED in the light of day without alcohol and without embarrassment or shame while she jitterbugged as though I knew what I was doing—black and white old-timers played traditional Dixieland Jazz. A couple even told us that they had "enjoyed so much" watching us dance.

We bought poster 44/50 signed by the artist, and got Chinese food from the Great Wall Restaurant on Old Metairie Road on the way back to her house.

Her fortune cookie (which I ate) said, *"In love you will be happy and harmonious."*

I smiled to think of the old joke that forces one to add the words "in bed" when reading a fortune, and smiled deeper to know that this fortune still had integrity. How it fit the woman I now saw. I silently prayed and wished her God's will with this fortune, with or without me. This special evening was filled with friendship and intimacy beyond words.

We made plans to go to the Jazz Festival at the fairgrounds that following weekend. She asked me to come over "sometime" during the week to watch movies and I knew that she was risking so much more than she necessarily wanted to.

I wanted to ensure that she was safe with me and knew that I also was becoming spiritually reanimated and on new ground in this strangely trusting and reborn companionship. I actually cared more about her than myself.

The Jazz Fest led to more Jazz Fest and this led to more and more evenings and weekends together.

Finally, as we lay together one night, I whispered to her softly, "Be careful that you don't accidentally fall in love with me."

She smiled, but did not respond, as she tucked her beautiful hair gently under my chin, breathed warmly and drifted off to sleep, cuddled trustingly on my chest.

We emailed, dated, talked on the phone, and grew closer in our friendship and in our intimate knowledge of one another's lives.

I got to know more about her brothers, their families, her friends, and her BIG extended family.

I cherished the idea that she loved and honored her departed parents and grandparents very deeply and that she had a loyal commitment to her friends that surpassed any I had seen.

She was extremely close with family, decade-plus old friends, nieces and nephews. Ladybug and I became buddies as well, growing closer, but with a clear knowledge and respect that I would NEVER surpass her in Mommy's heart.

The unspoken power of Lisette's strong nature tenderly permeated my soul and made me ponder beyond simple thinking the idea of loving *"better."*

With Lisette, I did not have the euphoric chemistry that I had been swept away with in loves before (and had thus crashed recklessly on the rocks of rudderless passion). Rather, I had a gentle and deep knowing that I now loved this person as a best and trusted friend and that I wanted to serve and support her in strangely selfless ways.

To my shame, I was absolutely unfamiliar with these motives and feelings. I knew that this entire affair had been uncharted sea when I listened to the little sponsor and called her instead of compartmentalizing this fragile embryo from the get-go. I knew that I could love her *better*, but I wondered now, to my amazement, if I might not also love her *more*.

I had never apologized for loving deeply, lest it cheapen the loves that followed, and I was too open, perhaps, in sharing that I had loved others very much. She was no less open, though, with her sharing, and that rigorous honesty interestingly became the solvent that removed our masks and the concrete that laid the pylons of deep friendship under this already strong and soulfully growing relationship.

It was one of those moments of awakening for me when she got a phone call from her brother one day. They chatted briefly and then: *"Ok, bye,"* she snapped sharply, and flipped shut the phone lid faster and with more deliberate urgency than any gunslinger could have un-holstered his weapon and fired a shot.

I instantly chuckled and recalled my empty *horror* the first time I asked her out (on her way to Houma) and after speaking heard, "Ok bye click." leaving no time for commas and me feeling totally unimportant, rejected, and shot down.

"So you hang up quickly on everybody the way you just hung up on your brother, huh?" I asked with a dangling pause.

She thought for a moment and then looked at me with amazement that I had just discovered this trait.

"My brother doesn't even *say* goodbye…and, if you haven't noticed, I'm not a very big talker. No one in my family is." She smiled sweetly and left enough paragraphs hanging to make closing arguments at the Darwin trials. Oh, how her eyes could talk, and strangely, I could now understand the words.

"Ok bye click" I reflected. It was childlike and only harsh to the *expectant* ear. Emotionless. Pure. It had no waste of time or words. It had no hint of editorial implication or codependency. It didn't say something hidden.

As a wise old German Jew once told me, "'Let's go to lunch sometime,' in America *really* means, 'this conversation is over.' In Germany, it means 'let's do lunch.'" Lisette was an absolute zero, vacuum-like chunk of pure element in language space.

I reflected for a moment where I had seen this gift before and I saw my daughter's piercing little eyes with her finger twirling absentmindedly in her thick curly hair saying, "Not now Beau," in some child's conversation. Point blank. Unwashed. Pure language.

I knew suddenly and without ability to unlearn this new knowing that both Darcy and I had been compromised by many wasted words and the commas that separated them. I had spent most of my life saying adult words in childish ways because I had too much learning rested on an insecure foundation to be childlike, like Lisette. I prayed that Darcy would rediscover this clear, obscure freedom.

One day, the no-commas girl signed an email, "Love, Lisette," and I asked her face-to-face why she had used the "L" word after so much time. She simply smiled sweetly.

I joked again about getting too close to the edge and accidentally falling in love with me.

"I already have," she smiled softly.

I had to update my thinking and conclusions.

I had always been polite in such discussions out of reverence for another's hopes, but in truth, had always believed that soul mates were a lover's fabrication, most practically conceived as a poet's bullshit to woo his next piece of ass.

I believed that perhaps, best case, they were naïve, well-intended, short-sighted, cleverly spoken, self-fulfilling prophecies of lover's vows, or perhaps a human longing to bond with God through two broken pieces of flesh believing in an undiscoverable myth which would not stand the test of earthly time through their ritualistic vows and thereby *certified* "joining of souls."

Perhaps, I thought, created in His image, man invented God the way God invented man. But that, in our seeking, we cut ourselves off from the simplicity of the Spirit and became wanton seekers of empty fabrications, creating only religious Frankensteins and revered specters, to which we erected temples and deluded both our neighbors and our faintest hopes into worshiping our formless creations and creating an economic pipeline with a building fund and a hireling as its shepherd.

I believed that these shepherds then anointed the *becoming of one flesh*, which people often construed as God's blessing and therefore the foundation to pronounce themselves "soul mates." They were castles, built on sand.

I had seen that man could quote scripture for his own gain and even believe it for awhile, until adversity took his faith and emasculated his concept of an institutional God—leaving him to rediscover his humanness in the lonely rubble of his misguided faith and while sitting alone in his faithless edifice. I was also once that man.

I had always believed that some things were just quests for man and for man's invented gods to know, the concept of a soul mate being one remote ripple of such a skipping stone on a lake of muddy mythology.

I now see that I was looking in anger and not in stillness.

The stillness of a quiet woman had changed my knowing. I see now that I was wrong about man, about God, about love, and about soul mates. I did not even know what I was looking at. I was wise in my own conceit and vain in my programmed arrogance. All that I saw cynically did exist, but it was not *all* that existed.

I accidentally saw flickering of my soul in this sweet mate and in the still deep waters of her wonderfully broken and now reborn soul.

I couldn't have seen it without everything I had experienced, loved, and lost in loves before. I couldn't have seen it in my much speaking or in the skilled battle, hopes, and dialogues of days and loves gone by.

I *glimpsed* at it once in the stripped, selfless and powerless void of seeing my brother and his son buried under the barren fall and winter of a brown-grassed Kansas prairie.

I saw it again when I accidentally paused and looked into the beautiful stillness and serenity of this crowbar scratched and pried deep pool of once troubled, and now calm and mixed, healing water.

Wisdom is indeed a woman who delights in the children of men and who helped form the universe with Her unseen Kinsman.

One day, as Lisette and I were following a car full of teenage boys, one of them opened the back door, tossed a can, and puked from overdrinking in the streets of New Orleans.

"What a pussy," Lisette chided with experienced disdain. "Can't hold his alcohol."

One day, her nine-year-old nephew and his parents came by to drop-off some furniture and belongings, and after we had worked for a while, I offered him a drink of my open pop.

"No thanks," he said politely, "I can't drink it because you've been drinking out of that can and you're not married yet."

His concept of purity was so childlike that even I understood the refining of his Aunt's honor.

She and I married March 25th of that year.

Chapter 16
The BIG Sponsor

The tent pole of my happiness would be given, not by college or a joint, but by a simple man who launched me into a life of sobriety—John A. The farmer in my heart bore flowers and fruit in the garden of an ole sailor.

The little farmer knows intuitively that everything spiritual is patterned and oft hidden in *nature*.

Some things look good, but don't make sense, while other things make sense, but simply don't look good.

Some things neither look good nor make sense: Is the Buddha beautiful? A black or white Jesus? How about Mother Theresa? Ringe's nose? Las Vegas in the daytime? Someone unhappy in a mirror?

How our minds are patterned is not natural and is often hidden only from us, but not from our neighbors. *"The fool goes down the road telling everyone he meets, 'I am a fool.'"*

Some socks that enter the world as a pair emerge from the laundry as orphans and are then worn by their masters as a pair that does not match.

Scoffers see the obvious and claim that the wearer is color-blind, poor, without style, without decency, or perhaps even without proper mental capacity.

Trite conclusions are drawn in seconds by well-dressed and well-educated people about people they do not even know. How much easier is it, then, to despise a family member who wears mismatched socks as an act of defiance?

Mismatched socks must surely be the mark of a poor man, of a hapless drunk, of a homeless person, of a person with low self-esteem, of a rebel or, naturally, of hand-me-down, yard-sale trailer-trash folks.

Old men are forgiven, young men are teased, and women reap the horror of being condemned as invisible to the onlooker—all from a sock, which has lost its mate.

The clever man deceives his neighbor by buying only one kind and color of socks so that he always has a matched pair. No one is the wiser for his trickery and only he bears the angst of fearing their rejection and the pain of wearing their approval. Only he is aware that beneath his perfectly matched socks is a soul in yearning for affirmation—all covered by a matching sock, which has lost its mate.

And, what of a man who is twice divorced or a woman who has slept with too many men? Are they not also socks without mates seeking someone who can wear them without shame or condemnation? Possibly their truest mate is someone just like them, or their opposite: Matched or unmatched socks that lack mates.

There is a *nature* of life in the farmer's universe: Things get dirty. Things break. Things get old. Things don't always match or stay shiny. Parts come off to fix other broken machinery.

Whether the chicken or the egg came first sounds nice, but chickens make chicken shit and chicken shit scatters with a mechanical shit-spreader to make corn grow, corn makes cows grow, cows give milk, milk feeds farmers and chickens, farmers raise corn and maize to feed the cows, and everything spiritual is patterned and oft hidden in nature.

A Farmer's socks frequently don't match and, there, no one cares. That is their acceptable *nature*.

Why this precursor? Simple. Without it, one cannot explain John A. His socks often didn't match and neither did the beauty of his life match with the crudeness from which it sprouted and grew.

Like the farmer, John A's life took time to make any sense, yet left footprints in so many people's sand that even God needed John's simple help to feed and carry the people he touched.

He was a hapless drunken sailor who ended up an alcoholic master chief and used these things simply to drink more until he could surrender with defeat and thereby master his own heart.

John's tale is a simple tale and John was a simple man who repaired and methodically re-matched old socks.

It was likely the year that we were sled ridding off the barn roof when John found himself serving as Navy shore patrol in Japan.

Likely about the day and the moment we were sliding and falling down the magic mountain of snow, John A was drunk, sliding and falling down the sculptured steps and green flowered hillsides of his soon-to-be-wife's hometown. He had not yet met her and, so, had not yet started falling down the sculptured steps and green flowered hillsides of her specific family's home. That would be later.

Destiny would intertwine their lives and his lack of culture would join with her abundance of it to make a lifetime pair of strangely matched socks.

John's wife waited in time's clear abyss to meet her destined husband and unfold their unlikely shared journey.

She came from a cultured and educated Japanese family with money and deep pride. She was the brilliant and defiant daughter who would fall in love with a simple sailor. She was a seasoned martial artist and was trained in culinary masteries. She was honing these skills and working at a navy office in Japan as John practiced his young, yet ascending, drinking career and plummeted toward meeting her.

John was a nice guy, and obviously charming in an earthy way, or beautiful Toy would never have given him a look—not to mention that he was American, white, and military.

The fragments of World War II were still fresh wounds beneath the forming industrial hum of a newly reconstructed, proud and humbled empire, which seemingly exported only *Cracker Jacks* toys to its new conquerors.

When they did meet, John and Toy fell quickly in love and knew that they had some strange trans-cultural, inter-and-transcontinental joining of souls.

Given his nature, his love for Toy, and abundant bottled blinders, it was easy for a man like John to ignore silent hatred and scoffing from the local folks while he went about living his navy life.

Her family was cautious and fearful, but John was young and happy, so his life-force inspired her to believe and their life together seemed euphoric, raceless, and without man's false horizons.

They believed that together they could close the wounds of history and build a history of their own. And so they would.

She worked in the Navy office as he progressed up the ranks as a Navy enlisted man.

His respectful, forgiving, and kind nature served him well in his job, and, although he was stout and had also been trained in karate to the level of Black Belt, he rarely needed or used physical confrontation to carry out his duties.

A typical night was when they were called to the site of a confrontation and a sailor decided to jump in the water and swim away from arrest and detainment.

John ran along the pier and followed the incredible swimmer to where he emerged, amazed at the strength and speed of his drunken perpetrator.

As a young Tarzan emerged from the water, John stood in his path seeing clearly now that he was strong, now sobering, able, and in shape.

John surmised that it was no wonder the *other* guy was laying in a heap, hurt, bleeding, beat-up—but teeth intact and healable. Drunk or sober, this guy could have done it to three people.

"You're not gonna make me get hurt doin' my job tonight, are ya, sailor?" John smiled. "I've got a date later, and she needs *all* of me workin'."

"No," said the sailor, responding to John's humility and humor. "I've caused enough shit for one night. I'd appreciate it if you can do anything to keep me out of the brig, though, Buddy. I know I fucked-up."

"You can count on me," John said with integrity. "The other guy ain't dead or dying and we're all just sailors."

As his drinking progressed and he fell down the hill enough to embarrass his new wife, she insisted that he get some help.

He intuitively sought counsel at a local bar and discovered that there was a *chant* for stopping alcoholism. All he had to do was become a Buddhist and perform the chant each day. John saw this as two birds with one stone, since his sweetie was Buddhist and tired of his drinking. It didn't work, unfortunately, but he became a Buddhist for 16 years, nonetheless.

He was now becoming the one who had to talk himself out of the brig.

His behavior got more and more out of control as he drank more and controlled himself less.

His wife was tired of his behavior, and was ready to netsuke his nuts as restraint. He embarrassed her family, and the Navy was out of patience, threatening to kick him out, even though he had invested a few reenlistments.

He didn't want to lose his wife and he didn't want to lose his career, but chanting had not worked and he was drowning in an uncharted, high-content, low-cost, foreign sea of alcohol.

His buddies had covered for him all they could when he showed up for duty drunk, or not at all, and though people still liked him, he was out of chances. He was finally shipped back to the States and that was when it happened.

One night, the drinking had become so severe and had gone on for so many weeks that he was hospitalized and found himself with a medical team and a stopped heart.

They revived him with God's help and told his wife that he was stable, but would never leave the VA's psych-ward where he was imprisoned. He had done too much damage to himself physically and mentally.

John had taken a couple of runs at sobriety; he knew that he had created a problem and he knew that the solution was to stop drinking. He just couldn't.

He even sobered-up with a little help from AA and others for 11-months and 3-weeks one time, but then relapsed into a motorcycle wreck and a split upper lip, which would leave a noticeable scar running from his right upper lip to his nose for the rest of his life.

He now found himself destined for life in an institution. Thoughts of his wife and the life that he had dreamed for them drew on his humble and kind *nature* and he cried out to God for some final help. Something happened. He began to get better.

He had damaged his system, though, with cumulative effects and with his latest run, and so, the doctors had to put him on a variety of medications to deal with what was now diagnosed as something like, "manic-depressive disorder with episodic paranoid-schizophrenia," plus or minus a couple of other impressive prognoses.

The Navy gave him a medical disability discharge to give him a chance at free life and to avoid paying in-patient care bills for the rest of his life. They shuffled the frail shell of a man out the front door to what should have been statistical hell in the streets of relapse, return to the VA's psych-ward, and institutionalization or death. But, that didn't happen.

John A's parents knew him to be a solid *natured*, but not literate, man and so they went about using character, the spoken word, and focused action to teach him something they were now both quite good at—sobriety.

John's dad and two of his friends sat John down on the couch of their living room and told him their AA "story" one after the other, marathon, nonstop.

One man sat snugly on each side of John while the other stood in his face and told his story.

John's mom and dad had each been sober for several years and they had strong programs. They were not naïve about their son's chances or about the power of alcohol to kill him. They knew that this was life's last chance to save their son. The year was 1971; the day was January 29th. John had turned 32 four days earlier.

On John A's sobriety date, I was no longer sledding from the barn roof, but was sliding down KU's *Hill* of early danger.

The affliction had grabbed me four years earlier and I was enjoying it fully. I never dreamed then that I would become an alcoholic or that our common master would lead us to a deep and eternal friendship over 25 years later.

John and I were mismatched socks. We would never look quite right together, but we would eventually fit like only old pieces of hand-me-down, hand-stitched remnants could. Timing is everything.

I was sitting in a meeting at *New Life Group* in Wichita. I had been coming there for perhaps 18-months. I was pushing two-years of sobriety and my first sponsor, Bob S, who looked like a lumberjack, had just moved to Chicago to follow his computer consulting career.

That night the topic was *"Serenity"* and as we went around the room, each person shared his or her experiences and thoughts on the topic. When it came to John A, he said, "I'm John, and I'm a alcoholic…October 25, 1986…" He stared blankly into space as a child who was looking at the night sky. Perhaps 15 seconds of silence passed, and then he said, "…and that's all I got."

I was puzzled beyond words.

John A looked like some Pillsbury prototype of a navy master chief mixed with the sitting Buddha.

He was round, shaky, clumsy, unbalanced, earthy, fragile, strong looking, and truly had the Buddha's character shape and countenance, including a measure of stomach showing from under his (usually untucked) shirt. His pants usually sagged because his belt had missed a loop or two while being threaded around his protruding waist.

He looked like a master chief because he had faded Navy tattoos, a three-day beard that covered his face and entire scalp, a scar that ran from his upper lip to below his nose, and a tandem roughness engrained only by alcohol's night school of horrors that felt rough, scarred, scary, and unapproachable.

He had never said anything mean or frightening, and I had never spoken with him, but he scared me.

His voice was high-pitched and had a dragging, slow resonance, which did not quite fit his appearance, yet could only be his to carry.

His words had a slow four-count delivery with each syllable neatly dissected for studied ingestion—likely his own. There was always a four-count of silence between the first two words and the next four. Then each syllable of the next four words would be chopped-up succinctly and rhythmically. Then two more words, a four count, chopped syllables. It was not deliberate or calculated, it was just John. I had never seen a being quite like him...terrifying and childlike.

I pondered for a few weeks and finally asked an old-timer named Bob O what the hell John meant the other night when we were discussing "Serenity" and just gave a date in 1986—and then said, "and, that's all I got."

Bob said simply, "When you've got as much sobriety as ole John, you can say pretty much any damn thing you want to." He smiled with a smile that said, "Hell I don't know...ask him," and so I did.

When I saw John at a meeting a couple of days later I gathered my courage, walked up to him after the meeting, recounted the event, and asked him what he meant.

He said, "Well, let's see...we were talkin' about serenity and I got to thinkin' about a time when I had serenity for almost a complete 24 hours...and then I got to feelin' what it was like to be in that day...and had nutin else to say about it."

Wow. I wanted that. I would settle for serenity for 5 minutes!

I told him a few days later that my sponsor had moved to Chicago and asked if he was taking on any new sponsees right now.

He said he would sponsor me, so we agreed to go to the noon Saturday meeting and then go to lunch for a kick-off chat.

I entered the idea with excitement, fear, and trembling of this man who was 27-years sober. I saw him as proven experience and hope to help me give up being uptight and childish and for becoming serene and childlike. I wanted to be serene and childlike instead of childish.

We attended the noon meeting at New Life and hung around for about 30 minutes after it, chatting with other drunks, whereupon John gave me his first piece of sponsorship.

"There's the *meeting*, the meeting *before* the meeting, and the meeting *after* the meeting, is how I was sponsored. I like to be at *all* of them. That's were you really get to know what's going on in people's lives and where you really get to know other people...and they get to know you." Then we left to go to lunch at Applebee's.

I had a secret "kickoff" speech saved up that I knew would impress even someone with his time in the program.

As I drove, I talked about how my sponsor had moved to Chicago, how I had worked through step 12 with him, and how I was really doing pretty well.

I then paused appropriately and told John that I did have something bothering me, though. (It really wasn't bothering me as much as I had indicated, but I wanted him to see that I was both generous and forgiving and that I was working a good program.) I needed him to see that he had made a good choice in sponsoring me and that I had my shit pretty much together.

"There's a guy in the program, Mike P," I recited, "that had his car break down in Texas, so I used my credit card to pay a $2,300 repair bill. I knew what I was doing, but now I find out that he also borrowed $2,000 from Paul W for some other stuff, and now he doesn't seem to want to pay either of us back, or even mention it. I'm concerned that Paul may even drink over it, and I don't plan to drink, but I do have a resentment and I'm wondering what I should do about it."

I waited for him to ingest 1) that I had been so generous, 2) that I had already been patient, and 3) that Paul and I had both been fucked by another well thought-of member of the fellowship.

John's response was amazingly fast for a man who predictably had a rhythmic, high-pitched, four-count pause in delivery.

"THAT'S BULLSHIT," he barked, suddenly looking like a 280 pound growling bulldog and not the Buddha! "You're talkin' about personalities and not *principles*. This is a program of *principles* and if you let shit like that eat you up, you'll let circumstances control you every day of your life, and eventually you'll drink."

I was stunned, embarrassed, and every like emotion possible. I was speechless. My impress-the-new-sponsor strategy had blown up on the launch stand!

"Oh, shit," I gasped silently, "He's an old-timer; a real one! Oh, fuck! I've got myself an old-timer. Shit, shit, shit! This fucker will beat me with discipline and work me to death!"

Then I got shock number two. He laughed. "You'll be alright," he affirmed. "Just stay away from the bullshit. That's not the stuff to let run free in your head. People like you and me can't let that shit take root in our head. I'll buy lunch."

"No," I said. "I want to buy lunch. I asked you to sponsor me; the least I can do is buy lunch on our first meeting."

"Well, fine, then," John chuckled. "But someone like me will get a resentment about buying someone lunch as fast as I will about them not paying me back $2,300 bucks, or bumming too many cigarettes and not payin' me back. You may be healthier than me, but it's not about the size of the thing, it's about the principle of it. I like to play the big shot sometimes, and that means that you need to let *me* buy...or I'll resent the hell out of you for not letting me play the big shot...but I'll resent the hell out of you when you don't pay me back later too. Doesn't really matter. It's my *nature*. Lunch, cigarettes, or $2,300...it's all the same. Principles...Ok, I'll buy next time."

He laughed out loud and I knew that he was the bulldog, the Buddha, and the child in their care.

I felt safe suddenly, which was not natural or comfortable to me, but with John, I knew that God had given me a gift and I loved him instantly with the trust of a reborn son.

He never yelled at me again in nearly five years of spending hours and days together. We became close friends and I learned more about living from watching this gentle man than I had learned from life on the farm and two college degrees. He taught me with his actions. He taught me with his stories. He taught me by being honest. He taught me by being human.

John was nearly illiterate, so, when he read or wrote me something, I knew that it was supremely important. His shaky, childlike, misspelled writing in the front of a book that he gave me told me of the pain that he had felt discovering it, and I knew it was important to me.

His quoting of the *"Big Book"* made me know that he had learned it because it was important to his life, and now to mine.

His pointing out that alcoholics are *"childish, emotionally sensitive, and grandiose"* from the *'12 and 12'* made me know that it was my nature, his nature, and the nature of every recovering drunk to throw fits and act like a baby, using grandiose words and booming voices to cloak it as *manly*.

Honest stories of his childhood and of his struggles to keep a marriage and a family on course made me see that it was not something magical that would simply fall into place after a few decades of sobriety. It was spiritual work.

His battles with depression and life in sobriety made me know that our once proclaimed courage-building friend, *Alcohol*, was not "in the parking lot doing push-ups" as some said, but was in fact in our *heads* learning everything about our programs that we discovered, waiting patiently with the four-horsemen and their growing legions to finish our lives at relapse junction.

John was powerful and childlike in every way and did more good in his simplicity of staying the course than most great men would do in a lifetime of preaching and teaching their chosen protégées.

I learned that Paul W was also one of John's sponsees, and chuckled silently to know that he had also likely been given the "THAT'S BULLSHIT!" speech when he bitched about his loss of $2,000 to our fellow member: Principles: Lunch, cigarettes, $2,000— all the same.

As John spoke one day, I knew that my mind could process his slow dialect and still ponder related thoughts, so my thoughts echoed others who had sponsored and mentored me and I felt a gratitude for recurring sponsorship principles, for God's loaning of shepherds and angels, and for His answering of questions that I did not yet know to ask.

I remembered Bill Cape, a college professor who saw something in me when I was thinking of dropping out and letting Vietnam have its shot at me. Bill looked like a 6' 5" stooping Richard Nixon because of his facial features, black hair, and bad back, but he had so much integrity and passion for politics and for life that each seemed respectable and redeemable in his presence. He taught me some things deliberately and some things accidentally.

Deliberately, he coached and guided me on through a bachelors and then a masters degree, and let me know comfortably that even a farmer who can't pass IQ tests is not alone or worthless while teachable.

Accidentally, he showed me the unspeakable horror that can befall a man when his brother's car runs without braking into a semi-truck that is lying on its side on a dark, rainy interstate, killing the entire family.

The look on Dr. Cape's face as he shared this nightmare's dirge locked into my mind forever and, though young, made me know that no amount of character, ability, or education can transcend the sudden dark power of a fully broken spirit.

He died within a year of that incident and never recovered his sparkle, leading me to intuitively save this sad loss and reflection for when my brother and his son would die, one of tragedy, one of a broken heart, like my mentor for his brother. Dr. Cape inspired me twice to keep living.

I recalled with more clarity now, coach Ringe's looming countenance and hole-instructing nose as he gently took me under his wing, coached me, gave me rides to cross-country meets, and banged my head in class for brief ADD awakenings.

I remembered his caring for me, strongly, silently, harshly, lovingly, and without words or grandiosity. I learned to see the world through his strength and through his heart, not just through the kid-popular giggle of mocking it through his nose. I began to learn that cynicism is mean and evil and that popularity has costs. Ringe inspired me to keep living.

I remembered Paul Larner, a large, lanky, quiet, gentle and sad, Ringe-looking old man with a large and hairy, yet complete, nose. Paul quickly sensed my fear and adopted me as a grandson-like friend when the ole man moved us to the farm in 1953.

Paul was our landlord and owned about 1,200 acres that we farmed on a sharecropper arrangement.

He would bring me fireworks on the 4th of July, would haul me around with him in his fleet of new vehicles, would let me shoot his rifle, and even gave me an occasional can of beer to drink while we worked on machinery at his shed or rode from place to place in the countryside—not wimpy beer either, Coors, 6% in a steel can that had to be opened with a *church key.*

These were the days before an aluminum, pop-top, sensitive guy, throwaway world, when a man who squeezed a beer can flat with one hand, or smashed it flat against his forehead was really a *"man."*

I remembered watching hired-men do this and thinking, "Wow...someday I want to be able to do that!" I barely had time, though, before technology replaced this American era with Japanese genius, and ironically, imported not only Deming's cars, but Sapporo in a 20-ounce, silver colored, tough to bend, steel can.

Paul Larner lived with a fiery redheaded, yet plain looking, woman named Bertha and made her keep a *"For Rent"* sign in her window so that they did not inadvertently become common-law married.

I heard my parents laughing about his shrewdness on that and other matters, but they did not know that children listened, nor did they know the man that I knew. I felt so safe with him and appreciated so much that this lonely old man treated me as a friend and as an equal.

I appreciate so much also knowing now that every ole man who hangs out with kids is not a child-molester or a reprobate. Some are simply surrogate grandfathers and unlikely angels, shepherding God's frightened lambs from the midst of troubled waters and a wolf-filled wilderness. Paul inspired me to keep living.

As John spoke, I thought of managers and mentors who had nurtured or frightened me along the way, yet taught me new and quantum ways of discovering life's processes and dealing with its uncertainties.

I thought of Don Hanna, a brilliant, athletic, cool guy from my hometown, and an elder classman at KU, who, perchance, saw me walking out the back door of the fraternity on my first day of school, wearing a BRIGHT red, collarless terrycloth shirt (with a white terrycloth circle at the neck) and PERFECTLY matching red, fluffy terrycloth socks.

"PLEDGE! YOU FUCKING DOUCHE BAG! GET YOUR ASS BACK IN HERE AND PUT ON ACCEPTABLE ATTIRE TO GO TO THE HILL," he barked loudly from 90' away! "YOU WILL *NOT* EMBARRASS THIS FRATERNITY BY GOING TO THE HILL DRESSED IN THAT MANNER!!!"

I learned best this way—honest, clear, and brutal. I began to observe how others dressed and mimicked them from that day forth. It was humbling yet freeing—A reproving *process*.

I thought of the City Manager and the County Manager, of the Major-General, of the retired School Superintendent, the Aerospace President, the Admiral, the Captain, the Commander, the Master Chief, the brilliant, harsh & horrifying Program Manager From Hell, the wise Transit Deputy GM, several Bills, Mrs. Paris (my WONDERFUL 1st grade teacher) and other teachers who pulled me from the bone pile of ignorance and foolish stupidity—sponsors who loved me enough to tell me the truth and, now, John A.

Some of these people I hardly knew at all, yet revered and learned from as naturally as a gifted word-slinger in a neologistic puzzle match.

Some I loved and knew simply as family. When in doubt, I often used my childhood experience to trade pain for knowledge, knowledge for experience, experience for wisdom, wisdom for principle. Others had learned likewise and I was drawn to them. Most were naturally brilliant, and would have tested so. I reasoned that I could learn from them, test poorly, and perform well. Each inspired me to live fuller and keep living.

I visualized ole man Wendler flying over in his airplane and yelling "wooorrrkkk," trailing vapor and profanities at me from a prop-churning sky, and I smiled.

As John A spoke, I cued from his words and recounted the days when I did not want to live. I also thought of the joy and experience I would have missed by leaving too soon. I remembered fringe moments that made me know if I did, or did not, want to live. Each was a vision fainted with time and dulled with chemicals, yet waiting patiently in its smoldering flashback chamber to be reaped. John A's stories awakened and clarified these sleeping memories.

I recalled a time when the ole man came home drunk and, of course, thus, happy because in the early days, he was only nice when he was drunk—later he was never nice.

On this particular night, his drunken euphoria and expectant warm reception clashed with the ole lady's PMS—and perhaps evening abandonment issues—so when he entered the front door of the house—which happened to be in the kitchen—Mommy swept back like Mickey Mantle and fired a doughnut cutter full-speed into the center of his slightly down-tilted, farmer-tanned, exposed bald head.

All I recall was watching a perfect, quarter-sized "O" of blood ooze out of his scalp from the inner "hole" of the cutter, and a shocked and frightened looking man fall backwards as though he had just received, not a small tin doughnut cutter to the head, but an upper cut from a desperate boxer. He was stunned. I didn't see that look again until years later when he was lying on a stretcher waiting to die. But, that was not where it ended, nor is that why it is tied to life-or-death clarity for me.

Mommy, being as bipolar as me, grabbed my hand as I gawked-upward at the scene, yanked me, and marched us across his falling, retreating, body and into the warm, muddy, rain-soaked summer yard.

"I'm going to take your goddamn *new* car and run it off in the ditch and kill us both, you son of a bitch. Then who's gonna work your fucking farm while you're off drinking and fucking who knows who!? I've had it up to my fuck hole with you!" (Oh, that saying! Like chalk on a blackboard, even then!)

I remember pulling back to keep living (even though I would be staring into the medicine cabinet a few years later asking myself which pills might kill me painlessly). I remember then weighing the prospect of living *ALONE* with him tomorrow against dying with her tonight, and then compliantly getting into the car, but I also remember not yet wanting to die.

I don't remember any of the details, or his appeals, or what the words were saying as I was weighing her sincerity and intent, but I do remember believing her and so feeling relieved as she backed the car around in Uncle Francis' drive a couple of miles down the road and took us back home. (I try to not associate this conditioned trauma with a woman driving us to Angola Prison.)

I recall the job that I had the summer after Daddy died and pulling out in front of an oncoming car while mowing ditches south of Dighton, Kansas.

I remember hearing the blaring horn, standing upright and *instantly* on the tractor's brakes, stopping, and feeling the large blue Chrysler's bumper bounce off the tractor's left front tire—just the rubber, not the wheel—and thinking that a micro-second had saved my life. I realized that I definitely didn't want to die that summer. That felt new, freeing, and hope-filled.

So, what had sponsors and mentors taught me? As John spoke, I knew that those who meant the most to me, and who had altered my perceptions most, had taught me principles, processes, and to face life as a great and unique discovery—childlike, not as something to fear from the waning crowd's approval or from a shadow's cloak. Life was *living* life.

Many of them had taught me with tones of the ole man, but with an honesty that helped me see better and "fit" better in life. Now, John was inspiring me to live, and not just live, but to embrace the adventure and live fearless in a secret knowledge of God's daily protection.

"Go to work for God," John would repeatedly say. His mother had told him that before she died.

I realized the unlikely forum of this unlearned man and an "educated" farmer fellowshipping for mutual growth because of a common malady of the spirit. I realized, through John, that nothing was wasted as long as one can keep living to perceive it.

"Time takes time," John said, quoting Bob O, who was probably quoting John A. Each block built on another...lesson upon lesson, stone upon stone. I felt an unlikely mating of scuffed thumbprints, mismatched socks, and tattered souls.

I recalled old-timers answering the newcomer's question, "How did you get so many years of sobriety?" with, "Just don't drink...and don't die," and I knew that the simple truth of it was simply true. John A was living proof to me and his experience filled me with hope, strength, and a will to live.

Chapter 17
Now that was weird

John A told me of a time in early marriage and early sobriety when he reverted to old behaviors, got angry, and poked his wife in the chest, while poking and shaking his right index finger at her. He described with a still-fresh, stark, and childlike horrified clarity, how Toy's small hand sprang instinctively, and almost invisibly, from stirring culinary master to stirred martial artist, grabbed his shaking finger, and dislocated it at the center knuckle, leaving it dangling like a twitching, emasculated penis.

"Shhyouuuu no poka me, sshJohn," she commanded sternly with her brown, brilliant Samurai-like eyes dancing side to side and burning a hole through his now-startled gaze.

They reset his finger, were silent for a while, allowed him to pout like a baby, and then made love. He never poked or shook his finger at her again and one of two brilliant sons was born nine-months later.

John struggled with depression and episodic schizophrenia all of his sober life. He was childlike and honest about these experiences and understood better than anyone the strained effect it could have on his marriage.

He knew that his wife watched him closely, monitored his meds, insisted on feeding him healthy food, and was a taskmaster about his daily routines. She was as impatient as he was patient, as grown up as he was childish. He resented her sometimes, but allowed her to set him straight nonetheless.

"She loves me so," he repeatedly told me, proudly, and with childlike amazement. "I don't know why."

John constantly taught me things about life and sobriety by using the word "I" and then talking about his own life's choices and experiences. "Sometimes I like to play the BIG SHOT," for example, told me that I was acting like a know-it-all ass and playing the Big Shot. I learned more from his simple stories and tales about his life than I likely had from my own experiences. To me, he was a watery mirror of Godly reflection.

He was a simple man and a simple sponsor. Some old-timers would beat a sponsee to death with the Big Book and other AA literature, quoting it and quoting it and quoting it and making sponsees read it and read it and read it. John did not. *We* didn't learn that way.

He knew that even though I had a master's degree, I hated reading, and we shared that contempt. Neither of us learned best that way.

He taught me through stories of patience, stories of acceptance, key pages in the Big Book—449 and 552 being the core— acceptance of life and two-week's of prayer for another who had offended me. It was that simple. To him *the book* was that simple and his program followed, simply.

John wobbled like an old penguin when he walked. He sometimes got out of the car and began falling off to the right, whereupon he would gain steam and then fall on his side.

Ryan H and I hung out with him most weekends, all weekend, and were thus there to observe these "leanings," pick him up, dust him off, and laugh about it with him.

Falling out of the car was a luxury, because Ryan and I nearly kissed the ground each time John *landed* his blue Ford. Curbs and stoplights were not for John. He could not perceive them and rarely paid attention to them. We routinely jumped one and ran the other. Arrival should have been announced like an arriving flight after a wheels-down landing. It taught us to trust John's God.

Ryan and I finally took him to the hospital ER one Saturday afternoon when this imbalance was unusually bad. We stood there while he shared his medical history in a totally inappropriate violation of confidentiality by the hospital.

I had heard it before, so it didn't surprise me, but it had to be an earful to Ryan, who was now three years sober and only 22-years old.

"Do you have any medical conditions that we need to know about," the admittance lady mechanically asked John.

"Well, let's see," John responded predictably in his slow, high-toned, two-and-four-count, pausing, delivery. "I've been diagnosed repeatedly over the past few decades as bipolar, manic-depressive with chronic episodic paranoid schizophrenia, acute alcoholism, in recovery, by the way, and arthritis, bursitis..." the string of items trailed on and on.

Ryan looked at me with the cynical smile of a guy who had just discovered a serial killer and said, "Jesus Christ, let's get the fuck outta here before he flips out and kills us and half of this place!!!"

We laughed and smiled joyfully to see our harmless old-timer friend still going on in rhythmic broken tones about his medical accomplishments. We were there for a few hours, and a couple dozen cigarettes, whereupon we took John back home to Toy and a healthy balanced meal.

"Tell me, John," I said one day, "how does your schizophrenia manifest, and how often do you experience an 'outbreak' of it?"

"Not that often," John responded. "But, it's tied to my bi-polar crashing and then I start to get weird." I looked at him with the curious invitation to talk more about that.

"For example," John said, "I'm a Christian, so I know that I ain't Jesus, but one time I thought that Jesus Christ had occupied the body of John A to do good on Earth, and I was off to the races. I started talkin' manically about this and that and orderin' Toy around like I was the Lord God, and before long I found her haulin' me back to the VA Psych-ward."

"Now that was a weird thing..." he paused, thinking. "As we walked to the check-in area, I actually sensed for a minute that somethin' *was* wrong, and I began to feel really paranoid that all of those ole guys linin' the sidewalks and halls were scowlin' at us with disapproval...I could feel their eyes followin' Toy and me, and it felt as though they didn't like us. I couldn't understand how they couldn't like Jesus and my 'condition' didn't allow me to decipher true from false. I concluded, though, that they had rejected me before to the point of crucifixion and so, decided, *that this* was why they were looking at me with contempt."

"As we sat in the waitin' room, I mentioned it to Toy, and she embarrassed me with a rational perspective...which she has always been gifted at." He smiled lovingly, turning red with memory.

"No, sssJohn, sssyou not Jesus and they not looking at sssyou like you Jesus. They War II vet, shot by Japanese and looking at us like old vet look at man with Japanese wife...It THEY hospital. They not like ME. It not about you, sssJohn! Sssyou too self-centered."

"Another time," he reflected, "I thought that I was runnin' for President and when I called up my runnin' mate at 3:00 in the morning to see how the campaign was goin'—another guy in the program, by the way—he and Toy had a short conversation and I was back in the hospital. He didn't think it was funny, and I wasn't jokin' anyway. There were a couple 'a other things like that. Toy's been so good to me and so understandin', she and the boys." He looked grateful beyond measure. "I ain't always easy to live with. I put them through Hell sometimes."

Now I understood why he didn't think I was crazy when I relayed that I had seen a UFO above our parked car once in western Kansas...but *I* really *had* seen it.

John became strangely silent for about a week later that year and, so, I dropped by to see where he had been and what he had been doing.

He was dark and morose. He had not left the house in a week. I had never seen this John and it was like seeing another being.

There he sat, slumped over in his back room with a 10-day beard, chain-smoking, no significant light, depressed, withdrawn, unbathed, dirty clothes, grossly mismatched socks, no shoes, and a tattered V-neck tee shirt. He was obviously gripped and soul-consumed with fear and paranoia.

"What are you doing, John?" I asked carefully and with concern. "I haven't heard from you, or seen you at a meeting, for about a week."

"They're gonna throw me out," he said despondently and in a whispering tone, without slow pauses and with his eyes shifting back and forth from the door to me, from the door to me. "They wouldn't give me any Celebrex, and they know that I went to 'a outside doctor to get some for my arthritis. Now they're gonna shut-down my VA benefits and lock me up for good." He was near tears.

"That doesn't make sense, John," I said cautiously. "Why would they do that over something as stupid as arthritis medicine? I don't understand."

"Because my VA doctor wouldn't give me any, and so I went to 'a outside doctor, and now they're gonna throw me out 'a the VA's program and lock me up." He breathed shallowly and quickly as though he were having an anxiety attack. "I'm fucked," he said.

"Let's get outta here and go to that greasy spoon on 47th street, ok? I'll buy us some breakfast and we'll play a few games of Keno. We need to get you outta here, John. You seem really depressed. Let's do that and we'll talk about it, ok?"

"I noticed it last week when the cable guy—well, he wanted me to think he was a cable guy—hung out on a pole and sat in his van in front 'a my house for at least a couple 'a hours. He was watchin' me...recordin' me. They may even be recordin' us now." He whispered in a low tone with his eyes motioning toward the street. "And those kids across the street...they were flyin' balloons and they had cameras or bugs on 'em to catch me, but I just sat on the front porch and smoked, so I don't think they got anything of value. Shit, man, they're gonna come and get me. Fuck; all because I couldn't do what my VA doctor said. I just couldn't do what I was told and let it go."

"John, go rinse-off your face and put on a shirt and some shoes and we'll go eat and play some Keno, my treat." I coached again.

"Ok," he agreed reluctantly. "They might as well arrest me out there as here where Toy can see it. You're probably doin' me a favor. You're not workin' with 'em, are you?"

"No, John. I love you, man...I'd never do anything to hurt you. Let's go eat."

As I drove us to the restaurant, John slid low in the seat and kept moving his eyes around to see if someone strange was pulling up behind or beside us.

We got to the dive, ordered greasy meals, him eating sparingly, and we began to play a couple of games of Keno, with John whispering softly that everyone entering the parking lot or room was coming to arrest him.

He responded most afraid when a large, just-out-of-prison looking guy with lots of military tattoos walked in, acknowledged us by nodding, with his own paranoid defiance, and sat facing us in a booth across the serving area. He and John's paranoia seemed to feed-off of each other. I felt frightened now, fearing escalation.

When a couple of rough looking, but likely sober, bikers pulled into the parking lot, John began to sweat and shake.

"That's them," he whispered hoarsely. "The three of them are going to take me." He motioned with his head and eyes to the guy in the catty-corner booth and the two bikers now walking up to the building. "I've really enjoyed our time together, and am sorry you had to get dragged into this," he added, with a sadness and resolve "logically" displacing raw paranoia.

When the bikers had sat in the other room for a while, I saw him sweating and looking at them, and grasped the depth of his horrifying delusion.

He was not responding to food, Keno, jokes, or reasoning. Asked if he had changed anything else, or simply took some Celebrex, he mumbled something about dropping one of his meds and taking half a pill of another one to save pills. I did not ask how he diagnosed this great idea.

The guy at the table across from us paid his bill, walked out, got in his truck, and left. John watched him carefully.

"John, I know you like to be simple, but I also know that under that you're smart as hell, so let me reason with you for just a minute the way you would me, ok?" I asked humbly. He motioned approval.

"John, you ain't thinkin' right. Trust me as someone who loves you and let me tell you that no one is out to get you and you ain't trackin'. It's in your *head*. These guys aren't here to get you; they're here to eat greasy food and play Keno, just like us. When we walk out of here and they don't arrest you, will you consider that I might be right about this?" I paused for him to respond.

"Naw, they'll just get me later...them or someone else; they're definitely watchin' me." He sat glumly with his head down.

"No, John. You ain't that fuckin' important," I winked and said in his sponsor tone of voice. "Ever heard of 9-11? You know, the terrorists blowing up the twin towers in New York a while back? Shit like that? You remember that?" He nodded irritated that I implied he was either checked-out or stupid.

"Well, they ain't got time for you, John. Trust me when I tell you that they are chasing *real* bad people and don't even have enough people to work *that* problem. They sure as fuck don't have time for you and your outside doctor or a Celebrex 'drug bust.' Trust me, John. You ain't that fuckin' important. I'm quoting *you* now...you recognize this speech?" I smiled playfully. It didn't help. He looked scared and, now, a little angry.

"Let's get outta here," I said, hiding my frustration. "Do me a favor, John. When we get home, call John B and have him come and talk with you about this. I think you need to check yourself into a clinic that you trust and get your meds regulated. I'd bet that Toy and John would agree with that, and we are three people who love you completely."

"Simply put, John...I love you. I'm worried about you. And, you ain't thinkin' right. You might as well take care of yourself as waiting for someone to come and do it for you." I smiled at him with a love that had to radiate. "Trust the people who love you, John."

I dropped him off at the door, smoked a final cigarette with him on his porch and said, "See ya soon, John. I love you."

He said that he loved me too, seemed somewhat more beaten into reasonableness and calm, and promised me that he would talk with Toy and John B to get their thoughts. I knew that, sick and paranoid or not, he would do as he said. It was his *nature*. I prayed for him as I drove away.

The next day I went to a meeting and found out that Toy and John B had driven John A to Prairie View, a very nice and respected mental health facility north of Wichita, and had convinced him to check himself in for evaluation and treatment as necessary.

I rejoiced silently to hear this and reflected with a new reality on his funny and not so funny stories about depression, delusion, paranoia, and schizophrenia. I knew meds were the key to John A's return to being childlike and serene. I prayed for him and thanked God for strong and no-bullshit friends like John B. He could reach John when no one else could, and again did.

John B was one of the most real and most focused individuals I had ever met in the program. He was about 6' 4", built like Superman, and gut-wrenching honest.

John A had always trusted him implicitly and they frequently sponsored each other. John B was the sort of person that let nothing dangerous go unchecked.

One night, for example, as he was leaving our AA meeting hall (which was ironically located above a liquor store), I hollered down the stairs, "Be Cool, John!"

I heard his giant boots walking slowly back up the stairs, whereupon he walked over to me, put his giant hands on my shoulders, looked at me with a mix of childlike and sober intensity, and said, "If you don't mind...I think I'll just be *me*."

I thought of the speeches of drunks being "hip, slick and cool," and knew that he had outlived and outgrown the concept of "cool"...it was too close to people-pleasing and too near to phony.

I thanked him for the lesson as he again walked away. "Be *YOU*," I said. He turned and smiled like a wizard. I loved John B too.

When I was able to visit John A the following weekend, I knew that he had returned.

His biggest complaint was that he was only able to get outside and smoke a cigarette once per hour. This was killing him. His color and childlike countenance were returning and his quiet sense of dry humor was back. He had traded-in fast-talking in low, paranoid tones for something resembling his chopped-tones and pauses. I felt so relieved to see *him* again.

"God, John," I affirmed over a couple of cigarettes. "You're looking great. I'm so glad you're back among the living. You were not you for a while. Do you remember what all happened?"

"They've got my meds straightened out again," he smiled. "Maybe I ought 'a quit fuckin' around with 'em and playin' doctor, huh?"

"You asked about my memories...know what's weird about that," he queried, knowing that I did not know? "I don't remember things the way they SHOULD have been...I remember them as they WERE *to me*."

"When I think of runnin' for President, I *was* runnin' for President. When I remember bein' Jesus, I *had* Jesus in my body. This time...I was fucked-up and it seemed rational, so that's just the way I remember it."

He smiled with friendship, recognizable trust, and personal acceptance in his again clearing blue-gray eyes. I suddenly noticed that he had shaved again recently.

"I'll be ok...Thanks for bein' there for me, man."

At that moment, I loved all of the Johns I had met so far and felt so safe and connected to this beautiful man. He was a sponsor and mentor above all others to me and probably did have Jesus in his body, talking with the Buddha.

John recovered and we resumed our daily friendship until I left for Louisiana to be with Violet. He taught me so much with his wise, gentle, and simple ways. He conveyed as many lessons with silent looks and humility as with words.

John called me a few days before hurricane Katrina hit and I didn't call him back. I could tell from his voice mail that his tone was despondent and that he was not speaking in four-count chopped syllables.

I reasoned that he had decided to play doctor again and, so, was on the edge of a bipolar crash. I knew that others could take care of him and focused on *my* pressing issues and *my* state of mind. I didn't realize that I was substituting Stephen Covey's *urgent* for *important*. Ryan, Toy, and John B could take care of him. I had done my part for a while.

A few days after Katrina had decimated New Orleans, Lisette and I sat exhausted and disheveled in Port Allen, Louisiana, where we had managed to relocate after a jaunt to Montgomery, and where we were blessed to rent an 1800s Old Store, which had been converted into an apartment on Old Store Lane.

Our phones weren't working yet and we had no computer access, electric, hot water, or television.

As we sat in the dimness of night, my phone turned blue and beeped with a rare text message. It was from my dear friend Ryan H.

"John A passed away today," it read.

I looked at it with disbelief and numb pain in the silent chirping of Port Allen's darkness.

"...Others could take care of him...Ryan, Toy and John B could take care of him. I had done my part for awhile."

<<<<<<>>>>>>

Calls one didn't make steal memories one should have had:

"Tell me about that UFO thing again," John A said.

"Well, it was 1967, freshman year at KU, before I'd ever even smoked weed and on a night when I had not been drinking..."

"I was home for Christmas vacation and my old high school girlfriend, Carla, was visiting from California."

"We were in my '63 Chevy Impala, parked by a large pond down below ole Paul Larner's shed, out in the middle of nowhere. It was a crystal clear, starry night in western Kansas, and we kept starting the car to defrost the windows and to stay warm, then we'd get hot and turn it off again. Off and on...you know what I mean."

"I planned to finish what I'd started in high school and she felt willing, so we were making-out in the front seat of the red Chevy. I was easing under her dress, gathering courage and feeling upper nylon, when I suddenly needed to take a piss."

"I got out, walked a few yards away from the car, pissed, turned, looked habitually upward into the night sky, and stood flat footed and breathless. It was surreal."

"Above the car, against the starry sky, was a red glowing light, or disk, perhaps 40 or 50 feet across—I couldn't tell because it was absolutely soundless and sitting perhaps 300 feet up, but against infinity, so I couldn't tell how high or big it was. I remember thinking that it was the exact same color and shape as a heat lamp that I'd broken once by shining it directly into a wet creamer can in the well house, except BIG. That's what I seemingly compared it with to get my mind around it at all..."

"I gasped and tried to grasp what I was seeing for a couple of long seconds and then jumped back in the car to see if she was aware of it. As I slid quickly into the car, I looked at her and said, 'Do you see...' but I didn't need to finish. She sat stiffly leaning forward and looking upward through the windshield, hand across her mouth, and clearly terrified."

"I immediately turned on the keys to run, but the instant the dashboard lit-up it disappeared...in less time than one could blink twice or snap one's fingers, it was completely gone. Only the starry sky remained. I didn't know if it had gone straight up that fast, and had thus become invisible, or had closed-up like a camera lens and became invisible. It seemed, unexplainably, more like a lens closing to me. But it was gone. Only stars remained."

"The next thing I recall in my memory is us riding around in the back seat of a friend's car, in Dighton, talking with him and his girlfriend about Christ knows what, but not about UFOs...and it was starting to snow.

I remembered vaguely thinking that snow was weird considering I'd looked into a clear night sky what seemed like only an hour before. I don't recall driving back to town...I don't recall talking about it... just poof, being back in Dighton and driving around in a friend's car."

"I didn't fuck her and we didn't talk at all about what we'd seen...didn't even think about discussing it...Except for the snow, I also have no recollection of thinking about time. It was as though it never happened and as though everything surrounding the event flew away instantly as a waking dream."

"It took years to realize that something weird happened and went unspoken. I've always wanted to see her again and see if she recalls it. I even tried to reach her a couple of times, but couldn't find her. Strange, huh?"

"Now, that was weird," John said, smiling, with broken syllables and a child's pensive gaze as though he actually believed me...or perhaps he smiled as though he believed in me.

Chapter 18
Look to the sky

After spaceships—and after my junior year in college—there was a summer of airplanes.

It was another calm and windless day in western Kansas as I stood on the end of a row of young, headless maize and listened to the hum of a powerful engine approaching from a half-mile or so away.

I had been guided there by heavy, pencil-scratched directions that told me which major roads to take, followed by stern, blue-eyed and specific *"where and how-to"* directions that said, "Watch for a post with a red flag tied to it...get out of your car...listen for me, and you'll be there. Start on the first row and pace off 15 good steps each time I pass. I'll do the rest. Don't start playin' with your dick and forget to move. Don't miscount your steps. Oh, it will help me if you wear something bright and definitely don't wear *milo* green or *dirt* brown."

I left early, as the sun was barely rising, and followed the directions that had been given me. "Left turn here, go a mile east, right turn; go a mile, left turn, half a mile...watch for the flag, park, get out, listen..."

There was the flag hanging sun-golden-red and still, tied to a corner post in the early morning stillness. I roared the Hemi just to hear its 383 and then got out of my (now-dusty) metal-flake blue '68 Roadrunner and waited by the fresh smelling end of the first green row.

By now, the distant hum had become a growing roar and within 60-seconds, the beautiful, white, low-winged aircraft blasted over me leaving a trailing mist of cool white vapor wafting gently onto the green upward-reaching milo leaves. A strong, machine driven, wind struck me and then quickly passed.

I walked 15 *"good"* paces along the end of the rows and turned around to see the low-winged giant pass a few feet over my head again and kick on its life-giving, life-taking, angelic, grim-reaper's mist.

I could smell the fresh purity of Sevin or perhaps Parathion, I didn't know which yet, but I knew that I loved the smell of chemicals coming from this roaring heaven.

I thought about pissing, but then decided that I had better get the routine of this "flying business" down before I lost track or focus.

"For now, watch, count steps, be where you're supposed to be," I thought. "You can piss later."

"Don't start playin' with your dick and forget to move. Don't miscount your steps," I recalled the old warmonger saying. He had obviously trained a few insecticide loving, anti-weed neophytes before. "Double spraying would be bad," I reasoned; "and so would missing a pass: Poison or living bugs; what a balance. Hum?" I pondered only briefly.

I could see and hear the plane becoming smaller as it skimmed along, barely topping the growing plants, and I paced off another 15 *"good"* steps, turned, watched, and waited.

I could see the white Pawnee making contorted sounds and motions on the other end of the field, but I could not determine what I was seeing or hearing. It sounded as though it was missing out or something and the turn-around didn't make sense to my totally untrained concept of aerodynamics. It seemed too fast and too jerky.

This time as the plane roared over me, I came as close to multitasking as young men can—I both paced *and* watched to see its maneuvers.

It rose to clear my head, barely missed the electrical lines which ran along the country road, suddenly roared with extra power, raised its nose sharply and pointed upward-left, arched further upward, sat nearly stalled, seemingly becoming perpendicular to the ground, nose up, tail down, moved its nose gently from left to right, became deadly still, dropped its nose, fell sharply to a downward left, spun 180-degrees as though it had been turned on an invisible stick, tail now upward and back, nose downward and front, groaned fiercely with raw power as a beast drawing new breath, leveled and narrowly cleared the lines again as it blasted over me and reengaged its white, crisp-smelling, floating cloak of bug-or-weed murdering mist.

I got delayed chills as I watched it become a white speck in the distance of V-shaped, straight-growing green rows. As I marveled, I paced-off 15 *"good"* steps and turned again to face the already returning white roaring dragon.

Its wheels were barely above the tender leaves as it flew its half-mile mission back and forth...Cut the mist, vroom, roaring power, upward hook, silence, falling to the right, dropping nose down, power, swish, vroom, mist...again and again and again I saw this unnatural, beautiful, and death-defying dance.

I suddenly, and without choice, respected ole man Wendler as no man I had ever witnessed and knew that the word "aerobatics" was a two dimensional, theoretical word for a four dimensional, theological phenomenon—pitch, roll, yaw, time, timing, and *God knows* what else! How could anyone be so good with a machine...a FLYING machine...or was it somehow alive too and symbiotically one with his jagged yet vulnerable soul?

"My God," I accidentally said out loud. "My God," I gasped with wonder.

When we completed this field and he roared over me for the last time, I jumped in my car and returned to the airport, where his plane was already sitting and his son Lain was topping its tank with crystal clear, high-octane, sweet smelling Av-gas. David was mixing the next batch of Sevin, using an open trough, water, bags of white powder, and a shovel to make it white liquid.

"Don't leave lumps in that fuckin' thing, David," said Clarence with the sternness and clarity of a mission commander. "I don't need lumps clogging up my nozzles when I get out there. Pay attention to detail, son...Pay attention to detail...and hurry up. In this business, time IS money and I don't need the wind to start blowin' too hard for me to spray."

It was like watching a squadron prepare for battle where getting planes in, fueled, reloaded with ammunition, and back in the air was logistical ground support for air superiority over weeds and bugs— enemies of the farmer.

I felt seeds of love for airplanes and began to understand urgency, teamwork, and focus, but it was something different than the ole man had taught me. This made complete sense.

"Here," said Clarence, efficiently handing me another set of penciled directions. "Get going. You'll see the flag. I put it there last night."

I jumped like a novice airmen and ran for my car to get to the next field. Within a few minutes of my arrival, here came the white Pawnee and we danced again—he, the plane, the crops, and I.

It was beautiful and filled me with adrenalin and a supernatural high. The morning sun now scorched me, but I felt only a focus on the mission. Keep flying. Kill the bugs. He was like the ole man, but didn't physically beat his kids and I felt safe in his unlikely classroom.

On good days, the winds in Kansas meant that 2 to 3 early morning runs and a couple of late evening flights were all we had.

Flights were broken up by hours of wind-blowing interruption and chances to go swimming, drink pop, play light-flashing, bell dinging, flipper flapping pin-ball machines, bowl, or play music and then run to the airport at Clarence's commanding beacon and work until well after dark.

At night, the residual "band" would fuel-up Lain's oxidized green '54 Chevy station wagon with Clarence's "free" Av-gas and chase rabbits around the airport until our bellies hurt with laughter and our shotguns were empty.

Usually, we left only dead cans riddled with pellets but we drove crazy, made sharp zigzagging turns chasing rabbits, rolled recklessly out of the car's open doors and shot at something. It was amazing that we lived through it.

This family was filled with defiant craziness and yet with natural teachers, brilliant, each of them in his own steely way, Mrs. Wendler the master. She was the sweet, calm voice of reason and even steadied the ole man. I loved the Wendlers like an adoptive family, perhaps more.

I couldn't assemble a model airplane, but seeing Clarence care for his flying baby made me realize that his job was in fact life or death.

I was amazed at how light the aircraft was the first time we "hangered" it.

The hanger was a "T" shaped tin building with room only for the fuselage and tail in the middle, and only for wings and some tools on the side. The tail was easily turned by only one of us, and two of us rolled it backwards only to ensure that we did not accidentally damage it on the doors. I could roll it easily by myself.

As I watched Clarence adjusting the airplane's cables and controls one windy afternoon, I began to understand the parts that I had always thrown away in attempts to build models. These things were important. Wow. Each piece fit neatly with other pieces to make this complex bird defy gravity. It was a loved mechanical angel.

I marveled at the giant engine that sat under the airplane's smooth white cowling, and watched how Clarence talked to it as he changed its oil and adjusted its operation.

I thought about how my cars each had a personality, and thought of how much more important this bird's attitudes were.

This engine was so much larger than the 383 cubic inch, high-lift-cam engine in my Roadrunner that it baffled me. Clarence said that the engine was designed to be light, that the pistons were deliberately "loose" and that she had over 500 horsepower.

Jesus...He loved this airplane like a daughter, or perhaps more like a second trusted wife or a spotless mistress.

"Let me tell you," Clarence said casually and in a low tone, as he watched me shyly watching him tighten down bolts, cables, and springs on his beloved Pawnee lady. "This thing and I are *one* being when we're up there. She looks soooo smooth and graceful when you're on the ground and she's gliding up and down that field leaving her misty vapors, huh? But let me tell you what...when we're on those afternoon runs and the sun's been cookin' all day, this baby's like riding a mean buckin' bronco and it *hurts like hell.*"

"When the wind stops blowing after a summer day on this ole flat, square, treeless pancake, the air that's sittin' a few feet above those crops is hot as the fires of hell. I'm sweating and so damned hot sometimes that I can hardly see out of one eye, and I can't afford not to see. My ass and knees are so fucking pounded some days that it feels like a hammer is banging on me, but this is the livin' that I love and I've never crashed a plane...*yet.*"

He looked almost prayerfully grateful, as though he might cross himself. "Yet," he repeated pensively.

I noticed, for some reason, his mix of slang and schooled English, and wondered how he decided when to drop letters, and when not to. I surmised that he was an educated man oft talking with farmers. John A would practice this also, as would I. He continued.

"I can't afford to get lazy, miss something, or make a mistake. Spray-croppin' is tough business, but it gives me lots of time to play in the winter, and I love that time too. I love fuckin' with the stock market all winter," he winked.

"I just have to live till winter to enjoy it, once per year, a day and a pass at a time." He smiled like a chemistry professor creating a bomb.

At that moment, I grasped his meaning with a solemn emotional gray that lay somewhere between black comedy, life, and death.

He looked sideways at me and continued his lecture.

"When my baby here is takin' that same summer beating, things get loose and I've gotta find them before they kill her and me both.

The last thing I need is for something to snap or burp when I'm in one of those controlled crashes that you see us do on each end of the field. I've seen guys hook the wires and crash. They died. I've seen guys pull into that question-mark looking turn we do and not have the right angle, the right timing, or enough power to pull out of it. They stalled or they nosed-in, full power...They died."

"Like I tell my boys: 'Details. Devil's in the details in this business' and I keep my eye on him is why I'm still here. It's that simple...no accident is not an accident."

He looked at me with that deep, piercing, blue-eyed, over the spectacles genius that I had seen so many times, but this time with a clarity and wisdom that I had never fathomed in another human being. I blushed to suddenly know that I loved this man as a father. He kept working...I now understood...working to stay alive.

It was a few days later that I was "promoted" into the role of mixing chemicals, and I saw the replicating genius of the Wendler clan from yet another angle.

Lain climbed into the airplane that day and took off with absolute confidence to spray a field. David could also fly, but was in the field spotting and I was mixing Sevin by hand, as I had seen David do in the days before.

As I mixed, refueled the aircraft, washed the windows, topped off the chemical tanks, and put Lain back in the air, Clarence showed up towing a big white cylinder tank on a newly spray-painted black flat-bed trailer.

"This ought 'a help," he smiled proudly with the look of a new father!

"What is it," I asked ignorantly?

"It's a little gimmick that I invented a few weeks ago. We just finished assembling it. It's a tank to mix Sevin and other chemicals...no more shovels, no more lumps." he smiled. "More time to play with your dick," he winked, cynically.

"I mixed together a few ideas and came up with this. See here...this motor is mounted on the end and welded tight to the tank on a platform so it won't move." He shook it hard and the trailer wiggled, but not the platform. "It's connected to a big-assed, three-bladed, triple paddle that runs all the way through the tank and this here is a bearing with rubber seals to keep it all from leakin'," he mused, pointing.

"See this glass gauge? It's so you know how much water you're puttin' in the tank from the top, here," and he started unscrewing about an 18" lid, tied to a chain, protruding from the top of the tank. "You'll put the water and chemicals in here 'till it's where you want it to make a load...or two..." He started a hose squirting into the tank, "see the gauge moving," he asked, pointing?" I nodded affirmatively.

"When you like the water level, you simply start the motor and add the right number of chemical bags. Got it? Now you'll be free to do something else while this is mixing Sevin...AND the mixture will be correct, disseminated, and simple every time!" He smiled as though he had just named the new baby and sold features on a new car all in one swoop.

He unrolled a fat extension cord from the hanger to the tank, plugged in both ends and turned on the motor. It began humming and stirring, flapping water, humming and stirring.

"Wow." I said gawking.

"Give me those bags," he commanded proudly, and I began handing him Sevin bags.

He poured them into the tank's big hole and listened proudly as the paddles mixed and splashed and stirred the powder and the water together. He poured the Sevin I had hand-mixed into the tank and said, "Close enough!" His toy was working!

Soon Lain landed, and although it was getting randomly gusty, Clarence was determined to load the plane for a maiden "chemical mixer" run.

He checked the fluid and smiled ear to ear to note that it was perfect, fast, and without lumps.

Then he pulled a big hose from alongside the new contraption and hooked it to a valved-protrusion near the motor and at the bottom of the tank. He looked at me, but obviously also wanted to share the christening of his new contraption with his son, who had now departed the aircraft and was taking an overdue piss into the edge of some nearby weeds.

He told Lain to stop pissin' and stick the other end of the hose into the airplane's chemical fill-tank, which he promptly did.

Clarence then flipped some other lever and swoosh, the liquid began to pump out of the tank and into the airplane. 20 speechless seconds passed as though they were prototype minutes. We could hear the humming motor and the liquid running through the hose and into the aircraft.

"Perfect," he gloated. "Just like it was supposed to work! Just like I designed it!"

When the tank was full, he flipped the lever, shut down the tank's stirring motor and hopped into the plane. He blasted off south to meet David in some field, somewhere, on the hot summer soil beneath the bouncy Kansas sky.

It was like watching Santa Claus in an orange hat yelling, "Merry Christmas to all and to all a goodnight!" as the plane left the ground and Lain and I stood smiling at each other.

"That's my Pop," said Lain grinning and shaking his head..."The mad inventor." He didn't even seem surprised.

"Wow." I said.

<<<<<<>>>>>

I started my airplane summer in Texas. I had a "personnel" internship in Victoria.

For a manic-depressive, summer in Texas is not as fun as summer in Kansas, but when there is love involved, it sucks.

I had gone straight from KU's junior year to Texas and had taken my girlfriend, Jan, with me, dropping her off at her uncle's house, where we stayed overnight and then went to her job as a summer camp counselor outside of Kerrville.

I had sometimes concluded that, although she had cheated on me the previous summer, she would be faithful to me with her renewed commitment and in a camp full of little kids. I was too naive to think that lonely character might replay itself and that the other counselors might be handsome young men.

I had also failed to be accountable for my childish and erratic behavior or for my frequent unleashing of verbal abuse to punish her for last summer's sins. I had failed to see that these behaviors might leave someone intuitively wondering—even searching to find—if there might be something or someone better for them.

I was trying again to balance the insanity of jealous reasoning with inexperienced romantic reality, and thereby, give our expressed and committed love a continuing chance.

All in all, she had plenty of integrity, and I did not doubt her love for me. I knew that she had hurt me with the prior summer's fling, and I knew that I wanted to get even, but I did not really allow myself to ponder my vendetta or the possibility of her cheating on me again—except when I went to visit her a couple of times on the weekend.

On these occasions, she felt distant, restrained, and different. We made love, and all the words were still there, but we didn't connect. I was too young to know what I was seeing.

I felt lonely and briefly dated a girl in Victoria, while I could, to embrace hypocrisy and avoid savoring my again growing and faceless jealousy.

I recall very little about the summer adventure in Texas except random mental photographs.

I remember making friends with a guy who was interning with the Victoria police department, and that he bought beer and showed me grisly crime scene pictures of murder victims.

I could drink in Kansas; I couldn't in Texas, so he aided and abetted me. He also caught a wild-Texas tarantula one day and amazed me with the gigantic size of it. I had never seen anything larger than a black widow or a trapdoor spider.

Some of the dead people had been gutted or cut from the back of their neck to the bottom of their spine, and worse. I had never seen things like this before. I knew, though, that this was what toad killing unchecked became.

I remember that gas cost 17-cents per gallon, that someone was found murdered in their car two blocks from my apartment, and that the battery of my Roadrunner kept going dead because the humidity of south Texas corroded the battery's connector cables.

I remember seeing a desk-sized group of daddy-longlegs gather on the end of a building where Jan worked at camp, and seeing them scatter when I threw rocks at them to unveil the hidden red building...and then quickly re-form into a black mass, masking the building beneath their collective mask. I wondered what else was hidden in camp from my seeing. I noticed that Jan did not introduce me to any friends, coworkers or kids, and I wondered why; but being self-centered, I rationalized that she was simply glad to see me, and eager to be alone at the motel.

I remember my policeman friend telling me that daddy longlegs were ants, not spiders, and thinking that as a farmer, three years into a degree, I should know that. I had not seen a live tarantula or a murder victim's picture until now. It frightened me to know that these things existed and to think of other things I had not yet seen.

In the night, in my small efficiency apartment in Victoria, I felt grown-up, but childlike, afraid, and alone.

I wanted to return to western Kansas and purge my head of new images, love's doubt, and dark experience, but I resolved to stay the course.

Then, in Victoria, one Friday night, as I was standing around with a bunch of people roughly my age waiting to go to a movie, this muscular, soft-spoken, early-twenties redneck-seeming guy emerged uninvited from the shadowed fringes of the gentle group and said, "You northerners educated those niggers and made them start to get so high and mighty that they think they can come back down here and work beside me...hell, even have my job!" His Texas drawl amplified his message.

In a complete lapse of grasping reality, I surmised him to be a straight-faced comedian, laughed, and said, "You're kidding, right? This *is* the 20th century and last I looked, even Deep South Texas was still in *America*?!"

He wasn't kidding. They actually had people that stupid and mean tucked away in the corridors of 1970. It was as though he had walked 105 years into the future, and hating me at that moment was all that he knew.

I felt the immediate and unbelievable horror of moving into one of my friend's crime scene photos as he broke a beer bottle on the side of an old stone building and ran towards me. I couldn't believe people actually did that, like in a movie, and it was as surreal as the UFO, but I knew suddenly and with grave emptiness that I wasn't in Kansas anymore.

I don't know what was said, or who saved me, but somehow the man stopped and walked off laughing. I crawled away, somehow standing upright, with him mocking and calling me "Yankee Toto Dandy." My kidneys were pounding, like fear hammers, with unchecked adrenalin.

His friends must have held him back to save me, as they may or may not have saved others, and I know that my words were conciliatory beyond humble, even while my left leg was raised instinctively to protect me against what I knew would be his oncoming deadly slicing lunge. It is a blur, but I know I was blessed that night and that I *definitely* wanted to live.

I felt so foreign and alone, and became so empty that I left the job early to complete my 220-page essay and get my five hours of

"A" from Professor Cape. That was when I went to work for the Wendlers.

The plane suddenly blasted over my head again. I realized that I had been lost in memory.

I had been doing this too long, apparently, because I couldn't remember if I had paced-off 15 *"good"* steps, or none. The plane roared back over me and a crisp smelling chemical vapor wafted down to cool me in the hot breeze.

My reflections of the rest of that summer are few. First, I remember Clarence telling me not to get raw Parathion on me or I would get sick, and me not believing him. I remember that the day I splashed it on my hand and didn't rinse it off led to 24-hours of puking and dizziness in a chemical induced flu.

Second, I remember starting the Sevin mixing one day in Clarence's contraption, as he flew off to spray a field and then, as Sevin mixed, playing with my dick in the cheap FBO trailer, after finding someone's black and white girlie magazine.

When he returned I topped-off the airplane, filled the tank with Sevin, and launched him back into the bumpy summer sky. I recall Clarence's anger when he returned and discovered unopened bags of powdered Sevin sitting in the hanger.

"Goddamn it," he yelled with his now reddish-blue eyes raging at me, and me alone, for the first time ever. "Now I'll have to spray that field again because you didn't mix the chemical strong enough. Do you *know* what that costs me in personal beating, airplane time, and fuel?! I can't believe this! Pay attention to detail, goddamn it...quit playin' with your dick and pay attention to detail!"

There wasn't room for humor. I felt so ashamed.

Third, and finally, I recall going to the lake one weekend and being attracted to a beautiful, sweet, non-promiscuous girl whom I had known for many years and who agreed to go to the drive-in with me that night. I hadn't heard from Jan in weeks.

I remember feeling off-balance and emotionally drunk late in the movie as we kissed and became surprisingly impassioned, as I gently slid her panties down, and as I felt her warm breath whispering that she wanted me. I equally remember being ashamed and embarrassed when remorseful chilling thoughts of Jan gripped me and I haltingly stopped.

"I just can't do this," I said pushing away and unable to explain why, even to myself.

The beautiful girl was humiliated and angry as I took her home.

I drove regretting one-sided loyalty, and resented Jan for fucking whomever she wanted, likely two summers in a row, yet leaving me so lovelorn that I could not be intimate with anyone but her.

Orbiting my *image's* apogee, the *mask* learned and protected, with and from youth and ambivalence.

<<<<<<>>>>>>

Fair stands alone in summer's passing and does not seek man's perception of life or time to give it context.

Fair is a manmade delusion, filed early and mechanically with man's concept of truth and religion. It is oft mocked in joking principle, yet remains as moral balance and delusional lie.

When the ole man died of heart failure, I knew that life was not fair to a strong man. When Clarence died of Alzheimer's, I knew that life was not fair to the mind of a genius. When John A died of cancer, I knew that life was not fair to a good man. When Brendan died of desolation, I knew that life was not fair to a young man. When "love" hurt people, I knew that life was not fair to those attracted to the bright light of whirling good intentions.

When what we know dies, grains of truth will remain in its undisturbed ashes and a gift may emerge for every accidental good deed.

Each death whispers, and each pain is an inoculation against something yet unseen. We cannot know what inoculations we are getting and we cannot accurately seek them with God-touched futures unfolding. It is oft assured that no relationship is wasted; yet with morose contradiction, one grieves and clings aimlessly to their passing.

Whether they live or die, weeds and bugs are fair, and silent death from a passing airplane is fair to them. They had their minute-long lives and likely expected no further measure of fairness.

In 1970, they lived and died as a summer glimpse of life's passing vapor.

I began to notice, from that summer on, that mosquitoes, gnats, and flies never bothered me again. In south Texas, they were giants and ate me alive, but never again. On a rare occasion, they have landed on me, but they do not stay and they do not bite me or drink of my blood. Likely they know that to do so is to die. I thank ole man Wendler and Jan each time they are repulsed by my now innocuous summer.

Chapter 19
the farm out of the boy

My family started well and my 1st wife made it so. Long-term plans by a bipolar husband, though, can turn magic into mud, careers into canyons, and hope into mania. I would have missed the greatest adventures had I not known Suzanne.

I had worked at the Bomber Plant for about 15-months when our reason for moving to Kansas found its appointed place and hour.

We were poor and tired of looking at properties which were now financially out of reach.

I propelled my family forward on grandiose dreams and plans that could not align. I told people that I wanted to move to Kansas to get a "little farm," but upon arriving, we found ourselves in a set of barn red, unpainted duplexes on Pawnee street across from a pool hall and some low-rent apartments.

Weekend drives in the country were like passing through Disneyland's "Small World." Things seemed more and more like a fantasy. Then a Sunday drive floated us to the dream.

As we drove down "Douglass Road," about 20 miles southeast of Wichita, we saw a thickly wooded and vine-ridden acreage with a badly faded, white painted, wooden sign drooping from a time-rotted post, and barely visible that SEEMED to say "For Sale." We had to back up to see it at all, and had to get out of the car to read it. It did…it said "For Sale!" We pulled into the heavily overgrown gravel entryway to peek at what this place might be. It was destiny.

Sitting in the driveway, around the turn, behind a falling down garage and near a white mulberry tree, were three cars parked and three people gathered talking.

It was the son and two daughters of an old couple who had died and thereby left the family homestead.

They were farm kids in their 50s and 60s discussing what to do about the rickety ole property.

It was so grown-over with vines, weeds, tiger lilies, and untrimmed trees that one could barely discern the giant red barn, two unpainted sheds, or the unpainted peeling white coffin-looking old house.

Suzanne, the kids, and I all piled out of the car and introduced ourselves, asking if the place was still for sale. They said yes, but added that they had trouble getting what they wanted, weren't sure if they were going to sell it as one parcel of 160 acres or as two of 150 acres and 10, with the house and outbuildings carved out into the 10.

They indicated that they could not get traditional loans because the water quality was currently "inadequate" to pass county standards—BUT that the water used to be "sweet water," and that, "there were still some platting and legal description problems with the property."

We instantly loved the property and knew what a rare and disguised treasure something this beautiful could be. We had looked at lots of properties. They cost a fortune and lacked farm character.

Our sense of emotion overrode our sense of financial reason and I blurted out that we would give them $50,000 if they would take that for the 10-acres with the buildings. I had no idea where that came from.

They looked at me as only a farmer can—three farmers—who saw a city boy coming a mile away. I saw their eyes exchanging looks and balancing honesty and dishonesty with destiny. They didn't expect this, nor did we.

They obviously thought that amount to be sight-unseen irrational, and said that they would have to think about it, that much was unsettled and, again, that the property "...could not get traditional financing."

There was a comfortable silence where birds chirped and flies buzzed around the mulberry tree. The unscripted serenity of this natural moment was an eternal feeling. It was as though God spoke in a comma of natural stillness.

Suddenly, in another unexamined idea, my mouth suggested that perhaps, if it were something that interested them, a private contract could be executed to give us time to fix-up the house and well and then gain traditional bank financing. Their eyes lit up and they said they didn't know, but they would call us if they decided to go that route.

I told them that they could draft the contract to ensure that it met *their* terms. We moved away and the siblings pondered and chatted as we peeked in the hole-riddled rusty screened windows of the ole house and noted that it was musty, ill kempt, and empty. In a few minutes, we returned to see if they had any closing thoughts.

"There's a cowboy living in the house right now," one of the daughters said. "He lost an eye riding bulls and sorta lives here to keep an eye on things."

I knew that she didn't understand her pun. I also knew that, in other words, "...it's only fit to live in if you're a one-eyed cowboy who's comfortable with a saddle for a pillow, a mean bull, a planned lifespan of eight-seconds, and a wide-open range." The farmer in me understood their message perfectly, but the carpenter in me said it didn't matter. We were tough too. We could tame this dilapidated mortal dwelling.

We left with only faith and faint hopes that a miracle might happen, and that we might be blessed to harness this grown-over wilderness. We exchanged numbers as we left and waited a long week. Then we called them...well, Suzanne called them. I always had grandiose speeches and ideas, but lacked the courage for simple action.

Suzanne was a brave and positive soul, subtly bright, the sweetest person I had ever known, and trimmed straight from Proverbs 31: *"She examineth a field and buyeth it."*

She had character and honesty that anyone would want in a friend, a wife, a teacher, and a mother. People were attracted to it, as was I. It would be years yet before my alcoholic void would begin to suck the light out of her *while resenting her* for the character that I lacked. In this hour, it was God-sent and prophetic.

After another month of talking back and forth, we signed a contract for $50,000 at 10% interest, paying $600 per month, with the understanding that we had a year to pay the loan in full through refinancing of the property. We knew that our work would be cut out for us and, *thank God,* did not know what we did not yet know. There were inoculations aplenty waiting here. Aplenty.

Living on the open range would have been a step up for the cowboy in some respects, but the roof didn't leak...yet.

We journeyed into our "home" in May 1983, and immediately began our first assessment of restoration and reanimation, with priorities finding us, not the other way around. We decided to move our furniture and belongings a little at a time and simultaneously fix items necessary for semi-civilized habitation of *this ole house.*

We met the cowboy. He was moving out with only a large, frayed-rope-tied green Army bag and a brightly decorated red, white and blue, scuffed-up, saddle. We determined that he was a nice man, made primarily out of grit, scar tissue, gristle, and healed broken bones and that, beneath it all, he was honest to the core.

His early 30s blonde straggly hair stuck out from under his dirty tan and blue "USA" ball cap and faded into a reddish colored, well trimmed beard that outlined his already sunburned face.

His good eye had the clear hunting focus of a blue-eyed eagle as he spoke. The black patch over his right eye seemed almost land-locked pirate-like and his legs were bowed with rodeo cliché.

"The ole place has character," he said knowingly. "It was built in three pieces, basically. The middle 'a the house was built in the 1880s, the two-story front 'a the house was built in 1939, and the back porch area was added on in 1954—all three pieces had different carpenters. It's a piece 'a work, alright." He blinked intensely and distractingly with his head tilting backwards, almost like a twitch.

Both the farmer and the carpenter in me knew what he meant and cringed.

"By the way," he said, alternating between scratching his ass and flicking at his nose, "Only the bathtub has water. 'Ah been both bathin' and doin' ma dishes in the tub fer the last few months. 'Ah patched everything else as long as 'ah could, but last winter took 'em all out and now only the tub has water. Plumbin's shot. Water's purty good most 'a the time though." He again blinked intensely and I tried not to focus too much on his eye.

The analytical in me cringed and the poet began to tremble. "...most 'a the time...What's THAT mean?"

Poet sniveled, poorly mimicking the cowboy's voice. I comforted him and assured him that it would be all right. "We knew this wouldn't be easy," I affirmed. "You're a fuckin' idiot," the sociopath interjected, shaking his head.

"Oh," the cowboy continued, "...and the well is 'a ole hand-dug thang. Both wells is. The one out back has sulfur water, so it don't work no more. The drinkin' one ain't as deep, so water's still good. You're drinkin' ground water from a ole sprang. Water rises and falls dependin' on how much rain you're gitin' but she keeps runnin' somehow..."

"Sometimes it's almost too much fer the ole place, 'ah recon." He blinked intensely again, tilting his head back and twitching the right corner of his mouth.

I smiled as though I understood, but in fact had been concentrating on not concentrating on his eye.

I extended my hand to say goodbye. He shook it firmly with the most leathery and powerful grip I had ever experienced. I noticed his silver, carved belt buckle and knew that this mighty hand had kept him on various bulls for a *full* eight-seconds. Likely that's what pissed-off the one that took his eye.

"Well, good luck," smiled the cowboy honestly, as he threw his belongings into an old brown, but mostly rust covered, 60s Chevy pick-up that looked like an elderly bull.

He turned for a final look at the ole house, touched the bill of his cap with his right thumb and index finger, nodded his head downward politely and said, "M'am."

He got in the truck, backed around, and drove up the driveway. He sat erect and proud, left arm out the window, and spat a final chaw of tobacco and brown juice on the driveway as he turned towards town and slowly drove away, looking taller than his 5' 6" frame. He had marked it eternally, like a dog pissing.

"I wonder where he's going?" asked Darcy with the concern a 5-year old would have for a homeless man.

"He'll be fine, honey," answered her mom. "He's tough and he'll be fine. He said he's going to stay with some friends."

"Wonder if he ate the bull like we ate attack chicken," the sociopath mocked cruelly. "Let's see, if you are what you eat...he's a bull. You, on the other hand...would be a...buckkkk, buckkk, buckkk." He walked around in my head with his arms flapping like folded wings and scratching like a chicken.

"You chicken shit," I murmured.

"Well, I might be," affirmed the sociopath. "You ate him and we live in here too. We are what you eat."

I was tired of his socio-sick humor, felt that he had too much time on his hands, and forcibly ignored him. He kept dancing like a chicken with one eye closed tightly.

"Asshole," I muttered.

"What," Suzanne responded?

"Nothing. I was talkin' to myself."

We began the assessment as soon as we entered the house.

It stood peeling and with a desultory creaking in the breezy spring warmth, yet somehow felt as though the old couple was still living there. The bushes and flowers in the yard felt especially of the old woman's spirit and hand.

There was no working heater, so we *concluded* that installing a wood-burning stove in the next four months would be a good idea. There were lots of trees and dried out branches everywhere, which could be used for wood. I would just need a chainsaw. God's natural warmth, I non-prayerfully concluded: Our first gift.

When we carried the portable dishwasher into the kitchen and sat it down, it immediately rolled itself across the floor and banged against the wood-rotted cabinets and counter.

"Not level," I brilliantly announced and grabbed a level and a tape measure to see how much. "Drops three inches in four feet. Not even *close* to level. I wonder what that is? Add foundation repair to our list of things to do, ok?"

I curiously stuck the level on the north, center wall of the old house (the wall that separated the 1880s house from the 1939 piece). I moved it out till it was plumb.

"Out of plumb...three inches in eight feet," I observed aloud. "I wonder what that is? Hum?"

Suzanne stood there scratching notes, looking brave and noting aloud that the kids had already fled to the yard.

"Watch out for snakes and things," Suzanne yelled out the back door. "We don't know anything about this place yet," she added with her mother voice still audible to the kids—but falling off with newly forming realities.

"Plumbing." I said, from the bathroom, tasting the water. "The entire thing needs new plumbing...and there's no hot water. The water tastes ok to me, though. At least the water tastes ok here in the bathtub. I wouldn't call it 'sweet' but it's ok."

"Plumbing." she wrote mechanically. "Plumbing." she repeated mumbling numbly.

"Entry and exit," I added. "It needs both water *and* sewer lines replaced," I was looking underneath the house through a bucket-sized hole someone had seemingly ripped in the bathroom floor.

"I wonder what that giant bubble is," I pondered aloud, pointing upward from my knees at a basketball sized, once wet and now dry-looking greenish-brown bubble drooping in the low-hanging faded green fiberboard ceiling of the bathroom.

"That ceiling all needs replaced...ceiling and walls. Sink too...oh, and the tub, plus there's no shower," I added, pointing at the sink hanging from one remaining rusty bolt on the wood-rotted bathroom wall and then motioning towards the rusty, chipped and cracked iron tub in its rotting cradle.

"Lots of work, huh?" Suzanne smiled with obligatory fake encouragement.

I took a week off from my job at the Bomber Plant and spent it installing plastic water and sewer lines under the entire house.

I cut out everything that was there, talked with Suzanne about where she wanted a washer and drier, and went to work demolishing with a wood drill, a hammer, pliers, and a hacksaw.

I liked that I did not need to be gentle and knew that I couldn't do any real damage compared to what was there. It was freeing and relaxing. The farmer in me was in heaven; the carpenter was back in school. The rest of *them* were along for the ride.

I found the incoming water line beneath the back porch crawlspace and dug until I could find, grope, grip, and luckily remove the connection, leaving good threads for a replacement pipe connection. As I sawed, banged and constructively destroyed the old house's past, my mind wandered.

Work at the aircraft plant was stressful and flew in the face of everything I knew in terms of common sense, quick thinking, or farmer logic.

It was bureaucratic, mechanically team based—minus the trust, communication, and comradeship—so let's say *manically* team based, filled with ex-colonels and generals and with generations of children who had been spoiled or abused, and then *cast* comfortably into the distorted pressure caste system of their fathers' and forefathers' teachings. Some of them were 4th and 5th generation employees, or more.

Entire families worked there and intertwined or mutated the politics and processes of aircraft manufacturing. It was based on strong personalities driving processes—principals, not principles.

It was common to be working with the child, the grandchild, the wife, the husband, the ex-husband, or the ex-something of a co-someone. Flings and affairs were something to talk about but FAR too many to number. One never knew whom they were talking to so had to be careful whom they were talking about. Silence was wisdom.

It was like an intellectual Arkansas, and perhaps not even that when one truly separated the genetics. It was a culture dominated by engineers and arrogant, egocentric male chauvinists who used to be in uniforms. If female, only *their* daughters likely had a true prayer of succeeding into upper management. Caste incest seemed far less damaged in female candidates.

There was a sharp definition between Commercial and military programs, and except for process overlap, the two would never meet.

Commercial products had airs of snobbery and home office blessing, but even the home office would never let a completed Commercial airplane fly from this hick-infested farmland. In Wichita, military was bread and butter, but felt low-class, not just second-class. I worked military programs.

I felt as though I had discovered a foreign land with a foreign language and culture in the center of my native Kansas. How could something so distorted plant itself and live in this simple state?

They spoke with disheveled urgency, anger, and acronyms, and I laughed aloud one day to see *"ACRONYM"* in my inch-thick acronym definitions book: "Abbreviated Coded Rendition Of Name

Yielding **M**eaning. Even acronym was an ACRONYM! And that seemed normal to people!

I knew that laughing at my own jokes would be some of the only laughter I would see here and I knew, deep down, that even I would quit *honestly* laughing in time. It felt so lonely, suffocating, and terrifying. Early on, I knew that I was a misfit and in trouble.

I felt such joy when I found friends as sick as I, one named James, another named George. As long as I was on a program with them, I was happy. We were an unlikely trio, but we all became grand friends. We were common people, not cut from the chosen.

James christened our friendship one Saturday as I crouched down beside him to look at a schedule of hardware deliveries we were working on. He patted the top of my head and said, "I love that. Somewhere I can sit my beer can while I woo you into giving me a hum-job." He was crude to the bone—brilliant, unschooled, vile, and a functional mad man. His large beer belly bounced like Santa Claus as he laughed and scratched his scraggly stoat beard. We were instant friends.

His wife and kids would become family friends and join us on the farm for parties and gatherings. They were honest and refreshing people.

George was tall, quiet, serious, and funny. He looked much like Chevy Chase, had a radio announcer's, deep, soft voice and sat at his desk making sounds like a galloping horse, intermixed with a flying arrow, then the believable, low-toned sounds of someone being hit by the arrow, shrieking with pain, falling off the horse, and dying.

One could hear the horse galloping away as he lay dying. How he did it, I do not know. How he did it, never smiled, and never looked up from his work, *baffled* me.

George also made electrical sounds and crowd noises that were inhuman and had to be joined by an unseen chorus of invisible, electrified, prairie beings. He and his fresh-back-from-England, musician brother would also frequently join us on little farm gatherings and adventures. James and George made the Bomber Plant bearable for a long season.

I returned to think of the plumbing's relationship to the unpainted block well house that I now struggled to connect with. It quickly transitioned into more corporate ponderings.

I was well sponsored and worked hard, but did not know what to do with sponsorship. I didn't know how to play the game. When all was said and done, down deep, I was still a simple farmer, a repetitive learner, and a western Kansas hick.

I knew secretly that I was already changing, that I hated every pay-period of my new corporate life, that I worshiped only the benefits, and that I already had a deluded sense of both career aspiration and self. I was gripped with fear to see it.

My eyes dilated and I flinched. This was an early trembling of catastrophic failure.

I failed to see that I was already responding to pressure and mass illusionary-bonding by twisting and expanding my flesh-grown *mask of blending countenance*, by drinking more, and by ignoring my instincts in favor of isolated family-killing and corporate fitting-in.

I didn't know yet that life would slowly become a dark, descending bi-polar chemistry filled with daytime pretense, cloaked paranoia, isolation, growing rage, and escapism in my off hours.

God was soon preached and prayed to by a stranger who lived in my body and He was soon understandably nowhere to be found. I did not know yet that this corporate experience would ultimately explode me into complete insanity, and from there, into numb panacea, and finally, awakening. For now, I was pretending with planes and plans.

I had planned escape and solitude in our newly acquired farm and resolved to build it into the dream that we had set in-effect. I really believed and thought that I could make the anesthesia last. I believed as surely in this ability to escape into the dream of re-sculpting an old farm as I did in my ability to drive darkness away with memorized and quoted scripture. What I could not build at work, I began to build into the old house and farmstead.

From this serenity, I would never have foreseen the unfair bludgeoning that I would give this sweet family in future days.

I faded back to hear them trusting me and playing in the nearby yard as I unknowingly joined hiding blacksnakes, rats, and daddy longlegs in our unlikely, symbiotic fellowship under the creaking house.

I was rational, faith-filled, and happy as I sawed, banged my knuckles, cussed, and threw plumbing pieces out from under the damp and musty cramped crawlspace of the ole homestead.

Suzanne went about sawing, weeding, and cleaning up the outside—working from beside the house, so she could hear me, then fanning outward, with the mission focus of a kind gunnery sergeant— weeding, planting, pruning, and taming everything in her path. It seemed that, in some way, she and the old lady had become instant communing spirits.

The kids could be heard laughing and discovering within their mother's random eyesight and constant earshot, occasionally being reeled in by her sternest sweet voice, but then off, capturing and adventuring again.

As I sawed and ripped steel pipes from under the house, I realized that I did not have room to move or even breath in some areas and so I went about cutting two additional shoulder-sized square holes in the floor of the kitchen.

This allowed me to reach pipes and lower myself into areas where I could connect and glue plastic pipes, based only on feel and faith, because I could not SEE what I was doing and did not have room to both see and glue adjoining, pre-measured pipes. I made many mistakes, but I made progress each hour.

It was a grueling three days of coming and going from our old apartment to the farm and back, early morning and after dark, but on the third day, I pronounced victory and we again turned on the well in the pump house. This time it didn't just run to the bathtub.

Water belched, squirted, hissed and finally sprang whole from new faucets and did not leak from the newly filling hot water heater or from an entire labyrinth of new pipes.

We had won the opening round and could now finish bringing our belongings to our new *home*. We had hot and cold water! We would spend our first night in the house tonight. I was euphoric. Everyone cheered!

I likely wished that my children were bigger so that they and their mother could carry me around the perimeter of the house on their shoulders and proclaim me their victorious hero and the "water king."

We thought that we had conquered the old house and that civilization was a coasting ride downhill from here! Little did we know that the ole farm had dozens of ancient and hidden tricks left to play—tricks aplenty.

As we lay in bed the first night, we drifted off to the tranquil chirping of early crickets and inhaled with sinking eyes the magic illumination of scores of gently floating fireflies. It was peaceful and calm as we floated off to exhausted sleep, us on the back "porch," with a fully screened view of the twinkling meadow, the kids in the "ugly" room next door. We were like campers in a musty smelling church camp. All was well.

Suddenly, we awoke to something. Both Suzanne and I heard it: A harsh, random and powerful scratching sound. It was directly over our heads through the green fiber-pressed pre-sheetrock ceiling where we couldn't see it, but we knew it to be aggressive and quite alive.

"What is that?" she whispered with false courage in the darkness.

I didn't know. Mice, perhaps?

We agreed that we would tear off the adjoining bathroom wall and ceiling the next morning to allow us to look at the attic space above our heads.

We slept little, and restlessly, the rest of the night. Fireflies floated and crickets sang, but now offered no respite from the continual scratching above our bed.

Soon birds were chirping their early morning song, crickets stilled, and lightning bugs snuggled into the meadow's fluffy grass.

At dawn's breaking I was drinking coffee and gathering up my pouch of carpenter tools. I would excoriate the bathroom ceiling and walls and unveil our scratching intruders. The sound made it clear that there were more than one of them, whatever they were. We surmised mice...large mice. We were wrong.

As I stood beneath the brownish-green bubble in the bathroom, I saw it as a logical starting place. It was round, it protruded for some ancient reason (I presumed roof leakage) and it was ugly. I would turn the bulge into a hole, don my gloves and rip fiberboard from there. Simple, right? Wrong.

As I struck it for the first time with the claw of my waffle-faced twenty-ounce hammer, the entire ceiling collapsed on me and there I stood covered in at least five gallons of fresh, moldy, dusty, dried rat shit. RAT shit!

It was in my hair, down my shirt, across my clothes and glasses, in my pouch, in the tops of my shoes and neatly heaped around my feet like a small Joan of Arc burning stack. It buried my gloves. I was somewhere between furious and a bunch of emotions that resembled throwing things, killing, and violently puking...emphasizing the violence. I was angry to the point of mute.

"Suzanne," I finally *bellowed*. "It's RATS! The scratching sound is rats. Motherfuckers! I'm covered with RAT shit! Fuck!"

I was now simply focused on destroying them and taking back our new *home*. How uncivilized this welcome was.

I sensed that the old people who once lived there were laughing uncontrollably at my hasty misfortune. I did not think it funny yet. Perhaps we could all laugh someday when I was also dead, but not yet, not today. It wasn't even eight o'clock in the morning and I was buried in rat shit.

"Wait till tonight, you fuckers," I muttered with premeditated murder entering my mind.

That night, as we slept, the rats—who had disappeared by day—found that they could *not only* crawl above our heads, but could *also* freeeeely glide down the inside wall of the bathroom and help themselves to some nice, fat, savory, yellow cheese I had left them on the bathroom floor. I waited patiently and with the anticipating euphoria of a trained sniper.

There was the scratching...movement towards the bathroom...scratching and sliding down the inner bathroom wall. **"SNAP!"** Nailed. A trap bigger than my hand had enticed the first dumb bastard and I was more than happy to don a leather glove and carry his warm, bleeding, still twitching body out the back door and give it all a mindless toss into the tranquil abyss.

I carefully baited a fresh trap, knowing that it could snap and break my fingers, and laid back down smiling with fulfilled vengeance and remorseless victory. We began to slumber: **"SNAP!"** Another one.

"This one's yours," I smiled cynically, looking sideways and unstirred through one eye and hoping to test Suzanne's courage and defiance. She had plenty of both.

She put on gloves, entered the bathroom and carried its fat, gray body past me and out the back door. Her face showed more remorse than mine, but had the look of necessary warfare by the time she returned to bed.

It was our second night of no sleep, but this night lingered not in sleepless fear, but in gruesome bloody battle. *"Gideon, thou man of valor!"* Man versus the Rat. Bait a trap. Close the bathroom door.

Start to slumber. **"SNAP!"** Five rats from the start and at 3:11 in the morning...the scratching stopped. They had retreated.

We couldn't believe the hungry violence that these gray enemies endured to find their maker. They were devils without spirit, flesh without natural warmth—A mistake that God had made in mixing flesh and spirit. An anti-soul.

Through a process of *elimination* or perhaps some form of rat communication, the war was over. They stopped coming into the attic above our bed...five lay dead. I vowed that the next day's priorities would be removal and replacement of the attic above our bedroom. I could only theorize that they were shitting *all along the watchtower* above our heads, and laughing at us. But they were not.

They had apparently saved all of their shitting for the five gallon "lump" that had fallen on my head the day before, or, they did it elsewhere. The ceiling above our bed was dusty, but not shit-covered as I gently pried off the first panel and inspected it for debris.

Removing the entire wall and ceiling covering took less than an hour and I saw a double fist-sized hole through the upper wall where the electrical connection came into the house from our power pole. It was the rat's doorway...their primary one, I presumed. I stuffed it with Brillo pads, glue and caulk and knew that I had resealed the wall to our fragile fort!

It was another victory, but this time without cheering. Only exhaustion and relief were apparent as I scanned the villagers' faces.

Beau's jutting blue eyes looked like a distorted tweety bird. Darcy's brown eyes were dark and focused, as a soldier who had looked death in the eye, yet was ready to fight again. Suzanne's brown eyes were the same as Darcy's, except relieved. There was no gloating victory in her spirit. That was mine to bear. Tonight we would go to the new little town and have a nice dinner as a family. They needed R & R after the R-A-T-S, and so did I.

I worked all day, making trips back and forth to the lumber company to buy 4" x 4" beams and other supplies for replacement of the horizontal V-shaped structure in the little "porch's" roof-span.

I ripped out existing support boards that ran parallel with the floor and those that ran up the back wall, and tossed them out the back door into a pile.

I noted that Suzanne had gathered up the rats and disposed of them. I changed the room's ceiling from a hand's height above my head twenty feet long and eight feet wide, to that height only along the windows, tapering upward to about ten feet at the northern inside wall. I knew that I would do this to the bathroom as well when we figured out what it was to look like as a final product.

I drank 3.2 percent beers to stay hydrated and carefully reinforced the remaining 2" x 4" roof "rafters" with the new 4" x 4" beams that I had bought.

I cut them at an angle to length, slid them into place on each opposing wall and nailed them to their companion 2" x 4" rafters, reasoning that a 4" x 6" spliced beam ought to hold about anything from falling through the roof...snow, people, anything. There was no more interior crawlspace for rats to occupy and I liked the open look of our new bedroom "porch."

The sun was hanging low in the afternoon sky as I cut and slid the last beam into its slot on each north-south wall and against its mated "rafter" on the outer western wall. I knew intuitively that I had done a great job because I could see it and the ole man had not yelled at me all day.

The analytical, the carpenter, the poet, and even the sociopath worked in harmony to design and build this structure. We felt collectively proud. The little sponsor didn't exist yet, and other neighbors had yet to clarify or announce their existence in my cranial high-rise. Daddy was my benchmark for success on jobs like this, and he was killing me at the Bomber Plant, so I appreciated his approving silence today.

I didn't realize then that I would stress test the structure within a few years by sawing an 18" diameter limb off the 100-year old elm tree with a chainsaw and dropping it on the roof—but that was what a 12-pack of logic and a desire to save tree-trimming money would do.

For today, I had reshaped the room and I was happy with my architecture, my engineering, my procurement, and my manufacturing. I was exhausted by the time we went to dinner, and felt a certain joy in aching muscles and cut fingers.

Dinner was small town magic.

As we sat in the little restaurant we soaked in the environment of a unique little town. We were surrounded by cowboys, farmers, dads, granddads, wives, mothers, grandmothers, huntin' & fishin' buddies, aircraft workers, drunks, preachers, teachers, and a kaleidoscope of children and teenagers.

I was glad that I was too tired to embrace my defaulting fear and its associated pre-planning of paranoia and defiance. There was plenty of that incubating for fear-triggered days and situations ahead. Tonight was sweet, peaceful, tasty, and serene.

At first glance, the townspeople looked at us as visiting foreigners from Wichita, but began to embrace us and even tease the kids after we told the waitress that we had just bought the old place three miles west. Everyone knew the place and everyone knew the family that had lived there...Mom, Dad, kids, and kin. The ancients vicariously delivered us.

We laughed, drank pop and ate the best Taco ever made. It had been invented, ironically, by an old *Korean* woman who worked there for years, and it surpassed any taco we had eaten in either southern or northern Arizona.

Mexicans built Tucson tacos; Navaho Tacos were in Page, Arizona. They were delicious, but these were without compare.

We felt like neighbors as we bit into the snappy salted salsa chips and the soft delicious wrappings of life in this wonderful new little Kansas town.

Chapter 20
the fight in the dog

Progress on the farm was going well. I had returned to work after the week-off to plumb, kill rats, and begin conquering the old house. Suzanne began looking for work in nearby communities—Rose Hill, Douglass, Augusta, even Wichita. We were still outsiders and there were 200 applicants for every job.

She was strong and upbeat by nature, but even she was feeling increasingly discouraged as she spent large blocks of a day loading up the kids, dropping off resumes, and returning home to work in the yard while simultaneously listening to the never-ringing phone.

We were "home" now so she was determined to reestablish a career foothold in teaching, to hopefully enroll Darcy in her school's 1st grade, and prepare the way for Beau, who was four and, therefore, close behind.

Suzanne was an elementary teacher, and unbeknownst to them, as good as they could ever find.

She had an excellent background and reputation in Tucson, where I had met her, and after a starvation dry-spell in Loveland, Colorado—where I learned to frame houses and she developed *"Frog E. Weatherly"as* a small weather cartoon for the local paper—we landed work in Page, Arizona, where she taught first grade and birthed our two children, Darcy and Beau. It all sounds simple enough on male reflection, but it wasn't by any reflection.

As I worked alternately patching and demolishing the house, I reflected that four years and one month earlier, we were cast into a family-forging season of life-and-death struggle. Four years ago, we could not have dreamed that children would be laughing on the farm of our dreams. Four years ago, we were too broken to dream at all. For one trip around the sun, then, life rippled and inoculated us with a painful season in the Maker's fire. Seasons indeed define life. Suzanne was 39 years old in Loveland when she miscarried a 5-

month baby boy 24-hours after dreaming that our hallway was filling with blood. Darcy was conceived almost immediately, was born in November of 1977, and Beau followed Darcy's birth by under 18-months, arriving in May of 1979.

His birth was nearly fatal to this sweet, smart, determined, artistic, distant-Israeli/ever-Irish blooded, auburn-haired, 4' 11" Sally Fields-looking woman—who had been carded in bars at the age of 36 when we first met, and who jokingly described herself as "about six-feet tall and blond."

There was the miscarriage, Darcy, then Beau, all in under 20-months. But it was tougher than that.

Darcy was 18-months and David (our stepson) was 17-years old when hell unleashed on their mother and, likely, mother/child love was all that kept her on Earth. Love bonded as powerful glue. Only David and his mother were perhaps more inseparable than she and Darcy.

David was 13 when his mother and I first met. He was a wild, powerful genius who would entertain and inspire his siblings as they grew by doing little things like memorizing and reciting, word perfect, and with literary flair, Poe's "Tell Tale Heart" on Halloween. Or he would recite *all five* chapters of the book of James at the Sunday dinner table. He would follow us to Kansas, join the Air Force as a crew chief, and later become a top-shelf power plant operator and mechanic. Stated another way, Beau and Suzanne nearly missed his entire performance.

Beau was born two months early—weighing *two*-pounds, eight-ounces—after Suzanne's appendix burst and went undiagnosed for another four days by her handsome, arrogant, chauvinistic young doctor, whose experience was apparently that women suffered poorly and complained a lot.

When we showed up at the emergency room, Suzanne was diagnosed, loosely, to be a hypochondriac with a pregnancy-induced bellyache.

I told the doctor that this woman could take pain and never complain, but he didn't listen and he wouldn't order blood tests—just bed-rest and observation. He admitted her for whatever set of compliant reasons, perhaps to humor us, or perhaps as revenue for the struggling rural hospital—perhaps both.

He offered no medical plan and seemed almost yawningly unconcerned.

The look the wise old Mormon doctor gave his young protégé when he returned to town, examined symptoms, and reviewed Suzanne's chart contained jagged knives and he *immediately* ordered a white count. It told the tale.

The end result was that Suzanne had an emergency appendectomy, was filled with gangrenous poison, delivered Beau 24-hours later, and then lingered with me in two additional months of hourly death row stress to see if Beau was still alive in Phoenix Samaritan hospital, five desert hours away.

Another doctor friend of mine who had been present for her surgeries said, "Damn, that was the stinkin'est gangrene I've ever seen practicing medicine. It was ripe, man! It'd been cookin' in there a looong time!"

He was no doubt inadequately sharing the miracle they had worked to bring her back from the grave, and we trusted each other, so I took it as a friend's encouragement. We would need a lot.

"Preemie" care has no doubt ridden on medicine and technology to come a long way, but was not a well-documented science in 1979. Preemie life is physically precious and practically precocious, but nature has ways of leaving some people in life; that's nature's *nature*. So, who can know destiny?

For context, a child named Al Smith was born on a farm, weighing three pounds, in 1914. His mother kept him warm in the oven in a shoebox.

He became an NSA agent who traveled Europe under cover of a traveling basketball team in the Second World War, and married my mother a decade after daddy died.

Al was tall, strong, quiet, nearly deaf, and had the finest memory I will ever encounter.

He ran a feed store in Scott City, Kansas, and billed *all* of his customers at month's end from memory: "Three 50-pound bags of protein pellets, two blocks of salt, a *block* of protein, three bags of 20% meal, one bag of dog food, xyz veterinarian supplies, 10 bags of planting-milo, etc., etc., etc. for farmer Joe." At month's end, items were listed, priced, and a bill sent to each and every customer from Al's *memory*. He never took a note.

Al would be the gentlest and wisest partner a mother could ever have. What the ole man had in mean, he had in kindness.

After two packs of menthols most of his life, he died of emphysema, gasping for air, babbling lists, formulas, sparking gibberish, and long-secret things that made no sense in his final hours.

We held his hand and were blessed to know him. Al showed that preemies may ultimately weigh-in small and leave as giants. Like truth, they are God's business.

Survival statistics still dropped with birth weight in 1979, and Beau would push science.

At my first sighting, he came out looking like a flopping red fish and hadn't even deployed his ears. I thought he had none to deploy. He didn't look human. He lay on the table with the squirm-like illusion of attempted swimming as the focused doctor affixed his barely budding lungs to continuous positive air pressure (CPAP) and his tiny veins to life-giving intravenous drips.

The doctor, Suzanne's doctor, was *amazingly* skilled at these procedures. He moved with precision and swiftness that was no doubt lifesaving to Beau. Arguing that Beau should still be in his mother was second-guessing life, destiny, and God. The now very humble doctor was absolutely an artist at premature baby handling.

Beau had an oblong reddish baseball for a head, including wrinkles for the stitching, a small white beard, peach fuzz textured white hair, legs and arms smaller than my index fingers, and functionally, no lungs...BUT he showed the strongest life-force and will to live I had ever seen in a living creature. He was being Air-Evac'd to a preemie ward in Phoenix within 90-minutes of being born.

We were too overwhelmed by poverty, healing, working, and parenting David and Darcy to simply break loose and go to Phoenix. The hospital assured us that there was nothing we could do anyhow except hold him occasionally. They didn't even encourage us to come. "He's in good hands," they assured us by phone. I dipped into my paranoid nature and faintly sensed that perhaps they didn't want us to get too attached or have too many memories.

A few weeks into our nightmare, some friends got together a "care package" with $300 cash, the City Clerk's car keys, and a hotel room and sent us off to Phoenix on a Thursday.

Holding Beau in my hand was like half a bag of crumpled sugar shaped like a small apple with tubes and a doll's body attached. His skin was thin and seemingly transparent, with vessels and veins uncomfortably visible. But, again I noticed that he was SO alive. That much energy would surely have exploded even a cat his size. I couldn't comprehend it. And there were rows of them just like him!

He, and the entire room of preemies, would continually alternate in not breathing. It was like watching a movie.

Blue cushioned transparent cribs aligned the outer walls, and each crib contained a baby doll attached to tubes and wires. Beepers would go off; nurses would calmly walk over, flop the baby on its side and thump it rhythmically on the back with two fingers until the alarm stopped sounding. It meant that the baby had restarted. "It" then remained a "him" or a "her" for another hour of desperate life. Strange magic. Strange physics. Strange medicine. Human touch.

Touch was SO important, they said. Bonding with someone was critical, because the baby had not likely experienced nature's burst of estrogen to create the chemical "love bond" if it was born more than three weeks early. Touch could replace that. Chemical love?

Shortly after our visit, when Beau had technically "died" a couple of times, he underwent open-heart surgery (to sew shut a valve on a heart perhaps the size of one's lower thumb) using Curare, the jungle poison used to hunt monkeys with blow darts, as anesthesia. They said that it was the only thing available for someone that small and was not an exact science, given preemies' metabolism, condition, and body weight. The "dark art" of medicine.

Two days later, with us calling every couple of hours to see his condition, we were told that he was finally awake, had experienced a small aneurysm, had dropped down to under two pounds, had yellow jaundice, and still, "*of course*," stopped breathing several times per day. They said that this was, "pretty much, all *to be expected*."

When asked about the impact of his cranial bleeding, they said, "We simply don't know yet. There are just not enough studies on preemies to project the impact of this, but it COULD, *could*, affect his learning in some way, possibly not; we honestly don't know." The sociopath helped me ponder the possibilities...comforting friend that he was.

By now, Suzanne had to have hernia surgery because the lower belly length scar where they had removed her appendix—and then later, reopened, removing Beau—became infected and was protruding painfully as a volleyball-sized hernia. She struggled, taking antibiotics as long as she could to wrestle with Beau's journey, and dangerously delayed her second surgery.

Doctors forgot to put her on antibiotics when she left the hospital after the burst appendix filled her with poison. Oops: A missed diagnosis, gangrenous appendix, a preemie baby born to escape the poison, no antibiotics, more poison, and now a hernia. The papers one signed acknowledging that medicine is an "art" and not a science was becoming *painfully* apparent. But the "Word" said, "*Sue no man at the law*," and *we* were peaceful people so we took our licks…well, Suzanne and Beau took our licks.

One morning, two months into the saga, the hospital called us up and said, "He's four pounds and climbing. Come and get him!" It felt like a microwave bell. *Cook…cook…Ding…the baby's* done! It was precisely on the day that was to have been his natural birthday, July 13th.

We hurried to Phoenix and asked lots of questions, the main one being, "Is he breathing right?"

The answer was no, but they said that he was "restarting on his own" now, and that if we hooked up an alarm to him, neither he nor we would ever rest. They seemed relatively sure that he would "*keep running*" on his own, so home we went…three fragile and exhausted people: Beau physically, me mentally, Suzanne physically and mentally.

We reasoned that if God had gotten us this far, and if Beau was still alive and kicking, we could depend on God to complete the work. We were physically and spiritually spent from weeping, from not sleeping, and from the natural human tendency to intermix worry and prayer, but we had hope because our baby boy was still alive.

He was so fragile and sweet looking as we made the journey back to Page and finally laid him into the crib that had been empty for too long. Seeing him free from needles and tubes was amazing.

Beau and I "bonded." He would lie quietly, like a little warm loaf of wrapped-up bread, on my chest at night as I stretched out on the floor with my fingers interlocked behind my head and watched TV.

He shared our poverty, stress, and work-fueled great adventure.

He *would* not bond with his mother, however, which staggered me. This was one of the most naturally sweet and bondable people God could create, yet I watched this tiny child reject, and even physically push her away from him, with hands the size of a thumbnail.

I don't know what animal chemistry underlay it, but it hurt her feelings and it made her feel completely inadequate as a mother. It was not her fault, and remains a mystery of nature to me.

She tried so hard, but he would not allow her to embrace his personal space for years, rarely as a baby. Socially, and by default, she accepted defeat and focused on raising Darcy while I focused on Beau. I had limited skills for this responsibility, but we limped along and survived the early seasons.

I had changed both kids' diapers, and got used to the smell of child waste products with Darcy. No big deal. But Beau? It is indescribable.

It is kind when I say that his piss was like a poignant mix of av-gas, ammonia, battery acid, and warm Limburger cheese. It was absolutely unbearable. His chemistry and metabolism were cruel and intense. He would also sweat profusely and the smell of it would gag me on a given day. I learned to gird-up and appreciate it as his God-given animal scent. No beast would have eaten him. I cynically wondered if aliens had genetically altered me in some failed experiment beside the pond below Paul Larner's shed.

When our mothers visited in rotation and helped us limp through this grueling season, we were inexpressibly grateful.

My mother was immensely attracted to Beau; her mother was not, and was never pretentious about it. She was not a pretentious woman—ever. This would become a divisive family pattern in years to come. Their help at the beginning was a strong respite, but then we had to pace ourselves and find the balance between working and raising kids. Social connection and bonding became academic luxuries behind surviving life's new grind. Any parent has felt their measure of this human race.

Future rats would not be our first night of no sleep with mission focus and rotation of duties. They did not know that they were tiny lightweights compared to Beau's predestined pilgrimage. The next block of time was blurred.

We traded nights of getting up and feeding Beau a small bottle of formula every four hours.

We were too poor to afford cable, so sat watching a Utah based, two-inch wide news strip with elevator music run across the bottom of our TV screen as the tiny child suckled his measured formula of white energy. His mother had tried to use a breast pump to save her milk, but quickly dried up as grueling physical afflictions ate her flesh.

One o'clock to two o'clock, six o'clock to seven o'clock. Off to work, back home. Do it again and trade days and nights.

We did this ritual every day and night until he hit about eight pounds, and then, with medical exceptions, he became "just a baby." I drank evenings and weekends to feel anything euphoric. We became physically and emotionally numb.

Suzanne lasted as long as she could and then went to Tucson to have the second mistake fixed. She aged ten years in one. She was still fresh from surgery and weak when she returned to teach 1st grade for the Page School District in August. *"Two surgeries, hell on earth, and a preemie baby later, how was your summer vacation, Mrs. Lincoln?"* But, one would never know with this woman's strong will and positive attitude that she was suffering.

She went through the pain, slowly regained her strength, natural color, and shine, even as she battled death's messenger and left *him* standing jilted at *his* sacrificial altar, unable to steal her baby or attain a double play by grasping her life as well...Likely from a will to live and raise her three children, she sustained. She had youth and spirit sliced and ripped from her, then slowly regained it as the planet wobbled once more around the sun.

One day, perhaps three months into Beau's life, a social worker came unannounced to our door to "meet" with us and we, exhausted, politely but firmly shuffled her out quickly as a government intruder and an unwelcome guest.

She had little time with us, but again mentioned the need for "bonding" in preemies and, pointing at some newspaper clipping in her folder, *casually* commented that *some* preliminary studies indicated that the absence of preemie bonding might be correlated with sociopath behaviors in later life.

Bullshit, fact, or not, I wish she had never told us this. It became a dangerous set of filters for viewing a child through an emerging alcoholic mind.

She left indignantly and passive-aggressively noting that child abuse was *common* in preemie homes. We then knew her real reason for showing up unannounced. I wondered if God or Satan had sent her to our door, but paused knowing that it was only the government trying to help us.

Beau grew very quickly for a while, then paused, then grew very slowly, then in disproportioned physical and mental spurts.

For a moment, he became a normal looking baby, and then he became a cute yet strangely disproportioned and dwarf-like child. He experimented with things in ways that taunted the gods of physics. He seemed to have intensely too much energy and seemed also to lack a *consistent* concept of consequence, time, or space.

He seemed to grasp "at" these principles, but then forgot everything we *thought* he had learned. He banged into the laws of nature again and again, then didn't, then didn't again, then did, then seemed to learn.

He was obviously obtusely intelligent, yet an odd little child— detached, passive-aggressive, defiant, bright, and analytical.

In his first year, he seemed at times robotic and inhuman in some way, like he was studying and manipulating us, as a being and not a child. Even his sweet mother felt this intercessory phenomenon. It frightened us.

Specialists said that we would have to routinely check him for hydrocephalic onsets and for rupturing of his belly button and testicles until age two. They also told us to check him at least annually for detaching retinas, until he was 16. We were religious in these precautionary rituals, and watched doctor after doctor hold a flashlight to his reddish, transparent, vein-filled nut sack and pronounce him "ok for now."

Beau was always attracted to the doctor's flashlight, stethoscope and other tools, and I sensed learning more of the world's operation than we suspected. He seemed ADD, but also learned intuitively, and in spurts, like a quick-drying sponge. We saw an odd learning *order*, but not a learning *dis*order—as feared from the aneurysm—so we had growing hope.

I can summarize his early behavior by stating that one evening I walked into our home in Page to see a 2 ½ year old Beau standing across the room *on a chair*, wobbling, teetering, left eye gazing and fixed in space, and looking into a lighted red flashlight with his right eye. He was pressing it against his eye and face with his tiny hands, leaning forward into the light and not moving it a centimeter until it bounced off the floor with his head still tightly attached.

It cut him below his right eye and left a flashlight shaped scar that they said he would "grow out of" during puberty. The large "cut" didn't break the skin, but sliced his muscle tissue deeply. Doctors argued that if we left it alone, his natural growth would overcome it, but if they repaired it now, he would always have a scar from the incision. He bore the "temporary" scar until after puberty. It went well with the growing slice that ran from his backbone and around his left side from heart surgery.

Beau was always Casper-pale white, bruised, and bled easily, and looked like tweetie bird. He had ever-present, quarter-sized baby-bird like purple circles under his eyes and constantly seemed hyper-aware of any activity around him, especially music and sound. His crystal blue eyes bulged from his sparrow-like eyelids and he had the countenance of an earth-battered, but God-protected little angel.

We always felt paranoia in public because he was always banged up and bruised and we constantly recalled the social worker's passive scolding. I would prove her right later, but not yet, and not because he was a preemie. I would arise to the challenge because Daddy imprinted child-raising on me and taught me how to deal with a lazy, absent-minded boy.

Beau hated pain and shook violently when food was sat before him—especially candy. He loved *any* kind of euphoria, but didn't like human touch.

I, consistently playing formulary alcoholic psychologist, reasoned that he hated pain because needles, knives, and poison-dipped blow-darts, at a very early age, had repeatedly stabbed him.

I reasoned that he shook for food because he existed for months, malnutritioned, losing 20% of his initial body weight, and eating from intravenous tubes.

I reasoned that he loved euphoria because his mother had been shot up with morphine the night he was born to control what was now the excruciating pain of being seven-months pregnant with an appendectomy and a drip hose for gangrenous marinated sauté. I was even willing to throw in that euphoria is 180-degrees from pain.

I argued that touch had proceeded being stabbed by nurses and rested my case. Little did I know that the opposite of pain was healing, not euphoria. I would learn that for myself much later. It all made sense to me through beer bottles and tokes.

Beau's strangest and most troubling behavior was his purely *random* reaction to pain. One never knew when it would happen, and it lasted until puberty.

Sometimes, when he would get hurt, he would stand there, get deathly quiet, stop breathing, pass out, roll his eyes into the top of his head and, then, fall (*wherever* he was), shake as though he had epilepsy, and piss his pants. One never knew when it would happen. It occurred only a few times per year. He would come-to about 15 seconds after each episode and recall nothing. Several doctors seemed interested in the behavior, but not alarmed: Something about probably, "outgrowing it and his being a preemie."

His learning "disability," if he had one, was perhaps that he learned complex behaviors, but failed to see the building blocks that got him there.

When he ran, he ran into things without slowing; when he climbed, he climbed up, then fell back down, when he *finally* talked, he never said words or short sentences again. He rattled like a pan lid on a fast boiling pot. He couldn't pronounce Rs and Ls and never *cared* to learn. He apathetically and defiantly wore out a speech teacher in elementary school.

His sister was as focused and articulate as he was unfocused and argillaceous. She molded him for daily battle and dragged him around like a waddling blue-eyed yellow toy duck on a pull rope—the kind that was the size of a football, went quack, quack, quack and followed its appointed child master, even if it were being dragged on its side.

When we tried to engage them together in conversation, Darcy would step in front of him like a feudal queen, hold her arms firmly downward, fingers spread with palms back, and engage us with challenging, intelligent saucer-like eyes and crisp answers to any questions asked, him listening and peeking from behind her like a hungry, gaunt, conquered yet trusting, bug-eyed peasant.

Darcy learned to control and protect; Beau learned to manipulate and be protected. At about the age of 3 ½, he began talking prolifically and never shut up again. This gave me confidence in his ability to later grasp the written word.

I could see his intelligence growing, but had already concluded in my early co-dependent and forming alcoholic way that, if he needed to spell his name "Bo" instead of "Beau" because of his aneurysm, I would allow that. How future compassionate I esteemed myself to be, and what a rev-up dad was scripting for his self-confidence! I would allow him to fail: Bo. When it was finally tested, it was I who failed, not he.

He couldn't write his A, B, Cs, or his name, one evening as a kindergarten school assignment, and then came home 24-hours later with a paper that I thought his teacher had written—letters were perfect. He stood patiently that night and created them again: *Letter perfect.*

The night before, when he couldn't write his name, he stood beside the refrigerator, (where I had unrolled and taped a large brown paper grocery bag and handed him a purple crayon), crying and writing letters backwards, upside down and...well, simply wrong in every imaginable combination. I had resolved, beaten, that "Bo" would someday do, then, POOF one day later...B-E-A-U, perfect and beautiful: The art of *nature*, or perhaps, the nature of *art*.

I could hear Darcy and Beau running in the summer Kansas "farm" yard, chasing things, building things, fighting, yelling, laughing, crying and being kids. Ah, Beau and Darcy—or by alpha gender, Darcy and Beau—what a pair.

Beau had refined the innocent look of a pliable tweetie bird angel; Darcy had retained the aggressive, focused, and hard look of a combat soldier. When THEY got into trouble, it was usually because of him, and his innocent face, coupled with her loyalty and unyielding defiance.

It took some time, but Suzanne finally connected with the Superintendent in Rose Hill and was offered a 1st grade team-teaching job. She was both humbled and elated. The little town in Kansas had hired a 1st grade teacher who would disproportionately influence the careers of dozens of straight-A graduating students, and others, for years to come.

Life was beginning to align to give us some "fix the farm" cash flow and, thereby, to allow us to get the thing refinanced within our one-year private contract requirement.

One day, an old farmer came by and Suzanne noted that rats were still a problem around the outbuildings. Specifically, large, gray, defiant *packrats* were the problem. They loved building a large nest of sticks, Beau's abandoned underpants, clothespins, walnut shells, other articles, and something red—usually one of the kid's toys. They *loved* apples, and Suzanne had even killed a couple of them with apple-baited traps. She was tired of being stared down by them when she entered the shed, and she was tired of being afraid to work with them watching her back from the rafters.

"Ya know what ya need," said the sage ole farmer. "Ya need a *cat*! Ya don't have any yet, do ya?"

"No," responded Suzanne, knowing the obvious link, but wondering about the reality. "We don't have any cats."

The next day the tall, rough cut, gentle-looking, quiet, balding, white-haired ole guy showed up with a gunnysack jumping around like a set of conflicted pre-and-post-OA butt cheeks on a stationary bike. He untied the rope and **WHOOSH**...two cats shot out of the bag and into the wilderness. We didn't see them again for awhile.

But, within weeks, one of them began to ease herself AND HER KITTENS near the house and we began to feed them scraps and leftovers. They quickly became domestic.

This restarted the childhood pattern of two-dozen cats thinning to half a dozen each year as our adventure continued. The rats disappeared from our seeing and we freely entered outbuildings to find cats, not rats.

"The small cat is the mother cat, but even the male cat is scared to death of her and she's also the natural hunter," observed Suzanne one day as she was having a drop-in conversation with the ole farmer who had brought the first two cats. She pointed at both cats.

The giant gray and white cat lay on the propane tank, casually licking his nuts. It looked at Suzanne and the farmer briefly and then went back to licking. She flushed when she noted that they were both observing this same scene.

As a distraction, Suzanne motioned towards the small, beautiful, calico feline who lay licking her paws near the propane tank in the noon summer sun. "She is constantly bringing her kittens mice, and she's already teaching them to hunt for themselves."

The kittens were pretending to hunt by pausing in killer stance and then attacking a rolling walnut. They quickly lost interest and began rolling around with each other.

"Well, there's a sayin'," the old man smiled knowingly. *"It ain't tha size 'a tha dog in tha fight, it's tha size 'a tha fight in tha dog."*

Beau came tumbling off the low branch of a nearby purple mulberry tree and lay there motionless and crying. Darcy looked down at him, and then came running and stopped before her mother, looking upwardly, grim and urgent. "Can we have something to drink?" she asked calmly.

Her mother looked at them both lovingly and smiled. "Sure," she said. The farmer nodded and drove away.

She helped Beau up and the three of them walked hand in hand past the sleeping calico cat and her brightly arrayed pile of now slumbering kittens: A gray one, a black one, a yellow one, a calico one, and a runt-like white one with gray speckles that defiantly lay by itself on the other side of its mother. It would become a Siamese.

Chapter 21
the beginning of tremors

The farm would not be complete without a consultant.

Brother Bill dropped by one Saturday morning near summer's end, beer in hand, and a recognizable lifetime-lasting smile on his face.

I was always glad to see Bill. He offered me a beer, which I of course took, even though it was 8:45 in the morning. We walked around looking at progress and challenges left in place.

I opened the access hole under the bathroom floor and proudly showed him the intricate, and still shiny, plastic smelling maze of pipes that I had built into the house, CPVC for the water lines, fat black pipes for the sewer...new pipes fading off into the distant darkness of the northern walls.

"I replaced it all myself," I said proudly, shining my flashlight to and fro and looking to him for accolades.

"Well," he smiled, barely looking, gulping his beer, farting, and then burping forcibly and dramatically. "Let's see? Plumbers. Umm? Act-up in class, make Ds, finally drop out or graduate so the school can get rid of them. Vocational course of study? 'Shit flows downhill and payday's Friday.' Nice job, Bro!"

He walked off deliberately, passive-aggressively, unimpressed while I reddened with embarrassment and hurt feelings.

My family had nearly carried me around on their shoulders. Fucker. Fuckin' trim carpenters. Arrogant prick!" Oh, well, I loved my brother and I knew he didn't really mean it. He was just fuckin' with me.

"So, what ya gonna do about this roof?" He was looking upward at the odd roof pattern with its mismatched layers of tattered, washed-out and near-hole ridden wooden shingles.

"I'm planning to reshape the middle of the house to tie in with the upper roof and set it on a windowed-wall that I build along the center peak," I said proudly.

"It is pretty fucked-up looking now," he added. "Anything will help." I could tell that he thought the house was a piece of shit, but I also knew that he had lived in places worse and didn't care a flip. He was examining the old building through the eyes of a carpenter and not through the comparative judgments of a neighbor or a man. "You gonna roof it yourself?" He motioned his fingers along the irregular and sagging roofline.

"No," I responded. "I don't know shit about roofin' and I thought I might find some *asshole* who does and see if I could catch him between jobs and cut a deal." He knew I meant him.

"I know just such an asshole," he smiled knowingly. "Let me know when." He walked off towards the outbuildings, grabbed us another beer out of the truck, and lit a Salem menthol. I followed him like a needy child.

"You got enough fuckin' cats here, don't ya," he motioned, looking at the pile of quickly maturing kittens playing by the shed. "They must cost a fortune to feed."

"Naw," I chuckled. "Ever since Suzanne's mom moved in last month, they eat our scraps. She cooks like a chef, seven course meal every night, and intentionally makes twice as much as we need, bitches predictably when we don't eat it all, and feeds them out the back door...talkin' to them like they're a bunch 'a damn babies. All works out fine. Plus, we don't have any rats now. We went from two wild cats to seven fat lazy ones in one little summer. Suzanne's mom's a good ole gal—tough as nails, and a great woman. I love her."

"I know," said Bill.

We walked past the garage with its broken concrete floor and into the 30' x 12', three-bay, hedge-pole shed covered with rusty nail holes and faded tin. It was surrounded beyond by acres of thorny hedge trees with a few walnut, sycamore, and young cedars mixed in.

"Beautiful place," he said calmly. "You're a lucky son of a bitch."

"I know," I said. "Soon as I get this place stabilized and refinanced, I think I'm gonna tear this shed down, remove an acre or so of those trees and dig a pond here."

I looked at a gully. "See how that ditch runs to the road? I'm told it runs like a river when it pours. We'll see. It hasn't rained much since we moved in."

I pointed at the jagged, 18-inch deep five-foot wide furrow that was cut beneath our feet, running under the northern end of the pole shed and out the southwest corner toward the grove of trees. It came from the road, past the well house and under the shed. It was quite a ditch, and *something* dug it.

"SHIT," he said, with pensive amazement. "I've gotta see what happens when it seriously rains. Hope I'm here. Might wanna have a boat." He winked with a squint. "This property's pretty flat from here to the house...does water go near the house?" He looked somewhat *seriously* concerned.

"I don't think so. It's still there," I joked logically. "I don't know where the water goes." We were walking now from the pole shed to the barn about 80 feet away. We stopped because we were treading face-high weeds.

"I've gotta get a BIG fuckin' mower soon, huh?" I chanted, turning back, pushing weeds out of my face and knocking weed burrs out of my hair.

Exhaling smoke, he squinted his eyes and nodded his head quickly, and in an exaggerated manner, to emphasize the priority.

"Damn," he said, amazed and pointing. "There's another damn shed, or barn over in that corner of the property!" He was pointing past the barn, past the seven-foot wooden corral fences, and into the northwest corner of the property several hundred feet away. "I hadn't noticed that when I drove by."

"Honestly," I responded. "I haven't even been to it yet. Too many weeds. Looks like an ole open-faced hay barn. I need a big fuckin' mower soon, huh?" I sneered again, mocking myself. He nodded violently again.

"Let me know when you mow this shit, and we'll go exploring," he said, losing interest for today. "Why don't you drop over later and we'll knock down a few brewskies."

"Oh," he paused. "You know my buddy Gary, the mean green rolling machine? He does all kinds 'a shit and might want to cut down those trees when you decide to build a pond. We'll swing by sometime soon and you can ask him. Save you doin' it yourself and he'd likely do it just for the wood. Just a thought."

I weighed trading the lumber for the work and thought of our Arizona-experienced family plan to use a wood-burner to heat the place, so hesitated mentally. Between now and the next two winters, I thought that I would cut the wood myself. I purposely didn't respond.

"Welp," said Bill, walking to his pickup and shooting his cigarette butt about 20-feet towards the chicken coup with his thumb and mid-finger, "Gotta run. Drop by later and we'll have some fun. We can swing by Gary's and see if he's got any fresh green." My addictions surged.

"See ya later, Broskie," I affirmed.

He backed up the drive and sped away. I went back into the house, gathered up the family and went to the little restaurant to grab some greasy good breakfast. Then I went to work tearing screens off of windows and nailing 4" cedar tongue-in-groove boards onto the back porch ceiling that I had now insulated.

We had called the Sears man and he was coming to put a set of custom built, bronze colored windows with screens as outer windows all around both the upstairs and downstairs of the house. Dilapidated, peeling and all, it was starting to look lived in. We would have the windows installed within several weeks, and that would begin the exterior warming and preservation process. Things like paint and roofing would be next year, or the year after if things didn't leak in the meantime.

I felt proud of our work, but knew that we would have to be careful with our priorities and our money if we were to refinance this place by next spring. We were already getting too many credit cards started, but we were making progress, and I knew that we could conquer it in due season.

Suzanne began teaching and immediately engaged an aircraft-working pig-farmer, the husband of a fellow 1st grade teacher, to come and mow our weeds for the first time.

He was a giant, strong, dark-haired man in his late 30s with dark eyes, a gentle spirit, farmer focus, and the most contorted last name I had ever seen. He came. He mowed. He conquered.

He showed up with a good-sized tractor, and a belly-mounted bush-hog mower, that growled and ground the giant, tough, green and now-browning weeds into a yard and meadow covered with piles of flaccid mulch. The weeds lay as dead as the rats. Gone.

For the first time, we could see the real beauty of the farmstead with only buildings and trees exposed. It was breathtaking as we walked around it freely that evening, drinking in the freshly cut-smells and sounds of true rural ambiance.

The kids basked in new freedom and discovered the wonderland playground of our old 60' x 30' x 28' peeling, but solid, and still red, barn. They entered it screaming and echoed exuberantly as Suzanne and I walked for the first time to the old hay barn that my brother had spotted.

It was tilting, held up by three mature trees on its east wall, but gigantic, filled with antique machinery, and open faced on the south and west sides.

It was attached on its west wall to a round, rusty, uncapped, solid steel silo cylinder about nine-feet in diameter and 20-feet high. It all had no apparent modern USE, but was a wonderful and magic antique appurtenance to the property.

THEN came the rains.

It was late August, likely some hurricane was brewing near New Orleans, Canadian air was floating from the northern skies and **BAM**, the heavens opened, and five-inches of sheeting rain came down. We now knew why large trees in the yard were tattooed with scorched lightning scars and why there was a virulent ditch running through the pole shed west of the house.

For a couple of inches, there was nothing to mention...just sheet lightning, flashes, thunder, lots of water puddles in the driveway and yard. It was calming. I sighed happily to think that our well would receive new benediction.

THEN, the farmer's field across the road began to burst with alluvium. It poured, ruthlessly and untamed, through the large square concrete culvert under Douglass Road, into the ditches, into the trench, along the well house, under the shed and into the meadow, which lay calmly two hours earlier.

Water began *burbling and banging; it* thrashed mowed weeds and debris against rusty sidewalls of the old tin pole shed. Its bays swelled with a swirling foamy torrent and I began swelling with apprehension. But it didn't stop there.

Lightning hit a tree about 40' east of the house and cracked with a deafening bang. The kids cried.

Soon the ditch and trench filled and the *driveway* began ALSO to run like a small broken river. Water ran perhaps a foot deep all the way from *near the house* to the pole barn, like shallow, yet fast moving, rapids. The squall of water cast itself around the old chicken coup that lay unpainted, perpendicular to the house. It flooded *harshly* into the meadow.

It began to creep even closer to the house, and our entire family watched with adult-cloaked assurance, and breathless horror, through the small, west facing, tattered and torn screen that covered the now noticeably fragile, peeling, once white painted window.

I had moved our truck and car up to the grassy area between the driveway and trench, but they alone sat on an island steeped in perhaps three or four inches of moving shallow water. The rest of the place was running at least a foot deep in water...more as it headed south. The pole shed stood in at least two feet of water and rising.

"Fuck!" I said out loud.

The kids looked as though they were gaining an adult understanding, as their mother said, "Want some popcorn, kids?" I appreciated her distraction, thanked God that the electric was still working, off and on, and went to the back door to behold water's muddy hell rushing through the meadow.

"Jesus." I whispered, somewhere between swearing and a humble begging prayer. "A boat wouldn't help, Bill." I could hear popcorn popping in the microwave and a hiss as they opened a 2-liter of Coke. I thought of the band and deck furniture on the Titanic. "Jesus," I gasped again.

"Hey, **Dick**! Ohhh, **DI...I...C...K**," called-out the sociopath, dragging out his words, and interjecting without invitation. "Maybe that's what the cowboy meant when he said, *'You're drinkin' ground water from 'a ole sprang. Water rises and falls dependin' on how much rain you're gitin', but she keeps runnin' somehow. Sometimes it's almost too much fer the ole place, 'ah recon.'* Remember *that?*" He mimicked the cowboy perfectly as the poet stood there wide-eyed, looking back and forth for assurance, and trembling with fear. Poet looked palely to me for comfort. I had none to offer.

"While you were busy acting like you were listening and trying to be *pooolite* by not noticing his one eyeee, I **was** fuckin' LISTENING, **asshole**! Mr. Cowboy was trying to tell you T-H-I-S! He wasn't blinking or, let's see, how'd you say it...umm...*'tilting his head back and twitching'*...Genius. That wasn't a *twitch*, **Dick**; that was a cowboy **wink**. A one-eyed, cowboy...**wink**. A **wink** from a **guy** who had his **eye** knocked out by a giant fucking...**bull**! THIS is what he meant by *'sometimes it's almost too much fer the ole place, 'ah* recon: *Noah's fuckin' flood II*, the movie! 'Ah recon, **indeed!**" He mocked me scornfully and wagged his bony head.

I was pissed and distracted enough by him for the moment to ignore the rain and go into my head to confront him. "Enough of this shit," I thought angrily.

He lived in the cellar by the compartmentalized people. He was skinny, balding, with shoulder-length straight and stringy rat-like hair, shifty-eyed, stoic, snakelike and mean as hell. He seemed to come at me when I was angry or afraid and I honestly didn't know how to shut him up.

He had access to most of my thoughts, emotions and perceptions. He used them to torture and humiliate me whenever he pleased. I sensed that he had broken off of the ole man's rage somewhere along the line and took root, like one of those hedge trees in the meadow that would grow its violent branches into another healthy tree, leaving even its prey with mutant thorny branches growing out of it, impure, raped and defiled. I hated him. He had a memory like a steel trap, likely because he needed no mental energy for other little things like morality, conscience, compassion, or kindness.

"What fuckin' good are you?" I barked, telepathically, looking down at him! You seem to shut up completely only when I give you weed or booze and you appear at times like this to make a situation worse. If I listened to you, all I'd do is scare the kids. What is your fucking purpose in my head," I asked glaring, and deliberately without blinking?

"Maybe I'm here to protect you," he answered. "Or, *hey*...maybe I'm here to teach you how to communicate 'effectivewy" with your gwowing wittle *boy*...you know, the pweemie who may not have gotten pwahpo...how'd she say it...oh, proper booonding."

He smiled like Satan's messenger as he mocked Beau's inability to use Rs and Ls. "And, by the way, I don't JUST live in your head...peek in your soul sometime. I think you and the kid both still have one? Or, did you each...*ever* have one? Hum?" He looked intentionally and sarcastically puzzled, with his finger twisting against his left cheek.

"That's below the belt, you mother fucker," I said, fearing that it had been my thought and not his, knowing we were one, but praying that, perhaps, he was a demon *possessing* me and not a true part of my psychic knit.

I felt fear, suddenly, more of him than of the rising floodwaters.

He fed comfortably off of my fear, and though I *thought* I hid it from him, he consistently breached the walls of my sanity and stole what he wished, scratching his initials on my mind's wall to mock me. He was simply a human mental rat, but I couldn't catch him. The more I tried, the meaner he got. I wondered where he came from and resolved that if I ever figured out how to exorcise and quiet him, I would.

He suddenly went back into his cellar, deliberately yawning and acting bored. "Rain's easing off, DICK," he noted across his left shoulder with his boots clicking and echoing and his words fading.

I looked again to note that the river was running strong, but the rain was indeed tapering. The house was not in the river...just near it. "Thank you, Lord," I whispered gratefully.

The kids were laughing with their mother in the other room.

I peeked in to see Beau shaking with imagined hunger and reaching past Darcy to grab more popcorn, even while he had a hand full of it already. She pushed him back mechanically.

"You mean, Dawcy," he said softly continuing without Rs and Ls. "It waining and I not wike this. It scaowy. It waining haw'wed. It waining." He was accidentally right. It was waning. The rain was finally waning.

"We've gotta do something soon and serious about this drainage," I said with atypically short summary.

"I know," Suzanne heartily agreed, smiling like she had been talking to Jesus too. "The cowboy warned us about this."

I wondered *how* she knew that! Jesus! An angel and a sociopath heard it, but not I. Perhaps she listened differently, or better. I had just never picked that up from the cowboy.

It was a few weeks later when my brother showed up late one Saturday morning with his friend Gary to drink a few beers, share some mean green weed, and survey the hedge forest.

It was turning into a perfect fall day and I was loading up logs from a tree I had cut in that area when they arrived.

There would be hard jobs and difficult jobs. I had to begin focusing on the difference; refinancing and wisely constructing the ole place depended on it. I could be easily distracted.

These were heavy logs, and it seemed as though hundreds of trees remained, though I am sure it was only a few dozen or so, in the area where I envisioned a grand tranquil pond.

I told them about the incredible rain, while Bill nodded his head and rolled a typical Billy-Bob joint...straight, tight, and smooth looking as a 100s-type cigarette. He was the master.

Suzanne and her mother were off buying groceries, looking for antiquities, French doors, used clothes, oddities, and other interesting items of little-known value. They were also keeping an eye out for a good deal on a wood-burning stove. Suzanne was as discerning as a ferret and sly as a fox at finding deals, and both her mother and she were helplessly addicted to yard sales...especially her mother.

Suzanne's mother dredged up word puzzles and romance novels. They saved us a fortune. The kids always found new toys and gadgets and loved the adventure. They loved the farm, but couldn't wait to go to town.

By now, I had purchased a yellow chainsaw and cut down two of the thorny, angry trees. I went through several chains doing it. Two-foot diameter logs and a myriad of lesser sawed-up branches lay strewn where two trees had been. I was loading them into my faithful rusty and white '68 Ford F-100 while Bill and Gary passed the killer green. I helped myself between tosses and opened yet another cold beer.

Gary picked up a checkmark-shaped piece of seasoned walnut branch and said, "This'll make a nice pipe."

Cutting two trees nearly killed me. Fortunately, Suzanne had found a man two miles away who was also an aircraft worker, but who freelanced, sharpening chains for only $3 apiece.

Hedges were like cutting sappy yellow limestone rocks mixed with sandy sawdust. They were full of whatever wire or implement was sitting near them as they grew. They simply ingested it and kept growing. They were hard and somehow felt like a spiritual tree-version of rats. They would burn hot and completely. It was not unusual to find barbed wire, bolts, or even an old wagon wheel grown deeply into them.

I knew that, stove or not, I had enough wood around the place that if Gary took every one of these trees; I would still have plenty. I prayed he would want this thorny pest of a forest.

I was ready to remove this pole barn, clean out and deepen the trench, and clear the trees for my future pond. It would certainly fill with water here; that was clear.

I surmised that removing the trees would be a proactive way of preparing for a pond—that we could not afford yet—and might even allow the water to run with less blockage from the trench, through the meadow and beyond. Anything would help.

"Want these trees?" I asked, knowing that Bill would have raised the question by now.

"Yeah," Gary responded. He was a man of few words. "I'll cut 'em and take 'em away if you want me to." He never smiled and his face sat hard and emotionless.

Gary was now easy to describe.

He was the cowboy with fewer words and *two* intense eyes: Different face, same hair, same beard, same spirit, same build, same gristle, same man. Amazing.

I knew that even hedge trees would tremble when he looked at them, knowing that they were not long for this world. He and Suzanne's mom would get along well, because they were both no bullshit and tough as nails.

"Ever hear of the Sahara Forest?" he asked unsmiling, and fully knowing that he was sharing a rote joke.

"You mean the Sahara Desert?" I responded, playing along predictably.

"That's what it is *now*," he finished, completely without smiling. "And, yes, that was me." He was ready to attack.

There was a seemingly non-stop chainsaw growling, trees cracking, then, crashing, and heavy stacking and thumping sounds below the barn as he sawed, chopped, and loaded rock-hard yellow logs every weekend and even some weekdays for the next five weeks.

I worked on other projects around the farm, always complaining about scratches and cuts, and needing approval and accolades for small accomplishments from my captive clansmen.

I would drop by just to pop a beer, but Gary was focused like a warrior. He drank quickly, talked little, and immediately returned to work with a hacking vigilance. He was sunburned and his face and arms were scratched from the vicious clinging and slashing of proud and stubborn half-century old trees and their offspring. His resolve seemed comparatively infinite.

Hedge trees had been planted during the dust bowl, in the "dirty-thirties," to battle wind erosion and its unannounced, airborne, and ruthless stealing of a farmer's topsoil and crops. Ancestors of these "pond area" trees were planted to protect this homestead's parameter. People often died from the "dust bowl's" illimitable dust, especially those with asthma, or like maladies. Hedge trees were drought resistant, and stood to filter and barrier against the hot summer's winds and dust, and her evil cold sisters of winter.

Over time, hedge rows took on a life of their own—rolling their green softball-sized seed clusters downhill or in rushing water—spreading to other areas. Their watchmen lined the entire parameter of our property like a giant square of protectors, now pausing, without a windstorm or a dust war. They stood vigilant like a Terracotta army. Most had imbedded faces.

Gary didn't wear gloves and, though the long thorny branches slapped, scratched and cut him with defiance, he didn't flinch and rarely even seemed to bleed. When he did, he wiped the blood on his dirty jeans with a silent contempt.

If he were made of human flesh, I knew that he was Viking or Scottish and that he had some strange ancient bond with spirit warlords and gods of the forest. He would have been one of King David's *Mighty Men,* and was surely kindred flesh and spirit with those who had dug the wells into this farmstead.

He kept to himself, worked sunup to sundown, drank Coors, smoked a little weed, and hauled off his beheaded, drawn-and-quartered arborous captives each evening in a new brown Chevy pickup with a flatbed trailer.

Suzanne's mom offered him something to eat or drink each day, but he always politely declined and kept working. We never saw him eat, though surely he did, or perhaps he drank energy from stumps of those that he devoured.

Gary would someday join five other good men in carrying my brother to his final rest in a barren prairie of quietly creaking cottonwood trees and gently blowing grass. Sahara.

Chapter 22
revenge of the rat

By now, I had paid more than passing attention to the subtleties of the property. We went about fixing and maintaining a little here, a little there. We put on a new cellar door, built a cover over the "sulfur well," to keep the kids and cats from falling in, re-hung and straightened the barn doors, things like that.

I had pondered, but not studied, the two hand-dug wells, and had admirably envied the manliness that went into digging them.

The ground was hard to dig about 18-inches into the earth, yet the two wells sat rock-walled and fortified with oblong softball and near-football sized rocks, one running about twenty feet deep—the drinking well—and one about 35 feet deep, but now filled with sulfur water. Each was about four feet across.

It was shabby, but the drinking well near the barn sat beneath an abandoned, four-legged headless windmill tower, and was covered with old boards and rocks so that something or someone could not fall in. The boards were pretty tight, seemingly to prevent the entry of animals or even casual debris.

There was a badly cracked, square concrete slab surrounding the circular well, poured crudely within the straddled legs of the old windmill tower. Weeds grew out of the cracks and I knew that snakes might enter them.

The other well had a 5-foot, round-base and 40-inch concrete walled *cube,* built around its top with an upside down "U" shaped pipe above it, over the well's center, and poured into the concrete. It looked like a *little* 40-inch version of our ole farm's block well house, but without a floor or a lid. It was actually cute. The new wooden "lid" made it cuter and left something for Suzanne to set flowerpots on.

This "sulfur" well had obviously been used at one point for drinking and, thus, still had the cliché rope-and-bucket mechanism designed into it. It was the "prettier" of the two wells, but poison.

Eventually, I would hook it up to a sprinkler system for the grass. Grass could handle sprayed sulfur water; we couldn't.

Things were running ok, coming together, and falling into place. We were marching towards refinancing. All was well, we thought.

I had managed to foolishly extend more credit and buy a "beautiful" showroom floor, new blue Ford 16-horsepower "Lawn Tractor" to mow the place—all 10.126 acres.

I reasoned that with the grass now mowed by a neighbor from face high, I could easily maintain it with this "powerful" machine and mow it every few weeks after the grass and weeds grew only several inches. Besides, I reasoned, the year was late and I didn't have to do anything about mowing in the winter…I could save that precious time now for house restoration and repair, resuming my yard maintenance in the spring.

The short story: The tractor was a piece of shit—probably not its fault. It would be a giant in the city, digging a backyard garden, or mowing a nice green lawn. Here, it was a pellet gun battling a charging rhino.

I would spend hours in 30-minute blocks changing belts and cleaning-out its air-intake system, even with the weeds only six-inches high. I mowed once more before winter, and knew I was in trouble for years ahead. Of course, given credit, it was *new* and we were now making payments on $3,200 so I had to make it work for a few years, no choice.

On other fronts, we had small victories, life again being kind to angels, fools, children, and drunks.

The ole farmer who had brought us the cats showed up one day with his tractor and used its front-end scoop to level, deepen and clean out the trench that led from the road to the three-bay tin-covered pole shed. This increased our chance of surviving another major storm.

He and Suzanne had struck up a farmer's friendship, and now he was always helping us out in little ways. It was a true blessing.

A neighbor and his sons came and hauled away the pole shed one fall weekend after Suzanne painted a sign that said, *"free building"..."Pole Shed: Take Me"...*or something simple and clear. *Poof*, it was gone: Good for that farmer; good for us.

We definitely couldn't afford a pond yet, but the house was coming together enough to present it for reappraisal and refinancing, so we felt good, and it wasn't even winter. It was fall. Even the new bronze colored Sears exterior, screened-in windows were installed and looked smart and "insulated." It deceptively communicated *civilization*.

Even without paint or a new roof, windows and other touch-ups began to make the house look modernized. The tongue-in-groove cedar ceiling was finished above the porch and we had installed a new sink, tub, *and shower* installation in the bathroom.

We were finally winning! Then we encountered ONE *first* little setback.

As I went in the house and guzzled water from the faucet one morning, I commented that the water tasted funny to me. I was parched from working, and I hadn't noticed the unsavory and peculiar taste the night before, perhaps because I had been drinking extensive beer.

Other family members agreed that it tasted odd. Even Grandma (my pet name for Suzanne's mom) commented that it tasted weird, and she was a smokeaholic with zero functioning taste buds.

Darcy used the word "bad" to describe it. Beau gawked and stood behind Darcy saying nothing. Suzanne used the word "nasty." I grabbed a flashlight, turned, and immediately headed to the well. The family followed like a tree full of Curious Georges.

For the second time since we had moved here, I disturbed the boards and rocks that protected the well from its surrounding environment. I looked downward with a new flashlight and there it was: A RAT, lying peacefully on its side, floating and bloating in the center of the well's tranquil water: Bobbing, dead, rotting. A dead smell wafted dankly out of the well. The family looked as though they wanted to move out TODAY, Right NOW.

I was grateful for the farmer in me and said, "Beau, get me a bucket and, Darcy, get me some rope."

We all stood there with the uncomfortable silence inflicted by knowing that we had been drinking decayed rat. There really were no words.

I could see Suzanne and her mother silently pondering if the family needed vaccinations against a hundred rat diseases, or even now against bubonic plague. Perhaps they even wondered if it were too late to be inoculated. I wondered myself. I suddenly pondered that the sociopath must be drunk in the cellar on his kindred's poisoned water and, thus, was silent in this humiliating hour of rat vengeance.

Perhaps it was a rat Messiah, dying for the sins of all rats and, thus, resurrecting the gray souls of five fallen believers. Perhaps it was their mother, casting herself into the well's abyss from a rat's delayed grief over losing her children. Perhaps she simply fell into the water and, like a human, froze slowly from a slippery hypothermia, while paddling hopefully to nothing. Whatever the drama, here lay a dead rat in our drinking supply.

"Here's the rope, Dad," said Darcy with a quick, focused presence. Beau was dragging a small metal bucket across the trench and Darcy was motioning for him to hurry up.

I recalled that I had no gloves and went to the house to get some, with the honest motive being a desire to guzzle two quick beers before I scaled the ancient rock wall of the rat's watery grave.

I drank one beside the refrigerator, without breathing or pausing, pondering how cold and good it tasted. I took the other with me to the well, for comfort and pre-planned grandiosity.

"Wish me 'well'," I smiled, emphasizing the pun, and with the obvious dragging look of a man about to enter the gallows.

"Hope I don't join the rat. If this thing caves in on me, or if I slip and fall in, please tie-off the rope and get some help, because you won't be able to pull me out of here and I won't have the strength to do it myself." That planted the grandiose seeds of fear that I wanted, and left me believing that I was an actor and not in any real danger. The family looked predictably frightened and anxious.

I tilted the beer about half way and felt the welcome rush of added alcohol to my brain. I tied the rope to the bucket's handle, with the flashlight dangling off an extended length of rope at the bucket's side, and sat it beside the large open hole. I placed one foot on the rock wall, eased down and placed the other foot across the well, a strong four-feet apart, feeling to see if the rocks were stable. They seemed to be.

I gulped the rest of my beer with a final free hand, tossed the crushed can out of the well's rocky circumference, and began picking my way slowly down the slightly-pear-shaped ancient rock wall.

It was cold as I moved downward. I couldn't see the rat, and Suzanne moved the light around to guide my footsteps. I had a moment of knowing that she was such a good and faithful companion—today, a literal light to my steps.

The 20-foot hole seemed to have about eight feet of water in it. My legs were shaking, but had sufficient energy as I evaluated them to ensure that I could make the trip down *and back*. My leather-gloved hands were feeling the damp, potentially slippery, cold rocky walls to evaluate whether they were *in fact* going to hold or collapse.

I suddenly realized the truth of my grandiosity and no longer felt like an actor.

The beers' euphoria was replaced instantly with a rush of survival adrenalin. My vision became keener and my legs gained uninvited, yet welcomed, additional strength. They shook more with the added energy so I paused briefly to calm them.

I wondered suddenly if the walls *might* collapse and, if so, now knew that rocks collapsing, plummeting and sinking me in eight feet of COLD water would almost certainly kill me while the family watched helplessly without resources to respond twenty feet away. The rat and I might ironically be removed together.

This felt just to me, in some way that balanced the universe. We were both life forms, I was merely bigger. I pondered if I shouldn't have perhaps felt some Christian remorse for the night of killing, but descended answerless. It was a battle of mind and soul that I did not wish to entertain now. I refocused, as time seemed to pause and drag.

I scanned that inner-knowing truth, or lie, that seeks to tell if this is one's appointed hour, and found the gauges to be green. It was not. I felt relief and continued downward, picking up the pace to avoid wasting leg energy. Any visions of grandiosity had evaporated now. I just wanted this task to be complete.

As I eased within reaching distance of the rat, I yelled for them to lower the bucket and, so, it came spinning and swinging downward on the yellow nylon rope. The light turned the water into a dark opaque mirror, which reflected me and revealed sporadically the rat's unreflecting body, as the light swirled and dangled on its descending pendulum.

As I grabbed the rat's carcass to place it in the bucket, I felt it's decaying skin begin to tear and knew that I did not want rat guts splashing into the water, so I carefully cradled her body, with a measure of unexpected respect and reverence, and gently laid her in the bucket.

"Pull her up!" my voice echoed, bouncing off the water.

I felt cold drops of rat-soaked water drip off the bucket and onto my face as the bucket quickly ascended upward. I shivered with disgust and immediately began ascending behind it.

Within 45-seconds, I reached the top and marveled at the feel of sunlight on my face as I birthed beyond the circle of rock-encompassed light and entered the outdoors. I silently thanked God for helping us with this task and wondered about our next steps to drinking water survival. I felt a deep love for the entire family and smiled at them without thought or motive attached. They had done a great job.

Suddenly the ole farmer, who had brought us the cats, dropped in and we simultaneously described our new affliction.

"Shoot," he said confidently. "When I run into that, I jest put a gallon 'a Clorox in tha well and leave it overnight; then I flush tha well rill good by leavin' tha water runnin' and she cleans rite up. Good as new in 24 hours!"

We stood amazed. God had brought him to our rescue in our very hour of frightened battle and he had suffered the same affliction.

"Happens all tha time, in these ole wells," he continued. "Jest tha way it is out here. We got critters and we share everythin' with 'em...Jest learn 'ta live on tha same place together. That's tha advantage 'a deep wells, but even they can get 'a critter, and round here yur likely 'ta hit sulfur water goin deep. These ole thangs work fine...just have 'ta keep 'a eye on em. Hell, I've had 'em and I got bad knees, but I ain't dead yet. You'll be fine."

"Gotta go," he smiled, backing around and driving off like an anointed preacher who had just dismissed church, snapped his buggy whip, and headed to Sunday dinner. We smiled in unison at perfectly timed messengers.

"Where's the Clorox?" I asked, but Grandma was already bringing it out of the house.

The next weekend the kids and I spent forming and pouring a retrofitted concrete slab where the ole boards and rocks had been.

I inserted a big metal garbage can in the mold to leave myself an access hole, and Brendan and Jason, Bill's sons, joined the kids in pushing their handprints carefully and slowly into the freshly poured Quick-Crete while Bill drank beer and looked on, waiting for Sunday dinner. We were ready now for other trips into the well, but with this tightly sealed addition, I couldn't imagine when or why.

The water still tasted a bit like chlorine, but it was fresh and almost "sweet" tasting. We prayed that it would somehow pass a County water quality test soon, because that was a requirement to refinance the farm. I added a swimming pool chlorine tablet to the well every couple of weeks from then on.

Somehow, we got tougher during that week and the farmer within me felt renewed and exonerated. Even the sociopath had nothing to say about this odd adventure, and we slept peacefully with our clean well, windows on our house, trees gone from the pond area, and weeds neatly mowed.

Fall's chirping dimmed, slowed, and finally stopped. Red cardinals lingered uncaringly as other birds began migrating for the winter. We could hear large flocks of geese honking a few hundred feet above the ground in the dark stillness of chilling nights.

We had bought a like-new, high-quality wood-burning stove from someone at a yard sale, and I was testing the wood I had cut to see if it would heat the house. It seemed to. Hedge sporadically popped, but burned hot in the still "ugly" room as little rotating fans pushed the warm air into other rooms.

I could hear the kids playing; Suzanne sat doing teacher's homework, and Grandma's unlikely laughter tumbled happily down the stairs and into the living room as she cackled at her sitcoms.

Now we were winning.

Chapter 23
a party and a tour of the house

Our family was ready for winter and, as a final hoorah, I borrowed from my farmer's logic, tore-out and used the old rusty wire fence along the front of the house for rebar, formed, and poured a sidewalk from the back porch to a long "L" shaped sidewalk.

There was a sidewalk in front of the house with "1939" etched into it, and that made a good starting place. It definitely made the place look more civilized and, I reasoned, might help our appraisal for refinancing. It looked nifty and the kids helped build it.

We could afford five yards of concrete AND, so, I also had them deliver a driveway full of road gravel to park our cars on, sparing us the mud.

David had transcended now from Arizona and was living in my brother's basement in Wichita. They quickly became best friends. David was 21 and preparing to enter the Air Force. Bill was a fun-loving alcoholic trim carpenter, who had found steady employment with a company that primarily rebuilt fire-damaged homes. He and Sahara Gary were working together, and so, the three of them joined with me to become great friends and serious drinkin' buddies.

We had decided to throw David a party before he went into the Air Force. We planned to invite only friends of his and Bill's, and their close friends, to ensure that it was fun, but not fully insane. We also invited James and George, the two guys that I had formed friendships with at the Bomber Plant and, of course, their families. A couple of Suzanne's teacher friends came as well. It was a grand inauguration party for her son and the first gathering on our new farm—picture perfect.

"WE" describe the house now, not because it's necessary to complete the construction story, though that's helpful too, but rather because it's necessary to understand a story that gives insight into David's eccentric persona under the influence of excessive drink.

Remember Beau's flashlight story to exemplify his oddities? This is the other son.

Sociopath's "short" version: There was a house with three pieces—the north side had a living room with two bedrooms upstairs, the center had a kitchen and an "ugly room" and the south side had the porch and bathroom. Oh, there's a front porch too. End of tour.

Analytical and Poet's shared version: The unpainted white house sat back roughly 100-feet from Douglass Road, with a yard already sculpted by Suzanne into a grassy well-groomed lawn, with rings of planted flowers tucked under large trees.

My version: (My version is drenched with sweat and suffering aimed at getting attention and sympathy). I built a house with pain, projects, concrete, gravel, and drinking mishaps. I'm too traumatized to go further.

Not all the pain was mine, however. "Uncle Bill" would replace the counters, and the cabinets were already painted chocolate brown and arrayed with carefully chosen decorative porcelain handles and knobs by Suzanne.

David's party was set against the perfect ambiance of a perfect home.

The evening of the party was perfect. People drank, wandered around the farm and laughed freely from sundown till leaving time at perhaps one o'clock in the morning.

Kegs of beer were strewn about and a smorgasbord of food lay artfully presented on two long, cloth covered, folding tables that paralleled the back porch and bathroom. The party was a smashing success by all accounts.

David, soon to depart for the Air Force, and man of honor, passed-out in Darcy's vacant bedroom as soon as everyone left, and (thank God) did not drive back to Wichita.

We all put away the leftover food, thumped the kegs to ensure that they were dead, cleaned up the garbage, shut out the lights, and went to bed. All was peaceful and quiet. Then it happened.

It was reminiscent of "Night of the Living Rats." We awoke at three-something in the morning to the sound of footsteps on the roof—not our immediate roof—somewhere further towards the front of the house.

Both Suzanne and I listened, un-breathing and intently, to see if we could pinpoint it. I suddenly wished that we owned a gun.

"It's moving this way," she whispered startled and sounding afraid.

It was erratic. Soft steps moved westward across the north roof of the 1880s house, then across the peak and down the southern roof of the old place. Someone was moving now across the roof above us, and towards the bathroom wall.

Footsteps halted in a place roughly above the kitchen door and then moved again along the wall separating our room from the bathroom. It was soft-footed, but it didn't sound as though someone were sneaking...it just didn't make sense.

It was as dark and only a starry sky could be seen. I could not even see the cellar or sulfur well out the back windows.

Time suddenly did what it could do in the well...it faded and stopped, dragged, yet seemed eternal. We breathed and lay frozen with no plan. I felt unmanly, but honestly didn't know what to do.

Suddenly, footsteps exited the roof and a crash occurred, near our window, below the bathroom window. Someone had dived, jumped, or fallen onto the folding-tables that earlier lay covered with food.

"Ohhh! Oh! Fuck! Shit!" We heard someone gasping amazed, stunned, and apparently more shocked than in pain.

It was David! We looked at each other, trying to speak with a sense of reason.

He walked a few feet away, pissed, and came to the back door. I let him in and he passed me unspeaking, with eyes that looked like someone who had a flickering porch light, but wasn't home.

"You ok?" I asked, still completely clueless and puzzled. He didn't answer. Suzanne sat in bed, quietly, and without words or questions to utter.

David shuffled, limping mildly, past our bed, through the kitchen, across the living room, up the stairs, and back into Darcy's abandoned room where he had been sleeping.

I remembered the time that I awoke to the sound of someone in the living room and, there, found David pissing while leaning casually in the northeast corner.

When I said, "DAVID, this isn't the bathroom." He turned his face, continued leaning comfortably on his bent forearm, smiled, released his crank, and waved in friendly acknowledgement, but continued pissing. I spoke again, but by now he was done, shook it, turned, ascended the stairs, and returned to Darcy's bedroom, which he had then borrowed for the night as well.

Even sociopath was stumped by his roof dive, but the analytical, who was getting arrogant and overbearing from all the work he had done on the farm, purported a theory: "He sleepwalks," he said. "When he drinks a lot, he sleepwalks, perhaps even other times, who knows?"

"Here's what happened...think about the pattern of his footsteps: He somehow went out the back window beside his bed, across the roof to the west, like he'd do if he were walking to the stairs, down the peek of the southern roof, like he'd do if he were walking down the stairs, back across the lower roof, thinking he was going through the living room and finally, SPLASH, off the back roof, aligned with the bathroom door...thinking he'd arrived at the bathroom, but stepping off onto the tables." We all agreed. It seemed...well..."logical."

David was a strange poetic and mechanical genius, and often poked holes in the soft eternal fabric that gives one's flesh life. This was a moment in that journey. Other moments he had barely survived.

He would, earlier in life, be pronounced dead in the water, iffy on the shoreline, and alive at the hospital, from a skiing accident that smacked him 50 miles per hour into a pink and purple Lake Powell cliff wall, and left his brain sack showing through a gash across the entire back of his head. Two days later, he was stitched, but back to full steam.

He would, earlier in life, borrow our brand new 1976 Dodge Colt, roll it down a mountainous incline near Loveland, be ejected through the *back* window, and live to have his ear sewn back in place and a large laceration stitched shut on this head. Next day...same ole David.

Later in life, and eight months sober, he would hydroplane and go airborne off a bridge in a brand new Trans Am on a rainy night interstate near St. Louis.

He would land upside down on the road beneath, slide until the T-tops and roof were ripped off, roll upright into a filling drainage ditch, and find a police officer sitting there.

The officer jumped in and held his head out of the water to keep him from drowning until help arrived. He would return to the living with his *entire* scalp sewn back into place and his face reconfigured, but still handsome, while missing a week in a mix of natural and medical-induced coma just to keep him alive. Then...same ole David.

Oh, what did he look like? That's simple. He was a mix of Paul McCartney and Rambo.

The next morning, he didn't want to talk about the leap from the roof, so we let it go and I helped him load up the empty kegs so he could return them to the liquor store.

I didn't realize that he would be smashed into that morning by another vehicle in an accident not his fault. Irony: A barely sober man with three empty kegs in the back of a truck, walking away from an accident not his fault. That's David!

He was banged-up, but uninjured, while the ole '68 Ford pickup took another lickin' and was towed away in its destined indestructible life of serving and protecting.

David would live to recite "Tell Tale Heart" and books of the bible to his own children and he would live to be the ongoing loved and revered big brother of Darcy and Beau.

Chapter 24
the laws of physics and other hidden damage

There was one more little *T-I-N-Y* sidetrack that was unexpected before we refinanced. It happened in our first winter. It was a small matter, where formulating alcoholic thought and "seasoned" reality didn't properly align. It's called a wood-burning stove and a Kansas winter. It was the heat equivalent of my lawn mower genius: A rhino and a pellet gun...actually much worse.

It went something like this:

David was visiting us after boot camp, and was therefore available to help his mother carry logs to feed the wood-burner, so I decided to take a couple of weeks off to have a double hernia repaired (which, by the way, I had likely caused while cutting logs and carrying our new *wood-burner* into the house!).

As I lay, post surgery, eating pain pills and drifting in and out of slumber, it snowed. Then, the gates of winter hell opened from a Kansas north wind and the wind chill fell to 50-degrees below zero.

There's no way to describe how cold our house got. It was struggling to stay 45 degrees and the walls were leaking icicle-air like a screen door on a submarine.

I had put pink insulation in the northern front door and windows, anticipating the cold, but nothing could have anticipated this—nothing except experience. We had lived in Arizona too long.

Even Colorado had a different type of winter, and had a thing called Chinook winds that were instantly 50-degrees (*ABOVE* zero) when they slid down the eastern face of the Rockies and spontaneously warmed Loveland.

Not to cuss needlessly, but it was fucking freezing in our little farmhouse! Whatever ambient temperature was present became academic when pierced through doors, walls, and windows by needle-like, invisible icicles of hell's bitterest artic air.

Suzanne urgently called and got quotes from heating and air companies, we extended more credit, and within a day one of them was installing central heat.

David, Suzanne, and Grandma curtained-off all outer rooms except the living room, kitchen, and ugly room and kept the water dripping and the wood-burner running at about 600-degrees night and day. Excluding airborne formless icicles, their efforts kept *those three rooms* of the house at perhaps 50-degrees—and the upstairs livable to an Eskimo at a flouting 40-degrees. Also, fortunately, the house didn't burn down when the wood-burner's chimney glowed persistently red.

In a typical David moment, I awoke disoriented and asked where his mother had gone, whereupon he responded casually, "I heard her talking to the furnace guy, and she whispered, 'Let's wait till the cripple goes to sleep so we can sneak off and be together.' I think she was trying to save you a few bucks on the furnace. I believe that's where she is."

I started laughing and couldn't stop with my new stitches jumping and pulling unmercifully. Cold air was secondary and irrelevant. With pain pills, I got the giggles and hurt like hell for endless minutes.

The heat was crudely installed, but running, that very day, with the contractor spending another day to run ductwork throughout the house and thereby to disseminate heat properly.

It no doubt helped our appraised value, but stood as another desperate lesson learned about old farmhouses, men who hand-dug wells, and one-eyed cowboys. With pain pills, Sociopath left me alone and was probably warm in his cellar.

Finally, we were ready. We applied for traditional financing, had a water quality test, and had the house appraised in April of 1984, eleven months after we had moved in.

Our water "EXCEEDED" state and county water quality standards and the appraisal came in at about $70,000, which allowed us to retire a couple of credit cards and access additional reconstruction money via a second mortgage for the next phases of our work. We got traditional financing, relaxed without the pressure of a timeline, and preceded with Phase II projects.

The first project, we agreed, would be the roof, so I took some time off, framed a soon-to-be windowed wall along the center peak of the 1880s house, and framed a new roofline to sit on it, running from the peak of the old 1939 two story house. This made the three pieces look like one house—just not yet shingled.

I extended the east and west sidewalls from the bottom of the old 1880 and 1939 roofs to tie into the new roof and lap-sided them to match the old house's 4" lap-siding. It looked quite nice and it was time to call "Uncle Bill."

By now it had snowed a lot during the winter and had rained again in the spring, whereupon water had begun to drip down the north walls of the "ugly" room and, also, into the kitchen from the failing 1880s roof attachment. That had helped us make decisions about fixing the roof first.

Bill took some time off, or was between jobs, and showed up at our beckoning to assess the scope of work.

We agreed that he would strip and re-shingle the entire house with new, top-of-the-line cedar shakes. He told us how to get them and we had them delivered. They smelled heavenly.

While we had him, I asked if he might install four skylights, or "roof windows," in the remaining south-facing side of the 1880s roof. He said "sure!" I was excited and off to work he went. It was Monday. He brought another guy with him to help with the project.

It was going well. He had stripped off the old shingles, installed the new shakes, and was reshaping the overhang above the (still-windowless) new roof peak that I had built along the old center roof. It looked great.

He ordered custom built windows to be installed along the peak. He had also ordered custom windows to install in four evenly spaced holes that he had now cut into the southern, 45-degree pitched roof of the 1880s house. It was going to look spectacular!

I went to work on Wednesday morning knowing that by Thursday night, the job would be done. We were elated, and wanted to show our appreciation, so I asked Suzanne to pay him something now.

Suzanne paid him half of his agreed-to wages that afternoon, and he called me from the bar about 3 o'clock, telling me to meet him there.

I went straight from work to the bar where we drank and toasted our respective roles in conquering and dragging a dilapidated old farmhouse from its inevitable grave into the 20th century as a visionary work of art. I finally left the bar and arrived home slightly after midnight.

The scene was quite ugly. I still have no adequate words to describe its harsh, sobering, effects.

As I walked in the back door and into the *unusually brightly lighted* "ugly" room, where the new roof window holes had been cut, there stood Suzanne.

The normally sweet and beautiful little Irishwoman looked like some fire-headed, rage-filled, living, wet version of the rat that I had pulled from our well, only scarier.

She was soaked head to toe. Her hair was wet and stringy. her clothes were muddy and wet; her clogs were wet and muddy. Her eyes were scolding with a scalding, death-casting look.

If she were not so exhausted by battle, and if she had sufficient violent will, and if she had owned a doughnut cutter, she would not have flung it, as my Mommy had done in similar circumstances. She would had clenched and thrust it directly and deeply into my head and removed a doughnut sized piece of forehead flesh and skull bone, simply to peek in and see if I had a brain...It would have been simple, understandable, instinctive, rage fueled, female curiosity.

Oh, I forgot to mention, by now we had torn the ugly green ceiling out of the "ugly" room and hauled it away. I had retrofitted the remaining 2" x 4" rafters with 2" x 8" support rafters (similar to what I had done with 4" x 4s" to the old porch) and left the room with a beautiful, upside-down, V-shaped, 14-foot high, cathedral ceiling. This had intelligently preceded my brother's coming to roof the house.

Suzanne had helped tear out and haul away the old debris, the support boards, the ugly green ceiling covering, and the dusty green-asbestos "insulation" that had overlain it above our heads. A chainsaw had done the rest.

The good news is that when the **FIVE INCHES** of rain came that night, the family didn't suffer, quake or fear to see if lightning would hit the house or if water would flood it.

The bad news is that they were too busy mopping, rotating buckets and pans, and tossing water out the back door from the cascades of water pouring into the room from four exposed and un-tarped roof window holes. In the bar, I had hardly noticed, but boy had it rained!

Being after 12:30 a.m., Grandma and the kids were in bed, apparently sleeping with physical and emotional exhaustion. Suzanne finished glaring at me, turned sharply on her left heel and, without speaking, went to bed.

When I saw my brother, as he arrived early the next morning, I described the event in some quick, diluted way and told him that he might tread softly around Suzanne, or even apologize and then stay clear of her. She loved my brother, but that would not save him.

I explained what they had been through while we were drinking. I explained her chagrin that we had not taken measures to tarp or protect the windows, when she had paid him as an act of good faith, and when everyone in the state knew that heavy rain was predicted.

I explained that no doubt she was angry with me because I went straight to the bar from the Bomber Plant and didn't come to tarp the roof, help with the disaster, or whatever.

I stood smiling stupidly, and with the same smile that Beau used when he and Darcy pulled an old woman's yard ornament out of the ground, and broke her window with it, in our pre-farm duplex days.

"Hell," said Bill, obviously unremorseful, not *even* defensively, and without hesitation as though he were reciting an ancient Masonic axiom, "...You NEVER pay a contractor mid-week." End of conversation...off to work. No further comment.

He may have talked with Suzanne later; I don't know. Neither of them ever said. But he left that night with double-paned gray smoked glass installed in each of the four roof holes and across the 1880s peak. It was absolutely beautiful. Even Suzanne could no longer hide her smile.

The saga continued.

It was time to tear the ugly, cheap brown paneling off the living room walls, and so we did.

It came off relatively easy, BUT as it was removed, large chunks of plaster fell to the floor behind it. This wall could not be saved for wallpaper. It needed to be replaced with sheetrock.

After a brief surgical consultation with my spousal colleague, I took a 32-ounce waffle-faced claw hammer to it and, soon, as Suzanne carried the stony carnage out the front, we had several pickup loads of lath and plaster joining dozens of sheets of cheap waste paneling in our front yard. The old (wider and thicker than new wood) 2" x 4" walls were now completely exposed.

I had been relatively impressed with the carpenters who had framed both the original house and the 1954 porch add-on. They used carpentry principles, spaced boards basically on 16" centers, overbuilt if in doubt, and put the framework together in an organized, sensible manner. This two-story piece of the house was not so.

Studs were every 6-inches, then perhaps every 30-inches, another one in 19-inches, 7-inches, whatever...all around the room. It was also not unusual to see a 9-inch or 15-inch piece of stud nailed on top of a long stud to complete its height to the top of the wall. It was hideous framing. But that's not the bad news.

I could see nine-foot cracks of sunlight running from the floor to the ceiling in both eastern wall outer corners, even through the exterior siding. The boards were half gone. I was looking at trees in the yard. But that's not the bad news.

I noticed some old termite damage, and pushed my index finger curiously against it on one board in the center of the room's inside south wall. RIPPP, my finger went *all* the way into the board, like thin, crackling paper. I honestly didn't know what combination of things was holding up the house.

Some studs sat old and tough, uneaten; others had been devoured almost entirely, standing as paper ghosts. The few "good" studs and exterior siding must have been supporting it. There were old and new wasps nests built into the sun-lighted, termite-eaten cracks of the two eastern corners. I felt raw despair. Suzanne looked sick.

"I will have to retrofit and reframe this entire room, one little space at a time," I commented numbly. "It's pretty much a hollow shell." My emotions were dancing between sick and angry as I struggled to find a target for my newest collection of fears.

I smiled blankly, with false encouragement, and then went into a cussing rage that took me straight to the refrigerator for several more cans of Beer.

"Jesus." I said hopelessly and exhausted from ranting and raving.

The entire inside wall was pretty much eaten, the outside—non-bearing—walls seemed untouched except for the corners, *and* about a foot of the bottom of the *entire* northern outside wall had been a termite meal.

I didn't know anything about termite eating habits except that they liked wood. Why they had eaten and stopped in these patterns I did not know. They had left a mess.

I grabbed a giant can of Raid and sprayed the shit out of the wasp nests clinging in the corners. I needed to feel that something could be conquered, *and* that I had killed something, anything.

I thought again of the Titanic and its deck furniture, and I could see a fading quarter-moon shaped "glub" as it all sank from the ocean's surface and left a giant bubble. I visualized this house being similarly swallowed by the Earth, and I shook with powerless, raging fear.

"Let's find a foundation guy," I said glumly. "I need *something* to get fixed in this fucking rat trap!"

Suzanne nodded sweetly and began her virtuous woman's search for this discipline—as she had done on the central heat and a hundred other items.

I grabbed the kids and we began loading debris from the front yard into our (again healed) ole white pickup, whereupon we drove it 26-miles to the Butler County Landfill, returned, and did it again and again.

I stopped to refuel with gas and beer on the return trip through El Dorado as we loaded, hauled, and dumped, loaded, hauled and dumped. The kids worked hard and I was proud of them, but was also totally preoccupied with the nibbled hell we had unmasked.

"What am I going to do," I silently pondered. **"FUCK!"** I roared, with the kids now used to this unpredictable pattern of rage. *"To the dump, to the dump, to the dump, dump, dump,"* we sang. Then, **"FUCK!"** I bought them some candy to eat while I drank another oilcan of Fosters.

It was time for something to go right—ANYTHING now.

After several contractors talked about jacking, bracing, pouring and leveling the house for thousands of dollars, a square built, kind faced, burr-headed, ex-marine looking guy came by who said, "$600. I'll level your house for $600."

We were suspicious, but he had a sage kindness that we somehow trusted and, therefore, hired. It was a thank you, Jesus, call. He knew old houses. It was as though he had been cut from them at birth.

He showed up again within a week with a small, wormy looking guy in a green army coat. He looked much like a harmless version of my little sociopath. He was wiry and strong looking, thin and short, fearless, and felt as though the contractor had found him under someone's old house, or perhaps, trapped in a cellar. His eyes had a greenish brown catlike look as though he might see better in the dark. To work they went.

The brick-shaped ole contractor turned his accomplice loose under the house with a flashlight, a jack, a giant rusty screwdriver and a short-handled, eight-pound, sledgehammer. The contractor then meandered slowly into the kitchen, stopping occasionally to look at and jump gently on the floor in the ugly room, the living room and the kitchen.

The contractor finally walked to the kitchen floor, next to the dishwasher's chalked tie-down, beside the doorway into the ugly room, and stomped hard. "WHAT'S **HERE**?" he bellowed towards the floor so that his words apparently penetrated the flooring.

We could hear the wormlike lad, crawling like a giant centipede toward that spot. I recounted, amazed, that I could barely squeeze in there or breath, yet he was coming toward it with great speed and agility.

The contractor waited until the crawling sounds stopped and then stomped his foot again. "WHAT'S **HERE**?"

A muffled, inaudible to us, sound came from under the house that sounded like, "Iz 'a roooc wiii 'a boarrrd aaatttaccchd."

"PULL IT OUT," the square man roared into the flooring. There was a tap, tap, tap, tap, thud, bang sound and, then, CRASH, the floor where the contractor stood fell about three-inches.

"Kitchen's level now," he said softly and confidently already moving towards a low spot in the "ugly" room, where water had likely puddled the night of the roof window cascade. He didn't ask these things; he could simply tell. He stomped his foot in the center of a low spot and we heard the wormy snake-man sleeking towards the boot's large thud.

"WHAT'S **HERE?**"

"Theerrs nuutinn heereee."

"JACK IT UP AND PUT THE ROCK AND BOARD FROM THE OTHER SPOT HERE," he directed. He stomped again.

The floor began to slowly rise, then stopped, rose and stopped, all intertwined with some thumping and banging. The ole man tapped his toe a couple of times and headed into the living room.

I knew that there was NO room under that floor, even though it bounced like a 22-foot diving board in the middle. There was a dirt hill under it. "This ain't good," he said slowly, still bouncing. I nodded in *complete* agreement.

"House is level now, and that's what you hired me to do, but you might wanna put a brace under the middle of this floor," he said, still gently springing in its center, like a diver, testing the board. "Whoever built this piece of the house left this span WAY too long for common sense; WAAAY too long."

"This entire room lacks common sense," I added, pointing at the mismatched, randomly spaced, studs with blocks nailed to their end.

"And, look at this termite damage," I said pointing to devoured full-length studs on the south wall, and then pointing quickly at the lower 12-inches of the outside north wall.

"I don't know what I'm gonna do about this," I shook my head looking humble, defeated, and stumped.

"Want my advice?" he said, kneeling now and poking at the northern studs first foot of honeycombed termite forensics.

"I like to keep it simple." He affirmed as a precursor to the advice he was about to offer. I had seen that simplicity from his earning of $600 in about 30 minutes, but knew that that's the value of wisdom and that it had been worth every dime. Now, here stood the man volunteering additional help. I welcomed his thoughts.

"Sounds crazy, but trust me when I say that you can do this. This house, you may have noticed, is holding itself up without these damaged studs. They're already like paper. If I were you, I'd go outside and rip-off half 'a dozen rows of lap siding and then just take a chainsaw to the bottom of these studs...all the way along your porch under these windows...cut 'em out and remove the termite damaged wood. Then, frame yourself a little short wall, to replace the piece that you removed, and pound it into place...stick a jack in there and jack it up some if you need to...then pop your new little wall into place and nail it to the remaining studs that ain't eaten here. It'll work. Well, gotta run."

We happily wrote him a check for $600 and away he and his silent partner went, driving west. I scratched my head and pondered, thinking about what he had suggested for the north wall.

I thought that the house might fall down in a giant heap of bowed rubble if something *were* still holding it, but the man seemed so sure. I decided to trust his advice and experience. He had fixed the dips and humps in our foundation with the speed of a seasoned craftsman. I believed him.

Trouble with me is, I never do JUST what makes sense. I am always *thinking* and then adding some spin of my own. Sometimes that's good; sometimes it's just too much.

I am going to fast-forward now and say that I took the foundation man's advice and it worked. The house didn't fall down and the new little wall, following a little jacking-up, fit into place and worked great. I then built little nine-foot (by whatever width) rectangles and reframed the entire living room...one little stud at a time...and that worked. Unfortunately, when I got the chainsaw in my hand to remove the termite damage, mixed with a few beers to take away the fear, I got to *thinking* about the bouncing living room floor that he had said to brace. I decided not to brace it. I removed it.

I became like a drunken beaver that gnawed without discretion or *natural* reason.

My chainsaw blazed and soon there existed a 14-foot by 14-foot square hole in the living room floor, because I had sawed it out. I then sawed that BIG square into four smaller square pieces and carried them out the front door and off to the Butler County Landfill, whereupon I bought more beer to celebrate. The floor wouldn't bounce now; it was in the dump, 26-miles away!

It was becoming a *process* now, and it made MY reconstruction life easier. Less stress, same amount of work, more mistakes that I cared less about: Beer, work, thirst, beer, work, beer, more beer, leave when it got too stressful and go to the bar. It was less controlled and deliberate than I liked, but it was working...for me.

I replaced the 14-foot square. Now, wire, reinforcement bar, and sand covered the living room floor. I buried that under a 14' x14' piece of concrete one-foot thick that I squirted from a delivery truck, through the lower stairwell window, and into our living room "pit." It didn't bounce NOW, by GOD! Ha!

Becoming a genius, and listening to the little analytical, who was also drunk, I went ahead and poured a 100-foot piece of circular half-inch plastic pipe into the living room "floor" with a *plan* to *later* install a hot-water heating system, using a fireplace that I would install *later—We* did install the fireplace, but never the "heated" floor. Analytical and I always wondered if it would work. No one else seemed to appreciate the kinetic genius of it.

I will fast forward again now, blurring order, time and money. Just think $2,000 to $5,000 dollars each time I list something, and hear the sound, "CHING," thinking "Credit." This will summarize the next decade of our life on the farm.

Understand that I was using an unplanned, but *progressive*, version of my "beer and boards" process to accomplish my part of the family adventure. I was drinking more, starting more, and finishing less, *but* there were *lots* of projects in work all the time. Fortunately, *most* contractors finished what we hired them to do, and Suzanne was supreme at picking honest and talented contractors.

Here's the "home" movie, more or less, presented in a mixture of moving pictures, blurred pictures, and random stills. I think I dropped the storage carrousel at some point is why these may *seem* random:

This is me tearing apart, jacking up, boxing-in, and replacing our wooden front porch with a concrete pad, and this is me pouring the foundation for a barn-shaped, walk-in bay window with hinged-storage "sitting" boxes along its 5-foot long front and U-shaped sides. The bay window is on the west "ugly" room side of the house, where we watched our first rainstorm in horror.

Notice that the bay window's front and side windows are smoked gray glass and perfectly match the roof and peak windows. Aren't they beautiful? It also has a fabulous cedar shake hip roof—a fine piece of work, all in all. CHING!

This is, by the way, *me* sawing a 10' wide by 8' tall hole with a chainsaw in the western wall of the ugly room, making Grandma and Suzanne gasp, pushing the wall out, with a substantial crash, and then building the bay window. *This is Suzanne* smiling gratefully when I actually built it instead of leaving a hole and going to the bar.

This is Suzanne finding a muscular, wiry, kind, focused and intense 85-year old—old-school—trim carpenter to finish the bay window, and about every other form of interior trim, while my brother was now living in California addicted to crystal-meth.

This is the house without enough breakers shutting down each time we simultaneously started the stove and microwave, and with a new central air conditioning unit attached, which shut it all down as well. This took more credit, of course, but was quite an improvement in the home's summer environment. CHING!

This is me discovering that the wiring *throughout* the house was as paper-like and brittle as the termite eaten studs...cussing, ranting, raving, drinking, disappearing to the bar for a couple of weekends and then seeing Suzanne engage a wonderful man named Gorman Wheatley to replace ALL of the wiring in the house, including a new 100-Amp breaker box at the pole in the yard.

I loved that name, Gorman Wheatley...sounded like a gunfighter or a buffalo hunter—handsome, Christian man too; salt of the earth. Breakers stopped breaking and a plethora of new plug-ins and gadgets emerged...even a lighted front and rear doorbell, and multiple ceiling fans, appeared. This is what an excellent job, which I obviously had absolutely *nothing* to do with, looks like.

This is us smelling the wafting, disruptive, stomach-rolling stench of absolute raw sewage in the fall, and realizing that our underground, sand-based, sewer system was now destroyed, spilling into open trenches and staunching us with stink.

This is Suzanne going to Butler County, getting a permit, and hiring Al Jones to dig us a sewer pond in the southern meadow, within a cloaking grove of beautiful trees. CHING!

This is Mr. Jones hooking my under-the-house sewer piping to his new lagoon and everything working fine from then on. *This, however, is a flood* coming through the yard, running over the lagoon as though it were a penny on a train track, and "cleaning" our lagoon out "naturally" by washing defecates of debris down the gully to God knows where, a few times per year.

This is me, ironically, after a couple of *purging* rains, fencing the sewer lagoon to meet "County Sanitation Standards." *This is toilet paper* clinging on the fence after its next purging. *This is a white duck* swimming on the lagoon for some reason. *This is a possum* eating the white duck. *This is me* killing the possum for killing the duck...oh, *and me*, filling a small hole with two-gallons of gasoline and experiencing an earthshaking explosion, while killing a bunch of underground sewer-lagoon bees—that attacked my mother and me, at a Sunday family gathering. They had a right to live...'till then.

This is me engaging a sheet rocker to sheetrock the entire house after I had FINALLY reframed and reshaped every ceiling in the house, insulated it, built a loft above the kitchen (that would become our "Master" bedroom), and added a walk-out balcony with double-glass-doors in Darcy's room. Isn't it lovely...See how it outlooks directly across, and into, the tree house that the kids and I built into the eastern tree? What fun that little pause of being childlike, instead of childish, was.

This is Suzanne and I getting a free antique walnut banister from her friend's abandoned old family farmhouse near Hutchison. This is me building a set of stairs along the wall that divides the "ugly" room from the kitchen, and thereby, allowing access to our master bedroom loft. Notice the "L" shaped landing at the bottom, and the large, hand-carved spiral end-banister...what a find! Perhaps the best things in life really are FREE!

Oh, this is me falling through the ceiling of the kitchen while preparing to frame the loft, and *this is me* landing on Grandma's pure-white, stooped-over, head as she was stirring and cooking...Oh, how she laughed, though it seemed to disguise murder, as I got another beer and she tossed the food that had been peppered with falling debris! Her hand seemed unusually shaky as she paused and then put the butcher knife back in its holder...Probably just getting old?

This is ole John, the carpenter, installing the walnut stair rail. Isn't it absolutely beautiful? Oh, notice the 14-foot bookshelf that runs across the entire south wall of the now *beautiful* "ugly" room, above both the stair landing and the antique, 15-pained, French doors that separate the room from our back "porch" bedroom? The porch where we slept with the rats has now become Beau's room.

Oh, see how the house's upper-glass pained back door is divided so that only the top half may be opened and how it lets the smell of flowers blow through our newly installed screen door? Ahhhh…I remember the smell of lilacs, honeysuckle, and spring rain with doves cooing in the meadow.

See how the bay window and skylights turned the "ugly" room from dark and cold, to warm and bright?

Oh, there's ME sitting on the top of the loft stairs looking out the roof window at the old elm tree beside the cellar. Isn't it enormous? It's gotta be 150-years old. That's me smoking weed and drinking a beer there while the family's off at one of Darcy's ball games. The open side windows of the bay window carry out the smoke. I so loved being stoned, listening to music, and being alone back then. Ball games were a hassle when drinking.

Oh, I love this! *Here's Grandma* hunched forward, chain-smoking Virginia Slim Light 100s, blue eyes bugging with salient anger, and being salted all day by sheetrock dust, as the sheet rocker sands his tape work. This is her cleaning up the house that evening and going to bed without even speaking. This is her doing it again the next day…and the next.

Oh! Here's Suzanne renting two-stories of scaffolding and spending the *entire* summer carefully scraping and sanding the peeling white, lead-based exterior of our house, top to bottom, side to side, end to end, one square inch at a time.

This is her, melting in 105-degree weather on the scaffolding, peeling paint off with a hair-drier looking heat gun and sweltering in the summer sun. Nice tan, huh?

This is me buying a 2400 PSI *airless* spray painter, opening a six-pack of Bud, opening three five gallon buckets of paint—in that order—priming the house with white primer, and going to the bar *four-hours* later. Didn't even break a sweat!

This is me drinking all weekend while the primer dried, telling and retelling the story about a friend who tested an airless sprayer a quarter-of-an-inch from his index finger and who shot white paint *through* his finger and up under his finger nail. He nearly lost his finger. "2400 PSI's a LOT of pressure!" I would repeat enthusiastically, *baffled* that no one ever seemed to care.

This is me opening a six-pack of Fosters the next weekend, painting the house number *420 light green* in four hours, and then going to the bar all weekend while the paint dried.

Here I am telling the "2400 PSI" story again, but this time with the paint under his fingernail being *green,* and me adding some near-loss-of-finger, pus and infection drama. That seemed to draw a better response.

This is me painting *some* of the trim a beautiful *dark forest green,* then getting bored, and abandoning the job for Suzanne to finish, while I went to the bar for several weekends, or months, I honestly don't remember which.

This is my first clear glimpse of Suzanne's eyes showing disdain and disrespect, and of my apparently resenting her for not appreciating all the work that I had done. See it here in this picture? Wow, I had never really looked at it that closely before. Hum?

This is me hiring the friend of the dad of a casual drinking buddy to dig our pond *the first time*, and *this is Suzanne* negotiating with Al Jones to undo the mess and dig it *again* two years later—yeah, a second time...this time perfectly, and beautifully, leaving a kidney shaped one-acre-plus, pond with an island peninsula sculpted on the west end. CHING! CHING!

This is funny, so I have gotta show it! *This is me* getting drunk, tossing 300-pounds of grass seed along the barren banks of the new pond, tying an old set of bedsprings behind the pickup with the yellow rat-rope, and dragging the seeds with an unruly cloud of dust to scatter them. Looked like the dirty-thirties! Probably 100-pounds would have done it.

This is the thick, un-mowable, mess created when it rained and apparently grew *every* seed. That little blue Ford sure wouldn't mow it now! Funny.

Subtotal so far: CHING, CHING, CHING, CHING, CHING, CHING, CHING...

(I was struggling. Either—Or, Neither—Nor...Presentation...I—Me? Ah, YES...all about me).

Oh! *This is David's wife* catching an 8-pound catfish out of the pond 3 years later. And...oh, *this is **ME*** finding my only remaining modicum of serenity standing by the pond and pondering nightly how I now hated my existence and my life at the Bomber Plant.

This is me selling the once "beautiful" blue Ford "Lawn Tractor" for $500, paying the balance of the $3,200 loan, and buying an orange, powerful, flawless, KUBUTA with a 5-foot mowing deck on the back. Here's me drinking beer while easily mowing our 10.126 acres from that day forward—including the unruly pond—with flawless Japanese technology. Thank you, Dr. Deming.

Oh, this is cute. *This is me* drinking beer and teaching David's nine year old son to mow, with him in front of me on the big KUBUTA tractor seat. *This is I, I mean, **ME*** a month later, simply drinking beer and watching Andy mow solo. He may be brilliant like his dad.

This is I, I mean, me, sneaking off to the barn, drinking an oilcan of Fosters, slightly bending the empty aluminum beer can with my thumb, poking holes in it, filling the indentation with weed and smoking it.

This is ME raging at Beau, and simultaneously acting like nothing had happened, when he snuck into the barn and caught me smoking. It was good that he admitted he had done wrong by sneaking...gave me hope for his integrity.

This is ME, being loud, getting angry, and acting stupid at Sunday dinners as this alcoholic weekend and evening behavior progressed and intensified.

This is ME, slapping the kids, apologizing, and regressing more and more to the bar, from the indescribable, baffling, acting-out of my now runaway anger. *This is ME,* hiding shame and loneliness under rage and growing isolation. Wow. I had about forgotten those days...umm, years.

This is the 125-horsepower, open bow, 21-foot, blue and white beautiful boat with a red, white, and blue vinyl interior, that we used for three summers (and that was *gutted* by rats when we parked it in the northwestern hay barn for the winter). Yeah, I bought it on credit, and then, perhaps, almost deliberately sold it for *a loss* when Suzanne implied that we were no longer setting a good example for the kids or having *family fun* at the lake. I was pissed. I showed her. CHING! CHING! CHING!

Oh, these particular videos don't have any pictures, and contain only an embarrassing amount of cussing and vile drug and alcohol-based discussion, because I accidentally left the video camera running when I put it away on the boat, after filming me making fun of Beau for being a "little pussy" for not being able to ski. But...in my defense, I wasn't always that way and I didn't do it all the time. I think I apologized, but I honestly don't remember. I doubt he remembers either. Come to think of it, he mentioned a fear of skiing when I saw him awhile back.

Oh, this is Beau, crying and pouting, but then working like a mountain man to break up the old concrete floor in the garage when I decided to replace it with new concrete.

He seemed as lazy as Darcy was motivated...never understood that, but I let him slide since Darcy was a better worker anyway. He was just too much work to motivate and, somehow, became relatively invisible over time. He says he watched me, and seems to have lots of stories to support that, but I didn't watch him very closely—too much work.

This is him, Darcy and me, running a 4-inch sewer line from the barn to the sewer lagoon because I was planning to turn the barn into a second large house. It worked quite well, but never practically, because I never finished the barn.

Ah, here's the barn filled with solar panels and equipment for its planned conversion to a solar house, with a planned full-length upper balcony overlooking the pond. It didn't happen, but the analytical and I enjoyed getting drunk and high and thinking these things up! We even borrowed money and bought lots of the materials to make it happen...there just wasn't enough time or money.

Oh, gee, I didn't know I had this...must be from a friend, or perhaps some bar's surveillance camera. Well, anyway, *it's me*...this makes me blush...but, it's me...um, I...no, me...drunk in a sleazy bar, *somewhere*, talking out loud with the sociopath and the analytical—making fun of the poet, actually—pissing in a dirty toilet that's backed-up, slipping on a piss-covered floor, and being unwilling to wash my hands because I wouldn't touch the faucets in that grimy, slimy, yellow and brown sink. Um, yeah, that's me, um, doing a "free" line of coke on that same sink's slimy surface an hour later just to "pick me up a little" before I drove home at 2:00 in the morning. Damn, I wonder where that came from?

This is ME quitting my job at the Bomber Plant a month later without another job because I was so angry that I simply couldn't deal with "those idiots" any longer. They had pretty much ruined my life and my plans for corporate success...an inbred caste system with no room for a hard working farmer with unappreciated genius. God, I hated those fucks. I stayed nine years, one month, and twenty-five days—but who's counting?

This is me blaming Suzanne for our debt while spending $300 per weekend now on booze, weed, and sometimes, meth.

This is her hiding credit cards and bank overdrafts from me because she didn't want to "upset" me while juggling the bills. This is me, stomping off to the bar and telling her in a fit of rage that if she ever does it again, I *will* divorce her!

"How can I trust someone that lies to me about our finances," I think I said, or words to that effect.

This is me, carefully and properly installing the fireplace, and her, hiring a contractor to install the rockwork.

Doesn't it look *fabulous*? Those rocks are from Colorado. Oh, gosh, this is funny; there they are again. Notice the two small pieces of protruding plastic pipe where I planned to install the water heating system and pump for the concrete living room floor near the fireplace. It's in the barn, pump and all, but I just couldn't seem to get around to it. It stands as an untested theory, and one of many harmless, unfinished, projects. Hum, I wonder if it would have worked?

This is my brother, now returned from California and nine months sober, installing a 13-inch by 6-inch by seven-foot, *solid walnut* beam that Suzanne found and bought for only $40 to use as the rustic and beautiful fireplace hearth. Is it perfect with that fireplace, or what?! It goes so magically with the rose carpeting and rich silver, blue and rose wallpapers that now border and sculpt our home...*um, house*. Does Suzanne have a touch, or what? She wallpapered the whole place. *(No one can touch me now, by the way. I am departed, living alone. I swear to God, that woman still doesn't understand or appreciate all the work I did. Fuck her; she can have it.)*

This is Suzanne, hanging Christmas lights and greenery in the bay window, across the bookshelf on the ugly room's south wall, up the banister, and along the staircase railing.

She is finally making the house into the true showcase of *"Small World"* beauty that we had envisioned, while crying and wondering what happened. But, she's continuing every good and noble work to keep the remaining family happy and to ensure that Darcy continues her straight-A career in college.

Suzanne was a straight-A student too, by the way. She will get over me, besides, I have nearly compartmentalized her, and I am already two months into a new relationship with Leslie.

This is Darcy, angry, beaten, likely even sad, yet focusing even her negative energy to excel in college, protect her mother, and build some new and healthy relationships. She is off to college now with a softball scholarship and several academic free rides, but I have no pictures of that. As I said, I was gone, and we weren't exactly on speaking terms.

This is Beau, figuratively still staring into a flashlight and falling. He is choosing bad friends, and so fucked-up now from a perceived lack of love, and from living for years with his raging and unpredictable alcoholic dad, that he lies constantly to avoid harsh consequences and can't find his brilliant and increasingly ADD-filled head with both hands.

Isn't he handsome now? Notice the scar is gone from his flashlight event. He outgrew it, just like the doctors said. He has some new scars now, but these pictures simply didn't catch them. I would guess, though, that he still has those pictures.

This is me, stopping in the driveway, humming *"A Small World"* and looking at the beautiful green home with its matching serene pond, its giant red barn, its purple and yellow flowered meadows and trimmed lawns, its strong and straight walnut trees and powerful elms, its rose, honeysuckle, and lilac bushes, its singing birds and cooing doves, its green-eyed owl, its bay window, its river-rock covered driveway, its sculpted sidewalks, its purple and white mulberry trees, its smoke-windowed house, its orange tractor. It's...Well, it's what remained after I left drunk and personally beaten in the green Saturn, with my clothes, a few family pictures, a fist-sized hole in my gut, and two guitars.

I fear that the *"Small World"* vision that once seemed so impossible was indeed created by God and a determined family, but became a shared nightmare that shattered hopeful dreams into bitter pieces from one man's descended dead reckoning.

Forget CHING, here. One really can't put a value on these next scenes, they are invaluable, or valueless, I honestly don't remember which impressive or lonely word describes them. I have no more pictures of the family or the farm.

This is a picture of me living in an apartment with "bag" furniture—bean bag, gym bag, and sleeping bag. Isn't that clever?

I am using two empty wine boxes and a guitar case for a coffee table...creative, huh? Oh, for image, there's a complex book on it from the University of Oklahoma press that I plan to read someday when I am sober enough to remember what I have read. It's about the chief founder of Wichita, James what's-his-name. Likely tomorrow. "Yeah, tomorrow I'll read it. I'm just too drained and tired tonight...too damned much stress."

I have another cold box of wine in the fridge, and there's a 12-pack of Corona too, plus the six-pack I'm about done drinking. I've got enough for tonight. I need to go workout; I'm getting fat and gaunt all at once. 'Oughta eat too, but I'm just not hungry and I can't get motivated to work out as much. Probably tomorrow.

No one will drop by now, and that's good, but Beau plans to move-in soon. Hell, he'll probably drop out of high school...'HELL/He'll'... that's cute. I don't want him to get confused and conclude that I'm some gutter alcoholic, so I'll keep stocked with import beer and stay in a decent apartment. *I'd* be happy in a one-room rat trap, but I'll do this for him.

It's been awhile, but I'm jogging sometimes to keep in shape. That'll set a good example for him. Maybe he'll run cross-country. He's pretty athletic, just not focused...and real insecure for some reason. I guess he doesn't see the brilliant, beautiful Beau that we see. When he gets here, I won't drink—in front of him, anyway—until evening and then, of course, on weekends.

He'll see that it doesn't interfere with my work. That'll communicate that I'm still in control. We'll be all right. Hell, I'm doin' alright.

"You *sure* are," agrees the sociopath with an amazingly positive tone. "Hell, I got tired of fighting with you," he adds like a trusted drinkin' buddy. "I'm glad we get along now."

"I thought you were actually going to buy into all that family and happily-ever-after, Small World, little farm, bullshit. You were selling your soul to that damn Bomber Plant to afford it. Good for you! You gave it what you could, and we did some pretty fuckin' good work, if I say so myself! Suzanne didn't appreciate it toward the end, but then, let's face it, relationships ain't your best framing—and, finishing, shitttt!" We chuckled together at his truth and I dropped a lime in the Corona to add some evening luxury.

The poet had disappeared. He irritated analytical, sociopath (whom we sometimes now referred to as simply "Soch"), and me.

Soch liked having a nickname, and he actually seemed to *like* being accepted. He and I were actually becoming friends. I couldn't believe it, after all these years. He seemed to be softening up somewhat, though he laughed that I was just getting *harder*.

He was looking healthier, walking more upright. He looked good, all in all. I felt happy for him. I knew I wasn't happy, but he seemed happier. He was one of the only few REAL friends I had left, and I appreciated that he had stayed with me through it all, given his *nature*.

Anyhow, the poet had stopped contributing. "Whinny little fuck! I don't miss him." He had quit writing music and poetry anyway. And, frankly, he wasn't that good. What a phony, egomaniac waste of time. It was all bullshit.

"Besides," chimed-in the analytical, "who'd listen to you sing anyhow, and guitars make a pretty good nightstand now for keys, cigarettes, and stuff, huh? Musical art deco...*AND* empty Corona bottles make good ashtrays, huh? And then, you just *throw them away*, huh! You can thank me for thinking of that!"

He winked, still arrogant from his work on the farm, but failing to acknowledge his total failure to help me at the Bomber Plant. He had snapped under the pressure, and hid like a little boy during the daytime, when I needed him. He just wanted to drink on the way home, escape, and work on the farm. Selfish fuck! I resented him. Being completely phony, now, I smiled with grim, yet numb and involuntary fading appreciation. He might be the next to go.

Something in me whispered that this was not our finest hour, but that it was ok for now. Analytical made me think too much and I resented him for that too. I was tired of thinking. I guzzled a beer, and washed down two extra Prozac and a Valium; it wasn't what the bottles said, but bipolar alcoholism was pounding me—though, I wasn't an alcoholic.

I drifted off to sleep, and slept typically restlessly, as airplanes flew back and forth from the airbase and as dogs barked in the empty concreted distance. I woke occasionally, prayed silently that God would bless Suzanne and the kids, and again passed out to sleep. I never got a restful night of sleep now. Likely, I was just depressed. Maybe I needed to talk to our EAP program about that.

"I like this simple life," I thought, still half-drunk.

I awoke again in the night and thought of the ole man, for some reason. I wondered if he would hurt other people. If so, it made me feel honored somehow, more loved, and not as personal.

We had never laughed, but we did in my fantasy. I felt a strange love and kinship for him, and knew that it was the first time in my adult life. I was 47 now; he had died at 51. Perhaps we were now able to understand one another as angry, equal, friends. He seemed to be leaving me alone now, and that somehow afforded me this euphoric bliss.

When I drifted off to sleep again I dreamed of the ole man and the farm...not the new, beautiful, farm...the old one...the one of my childhood.

In this dream, daddy and I were drinkin' buddies, and he decided that it would be fun to see if he could lasso Beau. It seemed harmless enough.

To my horror, he escalated the plan into lassoing him and, then, tying him behind the bumper of our old gray International pickup.

He bellowed at Beau in that familiar angry voice to "STAND STILL, GODDAMN IT," after he had roped him; he then jumped quickly in the cab of the pickup and took off, spitting mud from the tires.

Round and round he went, laughing more than I had ever heard him laugh. He dragged Beau, screaming and begging for his life, behind our old family pickup, through the yard of my childhood home that was now covered by deep puddles of thick, rain-soaked mud.

Beau was drowning, begging, and gasping for life as the ole man sped in circles and laughed insanely. I was frozen with fear, but finally ran desperately to catch the truck. As it sped by, I jumped into the back and cut the rope with a knife I had grabbed out of the well house.

The ole man was FURIOUS that I had interfered with his fun, and screeched to a halt, as Beau lay half naked, with new rope burns and bruises where his little heart operation scar had been.

The ole man rushed toward me, as he had done a thousand times when I was a child, and raised his backhand with expectant familiarity to hit me.

Suddenly realizing that he and I were now the same size, I grabbed his hand, slammed it behind his back and pushed him into the mud. I kicked him until he could not rise. "Stay down, *Mother Fucker*," I retorted in *his* own violent syllables. We've done enough.

I helped Beau up, cried, and hugged him.

I then awoke to the sound of a city full of chirping birds and low flying military planes. I was sobbing in my pillow.

As the dream faded into my damaged memories, I suddenly felt confused, remorseful, and lost. I intuitively sought out and reawakened the Poet for consolation. He was kind and ever forgiving.

After more blurred months of drinking myself into restless nights and nightmares—blended with days of hiding my countenance behind a happy face—my brother dropped by to see if I wanted to go to an AA meeting with him on Sunday. He had called the night before, so must have felt some urgent leading. I was ready.

"Sure," I said. "If *you* think it might help me…what have I got to lose?"

By now, the fist-sized hole in my stomach and chest felt as though it were going to implode my existence and seemed, somehow, spiritually tied to the vacuum of deepest outer space. I was hopeless and afraid beyond any human measure, and my brother didn't know it, but he remained as my only *true* and living connection to hope on the physical Earth.

"11:00," he said. "Tomorrow…Sunday. I'll come by and get you. Could be an interesting Christmas for you this year."

He jumped in his new white Chevy truck, waved, smiled with love, and left looking happier than I had ever seen him. I wondered how a man like him had done that.

Chapter 25
but if the light within thee be darkness

I once thought that hate was the opposite of love, but I now believe that, perhaps, numbness or apathy are more akin to its opposite. As the Earth experiences night and day, love and hate are perhaps sister lights that shine on the turning soul of man. Only love can grow in true light, but both can dwell in darkness. Each can burn with equal passion.

Burning together creates a flame so hot that the heart of man cannot endure it. The only choice is to embrace one fully, or move away from both and, thereby, find oneself removed from all spiritual power. This place is the opposite, or perhaps the epicenter, of both hate and love, and is the ultimate common resting place for those with addictions.

Man loves the darkness as he embraces hate, and hates the light, as his first instinctive, then accidental, then experimental, then deliberate, and finally inevitable—and perhaps involuntary—nurturing of angry and bitter vengeance shadows love. This is a turning point, often resulting in total isolation, lest he kill or die.

"God both gives and takes life. Which, then," he ponders, "is not an act of love, and which is only darkness?" "Be *ye hot or cold, for if you are lukewarm I will spit you out of My mouth,"* says the Bible.

Isolation becomes a world powered by the warmth of a natural drifting madness, yet filled with both the hot knowledge of a hidden, inexpressible, love, and the cold knowledge of a cloaked and bitter hatred.

Each lies buried, waiting to be rediscovered...one as treasure mines, the other as land mines. Memory or reality can *either* serve as a dim battery to power this existence for awhile, but mixing the two, via both reflection *and* renewed human contact, is quickly as deadly as simultaneously burning love and hate.

A man is likely, by now, too silenced by numbing pain and apathy to scream out and tell passersby that once valuable gold lies within, yet, he is also too silenced by buried hatred and well-meaning delusion to warn them of the corresponding explosions they will encounter if they embrace him and start digging for his gold. Eight internal beings are moving in now, trying him on for size, and announcing their kinship. They enter, deadly, yet unopposed.

His calmness is now a secret madness that humans likely misperceive as serenity or, perhaps, even wisdom.

Soul sick people are attracted to this man's illusive casting of light, and he to theirs. Their caring instincts wish to save one another, while their identical soul sickness is satisfied to find, mine, embrace, and then feed on more darkness. They coexist for a while as spiritual vampires, drinking one another's emptiness, and after this soulless feeding, they finally separate as larger beings, thirstier for the thick light of darkness.

Some such men simply die, filled with love and anger that has now decayed only into a putrefaction of muted sorrow. No one ever finds them or looks within. The sun rises and sets on them, but they see and know only the darkness. The sun neither bothers nor blinds them; it is simply irrelevant. They sometimes glimpse at a warm moon only to feel pain...to feel anything. Human touch is now a harlequin's wooing dream beyond their grasp and beyond their soul's dark, blank window so they wither within and pass unseen.

As John A described his memory of insanity, so do I recall these days of plummeting vacuous horror.

I reached, but could not recall days of light, sunshine, or happiness in this final season. Rather I recall only feeling a faint, helpless gratitude for the *mask of blending countenance* that operated to hide my demons and allowed me to grapple in daylight's obligatory walk while *it* transacted the necessary business of our day.

I recall only a morose, stomach-wrenching, compulsion to return to the drinkable remorse of another night of sinking further into unaccountable loneliness, and I recall crawling beneath my darkness and embracing the familiar growing ache of my now completing isolation.

When my brother again found me, there was no love or hate, no light, and no memorable daytime. There was only a spiritual darkness that sustained me while my *mask of blending countenance* performed its fleshly role and guarded me from another's searching gaze.

Darkness offered now the reflective illusion of a brightly shining light that had already attracted her with its needy, deceitful, hollow glow, *"...and great is that darkness."*

<<<<<<>>>>>>

"You are so filled with light." Leslie said, soon after meeting me. I was too empty to know, deny, or explain what she saw, but I was equally attracted to her. Having felt invisible for months, it was nice to be seen at all and wonderful to feel *anything*. The sociopath squirmed with an uneasiness that felt amazingly like opportunity mixed with jealousy.

She was filled with a raw and manic energy that mixed well with alcohol and loneliness to draw me back into a limited dance with humans.

Unfortunately, I was still reflecting on the whimpering death of a nearly 22-year marriage to Suzanne. Leslie was sorting out the death of an 18-year marriage. Reflection and renewed human contact were mixing as we attracted, and simultaneous love and hate would become its hotly burning, slowly cremating seven-year child.

Each time we met, initially, it was because she was visiting a mutual friend in my apartment building and each time we met, I knew that drinking was all that gave me life. Her unfaithful and duplicitous friend likely understood that also, but she did not.

When she asked early on what had happened to my marriage, I responded with an unmasked look that made her physically step backwards. For an instant, she saw the true energy behind the light, but she did not see that it was only one of many land mines buried with my inner treasure.

She waited until we were married and then kept digging, continually activating mines, yet digging more. Our dark energies fueled each other's isolation and ultimately drove us to separate married lives. That is the short version of my second marriage's hot life, chilling death, and euphuistic burial.

It was beautiful for a while, but only in momentary euphoric bursts. Wine made it better until I exploded with irrational jealousy, now immanently prepared for my brother's imminent visit.

I had dated Leslie for two months when I entered AA. I married her when I was ten months sober. She found land mines. Unfairly, others would find mines of treasure.

Today we have become good and trusting friends and light shines brightly in conversation. Today we know how to love one another with an honesty that can exist only in the light. Getting there took great illusion, tearing, darkness, and rebuilding. Leslie was a good wife and a wounding friend. *Blessed are the wounds of a friend, but deceitful are the kisses of an enemy.*

She was beautiful, energetic, smart, and strong. Her eyes were brown, blue, or green, depending on her mood or emotion— sometimes changing with her attire.

When I met her, she had long blond hair pulled into a ponytail, or cupped around her face, with a portion of it skillfully clipped back with expensive silver barrettes. When we parted, she had short blond hair sculpted against her beautiful face as subtle curtains for endless tears.

She loved her children with the fervor and watchful protection of a wild lioness, and I loved that about her. It was the heart of her power and the evidence of her heart.

Her children learned through loving consequence, wise interrogation, and free choice. They were strong-willed, defiant, beautiful, and brilliant like their mother.

She had hands that could create *anything* and deployed this wisdom to make elegant stained-glass pieces, stonework, furniture, baskets, needlepoint (TIGHT on the back!), quilts, bridal and bridesmaids' dresses, and a myriad of other creations. She could have earned a living as a master seamstress or in any three of a number of other arts.

I entered the relationship quickly knowing, and soon resenting, that I was her intellectual and functional inferior. She had struggled with academic life as a child, but got a degree in economics in only three years while working full-time to pay for school. She had a house full of unfinished projects, but was always working on several somethings. She was incredibly focused and unfocused all at once.

She owned and operated a management training and consulting company, which both fascinated and offered me incredible personal and business growth opportunities in my early sobriety.

She gave me hundreds of hours of self-help and business tapes to listen to while I was commuting and on the road traveling...and I listened. It was like drinking from a fountain of knowledge, and for several years, I drank freely. Then I indulged character defects, in lieu of drinking, and rebelled with a great and unannounced angst and stealth.

Leslie had spent time with a shrink, and prudently coached me to do so, yet neither she nor I had dealt honestly or effectively with past issues or damaged relationships.

We mixed our damaged past reflections with formation of a new marriage and the mix of hate and love burned hot and splashed molten history onto forming future. While the marriage was being scorched and refined, however, it burned as an uninvited catalyst for personal change.

Initially, I refused to deal with my failed relationship with Suzanne because I thought it disloyal and intrusive to this marriage. She dealt with hers similarly.

My anger was pointed within for my years of alcoholic destruction; hers was pointed without for years of alcoholic abuse. Sober or drunk, I picked up where her ex-husband left off and this was the battle scene for our little drama's second act.

I acted out; she rightfully scorned me. I retaliated, and it played again, and again. We dug at each other's darkness to enhance our feelings and to avoid looking clearly at our own. We believed somehow that conflict would lead eventually to stability and a stronger marriage. It did not. In fact, we mutated into veil-cloaked, life-sucking ghouls.

She escaped into her natural talent while I escaped into new years of AA and counseling, and there, finally, discovered and faced the unkempt secrets and practiced defects that had powered my cruelty for so long.

To strengthen our marriage, we studied the scriptures together. She, however, grew spiritually in a manner that dwarfed me, causing me the silent and age-old resentment that had possessed Cain to kill his brother.

Now my inferiorities were both mental and spiritual. I also knew—true or not—that I was, by far, not her best lover and she called me "pussy boy" *once* when we worked out. Mental, spiritual, physical: Complete insecurity to power vengeance.

I silently begrudged her growth and held her to the test of an angel to force her deployment of new scriptural learning. When I esteemed her to have fallen short, as any human would, I built on that cornerstone and began the first instinctive, then accidental, then experimental, then deliberate, and finally inevitable, and *perhaps* involuntary, erosion of our marriage.

I isolated not from others, or even from myself, but progressively, cunningly, and knowingly from my wife. Perhaps she noticed, perhaps not.

By now, she could not reach out, and in that fortitude of rebelling solace, I sought out Violet. Our unhealthy growth and relationship pain were not from a single catastrophic event, but rather from the weedy disease of damaged life and poisoned family trees.

Leslie carefully photographed my brother's funeral and reception, despite the scorn and contempt of his already angry children. They had lost their brother and their father in only nine months and they knew their dad had not liked Leslie. She became an easy target.

She told me that someday we would want those photographs, and she was right. She told me that she knew we were over the day I buried my brother, and she was right. Damaged life and our own unhealthy growth made *that* passing the figurative selfsame nail in *our* companion coffin.

I began a relationship with Violet 90-days after Bill died. I escalated an email friendship into telephone calls, and telephone calls into hundreds of hours of cellular enchantment. Both "me's" were hidden...one secret, one salient. A third was hidden from myself. Violet and I grew as Leslie and I died. Neither would know the real me, and even I had only relearned a transformational face.

The *mask of blending countenance* was so clever, and had grown into my new beliefs and me so deeply, that even I did not know its delusive power. I believed that I was making decisions on the clear and obvious foundation of now knowing myself fully. But, I was a child with a child's understanding and so *I acted as a child*.

I recall at twilight seeing Leslie putting blinds up in her daughter, Melissa's, new house in Austin while I was finishing a dog house fit for Melissa's growing baby Mastiff in the yard.

Exhausted from working and without mental defenses, I felt at that moment what she had known at my brother's funeral. As the sun was setting in the Texas sky, so, I knew, it was setting on us.

At that moment, I paused without breath and felt an involuntary deep Christian love and conviction, as I knew what I was about to do. No doubt Judas felt this as he kissed his faithful companion. The tearing and knowing was unbearable for an instant. It didn't deter me though; it merely served as another painful turning point in life's unseen path with its unmarked crossroads.

I was returning to life, and out of darkness, but was capable of great wrong in my enlightening journey. I felt a surge of deep regret and unquenchable pain, as though a bullet had penetrated my chest and logged in my redeveloping soul, but I felt powerless to change my course.

Three months later, I returned from my first trip to New Orleans and moved out. Our sun had set on summer's scorched flowers.

We would later pull the weeds and plant our friendship garden...something Violet and I would find only in a single bottle of sparkling red wine, made with faith's grapes, corked, cached, and ageing in the wine cellar of sacrosanct eternity.

How strange is the psychic path that pulls one's insides in, then back out, and finally into dusty dusk's irrelevance—how strange are the player's roles and the unseen *nature* of it all.

God's taking and giving of life, for us, became new life...an act of pure and simple love. My brother and I were each passed as a baton by unlikely sojourners, angels, and teachers along the Refiner's path, with Wisdom standing and crying at the crossroads, not just for us, but also for them.

When the high-rise community voted, we followed life's small example, brought Leslie's family back to life, and watched the crashing bus ascend backwards up the muddy Mexican canyon, onto the road and into the commoner's heart-felt hopes for a healthy and peaceful continued journey. I saw MY character defects fall from their faces.

Three years later, Leslie's mother and she went quilt shopping, did their hair and nails at an expensive spa, and began vacuuming the darkness from their own genetic past one smile and one conversation at a time. This would precede her mother battling cancer and dying.

Leslie became a black-belt Al-Anon and poured health and light into her children and her own sweet soul.

She is no longer a lonely enthusiast of darkness, but the resurrected and ascending angel that I once loved and hated into a sad and crumbled spiritual brokenness.

I loved her kids so much and knew that they and God would be enough for their mother…my someday lifetime friend.

<<<<<<>>>>>>

"Hey," mocked Michael, Leslie's middle son, as we sat together at our last family supper. "Who's this?"

He wiped his hand across his handsome face, pushed back his blond hair, and began trembling and shaking his fork in an exaggerated manner until it dropped food down his chin. He then picked up his water glass and spilled it likewise with verbose shaking.

"It's YOU!" He laughed playfully. I smiled, properly mocked and shaking, as I ate.

Later that night, Matthew, the youngest, came as his mother and I were watching TV, and flung himself with mime-violence against the TV screen, arms and fingers widely spread, making electrical buzzing and popping sounds and flopping with mocked electrocution.

"AAHHH…AAHHH…AHHHHH," He screamed in well-pretended pain!!! I belly laughed, enthralled and kindred with both his soul and his teenage humor.

"Shut up, Matt," said Melissa from the bathroom, as she was touching up her short silver-blue hair, and rotating her body piercing jewelry, to experiment with her natural Sharon Stone beauty.

I thought of Darcy with her brother and how she protected him with a bullying motion that disguised her maternal and matriarchal nature. They were the same.

I smiled in my soul, embracing two daughters and four sons, knowing they might never fully meet, but would all be incredible friends. They already were friends in my renovating high-rise.

Chapter 26
Who can find a virtuous woman?

Suzanne was a virtuous woman. She taught me the ingredients for a deep and lasting relationship, and drowned, innocent, still fighting for our life, in my swirling pool of chaos and chemicals.

She, like Lisette, loved and honored both her family and her children. That was how I knew later to look for that in a companion. Without her example, I could never have known true love or virtuous companionship.

She was broken with a bitter sadness that I would not know for years when her father died of lung cancer as we neared Arizona. I did not know how to comfort her. I did not truly know her pain. I know I am grateful to have known her at all.

A season before I left the *"Small World"* farm, and ascended the hill for a final time, thinking, "She's too good for me," I had a recollection that planted itself as another gift of eternal sight. A memory found me in the darkness and she was the candlelight of its substance.

<<<<<<>>>>>

"This water tastes funny again," I said, raising my glass toward the eastern kitchen window and the morning light. A Smurf-looking family nodded in unison.

Being increasingly grandiose, I swirled the tumbler like a wineglass, smelled it, sipped it, smelled it, sipped it, and proclaimed, "Snake...not rat..." I sipped and smelled it again, held it to the light, and discerned, "I'll say blacksnake, three feet long, dead three days."

It was guess and bullshit, except for the idea that it might be a blacksnake.

Blacksnakes were all we had seen on this little acreage: Harmless, rat and insect killing blacksnakes...and we had found one in the well before. My farmer taster could actually tell that it wasn't a rat and that quietly disgusted me.

Snakes apparently crawled through holes that led to the well, helped themselves to water bugs, and died trapped when the hole closed with collapsing draught and when the bugs ran out.

"Come on, Beau," I commanded, gathering up the beer, the bucket, the rope, the flashlight, and the leather gloves. "Let's go see."

Off to the well we marched, Beau now a lean, slightly clumsy and insecure looking teenager, still under 100-pounds. His blue eyes danced, his jokes flew, and his blond hair glistened in the fall morning light as we scuffed and rattled towards the well. He trotted beside me like a loyal puppy.

As I knew *my* daddy, so he knew any humor I had would soon be gone, and so, he tried to keep my spirits up with his own. He was using humor now as I used it—an insecure cloak—and though he was good at it, and quite funny, I shamed to know my role in planting its masquerading core.

I drank mostly now to forget my sins, and my sense of redemption was about gone. I had brutally damaged everyone in this family, especially Beau, the son that I raised through my own distorted filters.

When we reached the well, I saw the handprints that he and his cousins had put there. I didn't know yet that I would someday cherish memory's imprint.

I pulled an old rusty screwdriver out of the tower leg and wiggled it under the garbage can lid that I had poured and caulked into the concrete slab. I banged it with a brick until it popped out.

We looked at each other and, then, curiously into the chasm to see what we had been drinking. Beau shined the flashlight. It was a snake, perhaps 18" long, dead and floating about 18-feet down. The air rising out of the well had an acetate, vinegary, dead smell.

"Shit," said Beau with a disgusted look. "That's nasty." I felt empty, hung-over and tired. "Yeah," I agreed. "Fuckin' nasty." I gulped with impending reality and popped a beer. He stopped joking.

The water level was dangerously low because we were in the midst of a long-lasting drought. The wall of the well had shifted slightly inward on the east side, no doubt from drying earth. It looked unstable.

I suddenly felt a torrent of anxieties ranging. I simultaneously visualized running out of water or having a well collapse on me. I checked my internal death sensor and could feel no answer. I had numbed everything by now, and here was a downside: Even illusion was not responding with its intuitive lie. I flushed with fear.

"**FUCK**," I said for the ten millionth audible time. Beau smiled with a child's false encouragement. He looked afraid too.

I guzzled a couple of beers to prepare myself mentally, and then paused and said to Beau, "Ya know, you're smaller, let me tie a rope around you and lower you so you can just grab it instead of me wiggling down those ole rock walls and taking a chance on collapsing it on me." It didn't seem cowardly, just logical, and after a couple of beers, logical enough.

He never lacked courage and began tying the rope around his own chest, below his armpits. I respected his un-pausing courage. He seemed simply focused on the job, which I had always thought was not his nature.

I checked the knots to ensure that they were both tight, and not the type that would close and suffocate him with our pulling. I tied another loop around his ass and upper legs to balance the pull on his chest.

He tied the flashlight to a remaining dangling length of rope, as he had seen me do before, and stuck his legs into the hole to be lowered. I grabbed the rope and began to lower him into the well. Down he went a couple of feet at a time.

Suddenly, I felt exhausted. Years of drinking and sitting on my ass had left my arms with far less strength than when we had moved to the farm, and I knew that I could not hold him for long, certainly not long enough to reach the bottom, grab the snake, put it in a bucket (that would take a third free hand) and get back to the top. I panicked. "Beau, I'm pulling you back out! I can't hold you!"

"I can do it, Dad," he assured me with a positive, rippling echo.

"I know, Beau, but I can't. Come up NOW. I can't hold you! You're too heavy!"

I wrapped the rope around my ass and pulled as hard as I could in alternating tugs. I thought my arms would rip off, as weight transferred from arm to arm, while I reeled in the rope. My hands were choking without blood flow as I wrapped the rope around them to keep it from slipping. My arms trembled and my muscles were beginning to burn with agony. My fingers were purple with white rope marks and my back ached to the point of pounding.

I panicked and tried to tie the rope around the windmill tower leg, but lacked strength to do both things, and knew I was wasting precious energy and time. I finally watched Beau's arms grab the top of the little access hole and out he came.

I was pouring sweat and shaking so badly that I could barely grip. He emerged just in time, thank God. Any beer I had drunk for courage was fully gone, and the courage with it. Reality had felt as harsh as running the last few yards of a high school mile.

I knew that he wouldn't drown in two-feet of water, but felt ashamed and embarrassed that I had not been man enough to plan it properly or handle my end.

I was beet red—exhausted and ashamed. Failure and adrenalin rebooted my attitude for my descent, and even offered a sense that I would not die in this well today. I appreciated the Spirit's whisper or intuition's comforting lie.

I sat, drank another beer, and poured pools of dripping sweat onto the heating concrete pad.

"I'll have to walk down the sides," I said despondently. "Thanks for trying, Beau. You did a great job." These words felt foreign to me because I had used them so sparingly. "I'll just have to avoid the rocks that are sagging in."

By now I was re-hydrating from cold beer and warm adrenalin. My legs and arms suddenly felt stronger. Beau smiled with encouragement. He had been to the mountain.

I retied the rope to the bucket, made sure the flashlight was secure, dangled my legs and lowered myself into the 24-inch hole that was centered over the well's welcome chill. I spread my legs and secured a starting grip on the gray and black inlaid rocks.

I looked downward and suddenly understood that the bottom was 18-feet to the water, not half that as it had been other times. It looked far away. The drought was obvious and I knew that we were lucky to have water at all—ANY water.

Anxiety tried to surge again, but I shook it off like a bad pitch, and began my descent, shining the light and picking carefully to push my toes into solid looking larger rocks. It felt somehow, today, like another universe...a black hole.

I had on gloves and carefully monitored my leg strength to ensure that I could make the descent and get back out again.

My legs were spread by a widening four feet and I aligned myself so as to avoid the bubble of rock that was sagging into the well's east side. I could see up close, as I passed it going down, that it was much bigger and further indented than it appeared from above. I knew that collapsing rocks would make drowning irrelevant. I felt execrable fear, then oneness with the universe around me. It slowly turned from black rocks to reflecting lights. Calmness overcame me like a mariner's spirit.

I entered a dreamlike reflection of meeting Suzanne and of our early days together. My mind drifted backward as I carefully scaled downward.

I was grateful for this memory reprieve to my growing anxiety and fear, so happily went along for the ride. Suddenly, I was back in Tucson, Arizona, and not in a hand-dug well in Kansas. Down I went...back I went.

<<<<<<>>>>>>

"And that's our presentation for today," said the small, strong looking, tan, pretty, and businesslike auburn-haired woman in charge of our meeting. "Thank you all so much for participating. I think that we've shared a lot of great ideas here today. On behalf of the Pima County Career Guidance Center, we are sincerely grateful."

She was cute, but seemed controlling and stiff to me, so I immediately thought, "I'll bet she's a real bitch to live with." I don't know why I had that thought...but that was the thought I had.

After the meeting, a group of us clotted and flowed into the bar for a few drinks, and I joined them simply searching for a beer buzz and some new companionship. I had experienced a weird week and felt euphorically free, manic, and lonely, all as one emotion.

The week before, on Saturday night, while pacing in my apartment's living room, I had a strange, I will call it, "God" experience, whereupon a *heavy*, warm spirit settled on me and said calmly, *"Think about all of the girls that you have loved, yet called only friend."*

My legs buckled and I was folded involuntarily yoga style in the center of the room. I thought this weird, but wasn't able to get up. I felt completely stoned, somehow, and liked the feeling. I intended to get stoned later, but this was actually *better*. Wow. Weird.

From a poor-man's lotus, my mind automatically streamed backward into high school memories, and a message began to clearly emerge. I had been secretly sexually attracted to every woman except a few that I called friend, but there was one strange little companion, a bright, funny, beautiful, petit, brown adventure-eyed brunette, appropriately named Kathy Sparks. Kathy and I were best friends.

My plummeting meditations knowingly mind-mapped and cross-haired on a night when we got into trouble at 3:00 in the morning, as I dropped her off, and her parents asked where we had been...and not nicely! Both stood before us on the porch, and then in their living room, with fists clenched and pressed to their hips.

"We've been at the Fridged Cream...talking...since about 10:30," she answered innocently.

"We ran into each other while we were dragging Main, and then stopped at the Fridged Cream, sat on the sidewalk in front, and talked. That's all. We've been *talking*. We didn't realize how late it was. I'm sorry, but Dad, we're just friends...It's not like we're going together or something."

I recalled that her parents could barely comprehend that two people could be this sincere, this sincerely good friends, and not in a romantic relationship. Then my mind flew again into its corridors. I was along for the ride.

It moved through time and recollections in some fast-forward "knowing" state...not a dream, not a memory, not a thought...and brought me back to the floor of my apartment in a matter of about 20 minutes. I had been through time, as though it were spliced with all the senses—losing nothing and completely real.

My mind had grabbed clips and bytes, words, smells and sounds, from all of the relationships I had ever had, and had refined them into one pure vision, not yet shared with me. Pure pieces of impure relationships were refined out, and pure pieces of well-meaning pure relationships were refined from unintended impurities.

It wasn't about sex; it was about connection, commitment, honest motives, and friendship. If I had to give it a word, it recorded and refined out only the *truth* of each relationship—pure *truth*.

I felt physically drained, spiritually recharged, and mentally keen...yet the keenness was now without thought or desire for thought. I was stumped as to what had transpired. But, hell, I was only 25, and not some fuckin' Buddha! I didn't even have context for the experience, certainly not the discipline to enhance or study it. I got up slowly, splashed my face and strolled—smoking a joint—as was customary, to the neighborhood bar.

That was last week, six days before attending the "Businessman's Advisory Council to the Pima County Career Guidance Center" meeting, on Friday afternoon.

It was as though time did not pass from the living room "vision" to the hotel bar after the BACPCCGC (or whatever the fuck they called it) meeting six days later. Rather, I slept, I blinked and awoke to the feeling I had felt the week before. It hit me again in the bar as I opened my first beer.

I felt a deeply stoned spiritual presence that glued me to my chair and made me relax, far beyond alcohol. The environment stoned me. I was actually without anxiety or pretense and having fun. That "feeling" had me again.

The group of perhaps 45 had diluted into a drinking group of perhaps a dozen. I somehow ended up at the table next to the little Sally Fields/Marsha Mason looking meeting facilitator. She began to loosen up after a couple of drinks.

I rethought my first conclusion, and reasoned that perhaps she was simply focused, or even up-tight running the meeting and, thus, came across as…well, a bitch.

We talked and talked about the "mingling" meaningless of socializing until late in the evening. She used the words "mingle, mingle, mingle" in tones that drew smiles, and even head-nodding responses, from nearby people in the noisy bar, just to demonstrate that people were not usually listening…only seeming to. If I were to conclude from this, however, that she was cynical in nature, I would have concluded wrongly. She was, in fact, sweet to the bone, sweet of spirit, and sweet of soul.

We didn't really talk much about ourselves. I left the bar at about midnight. I was mildly drunk, content, and felt nothing particularly out of the ordinary, certainly not animal attraction, seeds, buds, or fruits of love.

It was perhaps *two weeks later* that I took my then pre-Julia Roberts looking, computer scientist girlfriend to Grace Full Gospel Church in Tucson and sat through a usual "Thank you, Jesus" fundamentalist service. All was normal.

The service was breaking up and people were shuffling towards the altar to pray, when the little "feeling" came over me yet again— first the floor, then the bar, now here. It didn't buckle my knees this time, only my mask of reasoning. I was about to utter a poor man's version of *speaking in tongues*.

Without thought or premeditation, I turned to my sweet, quiet, beautiful, girlfriend, who was now standing on my left, where we had been seated, put my hands gently on her upper arms and told her, "This is not right. We are over." That was about it. I stood dazed, looking at her.

We had navigated a few problems and bumps, but basically she and I had been going together since Jan and I broke up, for about three years.

Tonight, I was a foreign spirit in my own body. I hadn't thought it out. I certainly didn't go to church with the intent of breaking up. It hadn't even entered my mind. It just *popped* out of my mouth, without emotion, as though all of the pure truth from my sitting on the living room floor found this moment and came out as those seven words: "This is not right. We are over."

"Ok," she said, with a look of human love, but without emotion. "Can I keep some of the albums?"

"Sure," I said, too weirdly detached from reality to know anything sensible. It was all similar to the UFO night. Things should have been said, but never would be. I liked and loved this girl, but missed her next to none in the days ahead. She probably married some friend of Bill Gates and lived happily ever after.

The next week, my office phone rang in the late morning and a deep, professional, semi-auto-confident voice said, "This is Suzanne...from the Pima County Career Guidance Center...remember me?"

We had lunch, went to *Death Wish,* dated, had a beautiful weekend in Sedona, and almost instantly shared a nightly dose of the spirit that had overcome me thrice before. Her eyes trusted me more than any eyes had before. I drank of them like pure angelic spirits.

I married her less than three months later, a virtuous woman: Her 36, me 25, David 13. Darcy and Beau would show up roughly three and five years later.

"HEY, DAD! You all right," Beau echoed from above? I was standing over the water, staring at some hypnotic ripple, within reaching distance of the snake.

"Yeah," I answered, wondering how much time had passed. "Lower the bucket."

I heard him drop it and cuss, and then down it came...slowly lowering through a small hole of light, swinging gently back and forth on the yellow rope. I could hear Beau's shallow anxious breathing as he lowered the bucket. I must have been here for some uncomfortable amount of time. I sensed his fear and restlessness for closure of the job.

As I waited on the bucket, I squeezed another moment out of the washrag of reflection and recalled times when Suzanne's face had burned into my memory as that of a pure and undefiled companion.

"Viaja usted por avion?" She smiled sweetly, and with a bouncy happiness to her obviously practiced new syllables. She was greeting me at the back porch door of our farm upon my return from an

Hispanic Aging network conference in San Antonio. Her eyes sparkled and her face looked like an angel.

"Got it?" Beau chanted, bouncing the bucket before my chest and obviously wondering if I had checked-out on him.

"Yeah," I responded looking downward, surveying my body and realizing, amazed, that I was feeling refreshed and completely without tiredness. I wondered for an instant if I had been in the well all this time, or if, perhaps, I *had* been cast momentarily through time and back to Arizona's early awakenings.

Just then Darcy poked her beautiful and always intense face into the hole, and I shined the light upward to see what had blocked the dim light from above.

"How's it going?" she queried in her typically confident and mechanically scientific way. I didn't respond, which was unusual for me. Rather I paused in the moment, looking upward.

As the flashlight illuminated her face, I saw a young angel, with a halo of natural morning sunlight, looking down at me from above.

Her face was always beautiful without makeup, naturally freckled, thin, muscular, egg shaped, with a peaches & cream complexion that blended upward into her thick, natural, strawberry blond, hair. Her hair was clipped to the top of her head and, though she always looked beautiful, she never looked more beautiful. I could see her brilliant, flashing and questioning brown eyes even from a dozen feet below and knew yet again that in that 5' 4", 107 pound young woman was the calm executive presence of a natural leader.

I remembered suddenly her first Christmas photo, three weeks old, 21-inches long, 10 pounds, dressed in velvet red and lacy white, sitting in a shiny red hat box, her mother and her looking like two heavenly beings, one wise and eternal, the other a small, squirming cherub, both with innocent and identical, studying, brown eyes. The photo in my head remained even richer than that printed on paper, and I felt grateful.

As I reached and grabbed the snake...pink liquid dripped from its mouth into the round pool of rippling water below.

Like me, Beau had glasses, but Darcy had her mother's eagle-like vision, and I heard, "That's fucking disgusting," from above. She had her daddy's mouth trapped in her mother's lovingly sculpted mind.

I dropped the snake into the bucket and yelled for Beau to pull it up. I knew that a little Clorox and flushing would have our precious pool of life back in business within 24-hours.

I started up slowly and methodically, not forgetting that I might tumble the well on me, or fall, with a careless step.

I shone the light curiously into the rocks as I climbed to simply savor the joy of another conquest...and enjoy the luxury of still feeling strong and refreshed. My heart again applauded the man, or men, who had dug this stony manifestation.

Then Mr. Hyde appeared, as I was electrocuted with sudden and unexpected fear.

Relaxed curiosity was suddenly slammed into animalistic terror, and I exploded with volcanic cursing, and heavy breathing, as suddenly as I had before exuded complete calm and loving reflection.

"**FUCK! Jesus fucking Christ!**" I roared, with two heads no doubt appearing at the top now to see what had triggered the customary explosive change. I heard Suzanne and her mother murmuring as well and, for the first time, realized that they too were standing beside the old platform above.

All were used to this transformation and the kids likely knew that they should scatter and plug the well, but feared that the women might free me, and that I might live and find them, so they stayed put from intermittent love and punitive conditioned obligation.

"What's the matter? Dad," Beau's small cracking voice said, apprehensively. "What is it?" Darcy and her mother echoed. I felt Grandma's concern and hand wringing affection.

I was looking at my gloved right hand and seeing a thin, wormlike, multi-colored snake wiggling beside my fingers into the damp rocks to escape my sight. I wondered, rationalizing, if perhaps blacksnakes might not hatch multi-colored babies, as cats routinely had eclectic babies, but another side of my thinking was scanning to recall the precise markings of a water moccasin. I had never seen anything but a *black* blacksnake. With knee-jerk, rationalized reaction, I hoped it was simply a water snake. In any case, it had a mother somewhere. This was perhaps five seconds of thought.

I shined my light around with protective instinct, yet simultaneously with predatory stealth, to give it the illusion that it was not in danger while seeing if it might have litter mates or a mother sharing the well.

"It's a baby snake," I finally said softly. I no longer cussed or roared because I didn't want to startle the snake more. I erupted involuntarily into ten more seconds of recollection and thought.

I remembered, like flashback lightning, the day that I had seen a thumb-sized, foot-long, brown and white diamond-checkered snake on the sand road in front of our house, and had run over it with my bicycle. I was somewhere between sadistic playing and capturing the story with hard evidence.

It curled pathetically to protect itself, whereupon I gained speed, hit the brakes and slid sideways across it as it struck impotently at me because of its inadequate size. Two more runs and it lay dead in the road, flattened some and nearly torn in half.

I ran to the house to show daddy and got an ass chewing that made the top ten. "That's a GODDAMNED RATTLESNAKE," he roared, vicariously afraid and predictably angry.

"See that little stubby button on its tail...it's not pointed like a bull snake, you fucking dolt, because it's not one! It's a fucking RATTLESNAKE, and if he'd bit you, you'd have been fucked! Their poison is more potent than grown snakes and he'd 'a fucked you up good! They grow one button per year when they shed their skin, but they're all poison."

He pulled his 23-rattle booty (from a 23 year old snake) out of his pocket, shook it till it rattled, glared at me again, and stomped away, snorting. Lesson learned. Ten seconds of recollection and a second of changing instincts. Yet, here I was, drawing inadequately on experience.

"Now what about this little multi-colored thing...water moccasins didn't have rattles...only fangs."

"Shit. Are they sharp and long enough to cut through your glove?" The analytical was now chiming in.

I gulped silently. I wanted to cuss, but held my tongue for self-protection. I looked analytically at my thick new leather gloves and told the analytical to shut the fuck up. Right now, he was distracting.

I felt my heart and kidneys pounding and knew that horrific measures of adrenalin were again being manufactured and released into my system.

My eyes no doubt became snakelike because they were suddenly able to see sharply in the shadowed dark. Ten more seconds passed. I had not answered further. No one asked more. Several heads were alternating and sharing the 24-inch hole at the top of the well.

As I shined my flashlight around in an intuitive searchlight pattern, I quickly spotted two other snakes, one about two feet below and a quarter of the way around the well, another half way around the well, near my left foot. Both were four or five inches long, black, pencil sized and tapered. "How many were there!?"

Something silently flipped in me as when one turns on a light switch. I didn't do it consciously and I didn't authorize it...it just snapped. Flight became fight.

I felt adrenalin focus and convert to demonic rage. Death defying killer instinct possessed and filled me suddenly with the hungry nature of a soaring eagle. They were in MY family's water supply—MY well. My fear ceased and silent cussing rage emerged. I would kill them ALL!

"It's snakes," I finally answered louder and with more clarity. "Snakes, with an **S**. Goddamn, fucking, baby snake**SSS**. Lower me the bucket again." I hissed and roared in some mix of snakelike evil and the ole man's voice.

"Lower the fucking bucket, NOW, Beau." I barked. Darcy quickly took over the job knowing that her focus and efficiency would leave no delay and no room for error. Down came the bucket, quickly and without pendulum arching. Pure. Efficient.

First I grabbed the multi-colored snake with my gloved hand. It tried to wiggle into the rocks, but I used my pinky finger and trapped it…then closed in on it with my thumb and pulled it wiggling out of the rocks. It weakly struck…it mainly wiggled to escape. I bounced its head against the side of the bucket and dropped it in; it was dazed but alive, and too small to crawl up the sides to freedom.

Next I eased like a lizard to the one a quarter of the way around the well and grabbed him head first, squeezing his skull and tossing him into the bucket. Then I eased downward and grabbed the one who had perched by my left foot. I was a hunting machine. "Pull 'em up," I commanded. "Don't let em get out till I get back up, and don't let 'em bite you."

I scaled back to the bottom and hunted in a Nazi camp-searching pattern up all sides of the well to see if I could find others. There were none. I scaled the walls like a worm-hunting lizard mixed with an eagle and a madman and found no more intruders. I finally emerged out of the top of the well with what should have been exhaustion and fear, but instead with focused predatory insanity and barely squelched killer rage.

I should have changed gears and told the kids that they had done a great job. *I should have* told Beau again that I was proud of him for his earlier grappling into the well. *I should have* told Suzanne that I had visions of our early days, of her and Darcy's angelic beauty, and of the deep love I felt for them all. *I should have* thanked Grandma for praying and watching over me. I did not.

As I grabbed the snakes out of the bucket, and smashed their heads with a brick, casting them into the weeds near the drainage ditch that ran to the pond, I told someone to get me a beer. They all looked at the empty plastic six-pack holder and interchanged words that agreed that I had drunk them all. I was enraged.

I stomped off cussing and raging to the truck, barked at them over my shoulder to plug the well, and threw aside the tools.

I backed around in the driveway to escape to the bar, to find some weed, and if I were "lucky" to find a nose full of meth by midnight. It was still before noon.

"Pour some Clorox in the well and stick the cap back over it...I'll caulk it later, Suzanne," I hollered out of the truck window, a coward, acting like a calloused gunnery sergeant.

I drove off with subsiding murder and a transcending, shaky urge for more alcohol and hopefully, some drugs. This had now become too often the scene that I offered my trusting family as I sped away into isolation and returned nearer morning than evening.

If the farm and the pond were beautiful now, I could not see it. I was the well that I had just crawled out of, hand dug by my own self-will and mean defiance, filled with drought's alcohol and with unwelcome snakes.

As I drove, and as rage waned, I again felt deep and inexpressible remorse bubbling into my stomach and heart. It wouldn't do any good, I knew, because I had apologized and promised better behavior before, again and again and again, only to speak and act again in the manner I had today.

Fear acted out and then paralyzed me with wiles of the devil. Only spirits could offer me temporary respite, and temporary was becoming ever temporal.

I was no longer fun to live with. The sweet eyes I had seen in Suzanne during our first years of marriage, and fully the day she told me she was pregnant for the first time, were now looking down and away more and more, growing dimmer and dimmer.

I now hated myself even more than I resented the mirror of her unfathomable character and control. I was beyond falling and beneath redemption. She was certainly too good for me now.

The runner in me knew that I would soon employ his services to save the ones I loved. I knew this script too well. God help me. Two decades later, I knew it too well.

It was like planning a car wreck, yet I knew that I needed to finish it, and I didn't have the guts to help the grim reaper feast upon my fermenting carcass. I couldn't kill myself from cowardice knowledge of the scriptures, but I was surely killing the spirit of the woman who once loved me with a oneness sent by God. I was killing Suzanne and the kids...our family was dying.

Tonight I would kill pain and tell my newest story to seemingly interested, self-proclaimed geniuses and cow-brained drunks.

I would tell it with animation, hand, arm, leg, and face motions, with a loud and grandiose glory...omitting the personal issues that formed its true substance. When it came to strangers, I could tell a story. I could sure tell a story.

Darcy walked in that morning with a soft brown bird cupped in her hands. It was turning its head side to side, each time, 180-degrees. Its eyes were too big for its head and were indeed the greenest eyes I had ever seen in a living entity. There were thin yellow circles surrounding the brilliant green and huge round black holes seemed to blink within a yellowish transparent lining that randomly opened and closed. It was a baby owl.

I had never seen one and wondered how she could find and carry one into the living room in such a casual manner. We were stunned and speechless in unison. Beau followed her like a faithful second owl.

"Isn't it beautiful," she said, smiling ear to ear.

Darcy's little eyes sparkled as she sat it gently on the dining table and backed off, staring at it with her head slightly tilted in a studying motion—looking at it from various angles, as when an artist inspects her work.

She began twirling her finger in her short strawberry blond curls. Her hair was short and full of curls and both she and Beau were deep brown from the sun. They looked at each other, then at the baby owl, then at us, then at the baby owl, at each other, and at us. There was still a stunned silence...it simply didn't make sense that they would walk in with an owl. Was it an omen?

Suzanne finally verbalized our question. "Where did you find it, Darcy?"

"In the meadow, just across the ditch, sitting under a big tree...just sitting there." We still grasped for context. They might as well have walked in with an alien baby. Perhaps it was a shaman corridor?

"Just sitting there?" Grandma queried, trying to offer her input to adults grasping the brown feathered, super ostrich egg shaped and sized little creature with its flat, slowly twisting head.

It sat with its eyes blinking, irritated, looking at us; its little head turning from side to side, looking far more wise and intelligent than the entire family put together. It looked as though it wanted to explain something, but wouldn't bother.

"What shall we feed it," Darcy asked, as though she assumed that it was now a member of the household?

We all continued looking at each other and then the owl. Perhaps it was a cure for my drinking in some belated fashion? Maybe I was going to die, or perhaps Grandma. She was old, but I deserved it. A young owl...the kids...I couldn't think about that. It's all folklore anyhow.

"You found it...just sitting under a big tree?" I clarified like an idiot mocking an echo.

"*Yeth,*" *affirmed Beau.* "*Thitting undoe a twee. Just thitting theyo.*" *He nodded excitedly.*

"*I assume they eat worms and vegetable things,*" *said Grandma, the cook.* "*Maybe some tuna or even milk, though I doubt that. I know they hunt field mice and can see really well at night. With pussycats, we have no mice. I wouldn't even know where to look. I think they eat snakes too.*"

"*Snakes? Maybe we can put it in the well,*" *suggested the sociopath cynically with the analytical looking like it might actually be a good idea. I brushed them aside with my mental censure's hand.*

"*It'll probably die if we try to keep it in captivity,*" *Suzanne said.* "*I'm afraid we can't keep it, but I don't know what to do with it. If it was just sitting under a tree, it must have fallen; I don't think owls lay their eggs on the ground...in fact I'm about sure they don't. We don't want it to die. Hum...geasel weasel?*"

"*We have to simply put it back under the tree,*" *I offered, speculating.* "*We have to hope that the mom doesn't smell us on it, like some animals, and abandon it; but, its best chance of living is to put it back where you found it and hope for the best. We'll have to pray that coyotes or cats don't find it before mom does, but we have to put it back.*"

"*Can't we keep it...Well, let's feed it something first,*" *Darcy suggested.* "*It's probably hungry from sitting there all by itself.*" *She looked to Grandma for a suggestion.*

After trying in vain to feed it tuna, green beans, lettuce and water, we decided that time was ticking and we would transport it back to its point of origin. "*Do you remember where you found it,*" *I asked.*

"*Sure,*" *said Darcy, as though she were an insulted cartographic explorer and not a child.* "*The biggest tree in the meadow, beyond the ditch.*"

"*Mom and I'll go with you, in case momma owl decides to get mad. They have ferocious claws and beaks and I don't want you* getting your eyes clawed out." I thought of a focused, flying, protective, capable, and angry attack chicken.

We began walking towards the back meadow with young Athena now in a shoebox tucked with lettuce, tuna and water.

I watched the sky carefully, but did not see the mother owl. For some reason, even though they were night hunters, I frequently saw an owl gliding during the day. I had never pondered this before. I heard them at night…an eerie screeching sound tearing the dark.

"There's the tree," Darcy pointed as we found a crumbled area and crawled out of the eight-foot deep, 10-foot wide, straight-walled canyon that cut and snaked through our lower south meadow beyond the pond.

She took the shoebox from her mother and headed for the giant cottonwood that loomed tall and wide above the deepest meadow. Other mature trees surrounded it, but it dwarfed them all. It was seemingly dead and without leaves. A redheaded woodpecker was rattling with an echoing percussion séance nearby.

Darcy and Beau sat the baby owl on the north side of the giant trunk precisely where they had found it. We left only some water, some tuna and lettuce, but no shoebox. We reasoned that the box felt very unnatural and might scare or detour the mother if she returned, which we prayed she would. We had no idea how she would re-ascend the tree with it even if she did come, but knew she was little Athena's only hope…in the form of a wing and a prayer. We could provide the prayer.

We slept restlessly that night in a solemn state of worry and prayer for this helpless and beautiful little creature.

The next morning we ran to the meadow to see if the owl were there, gone and not visible, or…something. We didn't know what to expect.

HIGH up in the giant tree sat a small, humbled, and obviously strictly disciplined, feathered being, perched on what appeared to be a nest made of about five interwoven sticks. The nest reminded me *of a large version of the breakable boomerangs I used to make from Popsicle sticks.*

We looked with wrenched necks and saw our one-time visitor sitting in solitary confinement in her natural habitat. She had no doubt been briefly and sternly lectured on her age and place in the food chain, coupled and moored with powerful claws, and lifted by express elevator to her austere efficiency home at the top of the tree. We all smiled and thanked God for answered prayers.

"It's sure beautiful," Darcy said softly, looking up at the marvel of nature. "I wish we could have kept it."

By now, Grandma had navigated the meadow and joined the spontaneous little Audubon society. They all stood looking upward with splendor and awe. I stood looking at them with splendor and awe.

"What a beautiful family," I mused with censured conclusion, drinking my first beer of the day. "I wish…"

Chapter 27
by their fruits shall ye know them

Katrina stands in the annals of American history.

Lisette and I evacuated together and then weaved around limbs and ruin to find a decimated community upon our return.

I was re-roofing our New Orleans home. I was also sawing limbs that had bombed, injected, and pelted our home and yard. As I worked, a northern-appealing white preacher spoke in southern-schooled language and proclaimed that Katrina was "God's judgment on New Orleans and upon the *sins of the land.*"

There were no laughing children in the background as I worked; there was only silence supplanted by blank screeching crows, the air-pounding-chopping roar of helicopters carrying large sandbags across the city, the gnarling random tearing of chainsaws, and a mechanical dirge of trucks and front-end loaders removing people's lives as *debris* from the 300-year old community.

It was the saddest song I had ever heard, insulted by Tokyo Rose, preaching from a hilltop far away, and then playing gospel tunes.

Common people with shoes, boats, trucks, chainsaws, gloves, food, bottled water, raiment, medical supplies, and giant hearts were pouring into this broken community from all over the land to help afflicted *neighbors* in an hour of need.

Others were opening their homes, communities and church doors across the land to welcome beaten NO Samaritans. A flood of human kindness overwrought the tingling cymbal that broadcast from afar, and underscored the deceptive nature of spiritual battle.

I burned with anger at the preacher's arrogance in judging a people he did not know, and wondered at someone *amplifying* my once untreated dark nature and proclaiming it light—a*nd* with a "church" feeding his power-hungry glory. It frightened me to know that people often flock to mad charisma—darkness disguised as light, hate disguised as love.

I wondered about the *nature* and image of God, and knew that we would each someday surely receive judgment from *a just* God. I pondered Jesus' description of the Pharisees and Scribes, and knew that the essence of man remained unchanged in an electronic age.

"It is the nature of a hireling to sing the song of those who provide his table and raiment. Sadly, they are people falling in love with their own kaleidoscopic reflection, and others falling in love with that reflection in turn," yawned the sociopath. For once, sober, I agreed with him, again remembering, *"As in water face answereth to face, so the heart of man to man."*

"Whose bread I eat, his song I sing," boomed the deep, precise voice of Dr. Bremner in my mind's breadbox. He was my first journalism teacher, and an unwelcome, powerful mentor. I *cherished* the "C" he gave me and now, finally, heard his simple message. He used his voice for journalism, not preaching, with journalistic ethics guarding "truth" more honestly than most men's theology.

I recalled Leslie teaching a management class to a fundamentalist organization and confronting harsh critics, who were saying with disdain, "'Ah don't need this *stuff*...All ah need is the BIBLE."

Her response, recognizing that she, herself, had studied and learned massive amounts of scripture, was simple: "REALLY?" she said casually, and with theatric mocked shock, "Well, then, perhaps, if you ever need brain surgery you'll want to ensure that the doctor has *only* studied the Bible."

So, what had I seen in New Orleans? Bourbon Street? Yes—sober. Crime and murder? Yes. Excellent food and music? Yes. Deep humility, strolling cemeteries centuries old, placed as true north, filled with reminding neighbors, and ever whispering of our mortality? Yes. Life balanced by diversity and the strongest sense of *"community"* I had ever seen? Yes.

I wondered which American utopia *the* "Christian" was broadcasting from.

I was welcomed to New Orleans by an organization where all but 120 of 1350 workers, managers, and executives were African American. I was embraced by some of the kindest, wisest, and most Godly people I had ever met when I joined this long-tenured group, and again when Violet and I crashed into oblivion and I found myself alone and friendless. Nearly all of them lost *everything* under Katrina. The "Big Easy" was not.

I was never treated as a white man or a northerner in this beautiful community where I could have been sponged dry with dissimilarity and left as spiritually dead without care or notice. I wished I had seen people of color treated thus in other branches of my journey but, as a rule, I had not.

Color separated humanity and clouded natural human beauty, cloaking God's "image" with education, economics, geography, and carefully worded reasoned rubbish. Culture, however, joined art as paint to renaissance.

My mind reflected on the color of man and I realized the angel of light's programming that leads a man of any color to self-righteousness and bigotry, cloaked even from himself.

I wondered how well dressed spiritual giants would fare to find *their* kingdom blown away, their microphone under water, and their lives under the world's microscope.

Likely God knows the day and the hour of each reckoning. But, along the way, there is scripture to point to Job, Moses, Joseph, David, Jesus, and others. Anti-giants esteem themselves to be aligned with *these* people, not surgically precise targets for the javelin of Phinehas—though I borrow it, un-anointed, now to poke at them.

No doubt, the same disaster in an anti-giant's community will be "the *DEVIL*" attacking *their* ministry. They will not see it as God punishing the "*sins of the land*" when their town is frozen, burned, shaken, drown, dried with drought, or blown away. It is the *DEVIL!*

By then, New Orleans' little giants will have emerged from the ashes, and they won't scoff or simply say, "Brother...you just need Jesus."

They will feed them, clothe them, laugh when they laugh, cry when they cry, and give them something to drink when they are thirsty. That is the final exam and the mark of righteous people.

That was what they did after Katrina; that is what they will do again tomorrow, even for an anti-giant who has fallen. It is their character. Of many colors, these are the people I met in New Orleans...the people who welcomed me, and the people who were decimated by Katrina.

Slight of hand goes unnoticed, and money flows, if an anti-giant can keep one's attention on another in trouble. No doubt the grandiose seminary mind affirms that, "Ummm, aaaaaahh...Noah's world was destroyed by flood: Bad people. A flood destroyed New Orleans: Bad people." Perhaps it is logic caused by praying too little and reasoning too much.

It is frightening to a farmer the bullshit that an expensive suit and a sociopath can generate when they are together on a lighted hilltop preaching to the *cattle* of a thousand hills. Unfortunately, it splashes on the rest of us. God's surgery is consistently very precise. Go to the desert floor, dig up Dathan and his followers...ask them...and beware.

The biggest danger is to be a member of the flock of an anti-giant. Plague may afflict the flock because of their *hired power* and his consistent irritation of an honest God. When they willingly pay his check, they are willingly under his spiritual authority.

Historically, it wasn't drunks and hookers that led the disobedient mass to destruction, but Godless leadership, evil men and false prophets. Nothing has changed. One can find Jesus on Bourbon Street anytime, looking for lost sheep. I have met criminals from New Orleans who found Him there—even some who found Him in the gutter by the food line. *Now, ain't that some shit?!?*

Sometimes even anti-giants, their flock, and their children have roamed Bourbon Street...the mass of the crowd are not from New Orleans.

Why...Tele-giants have been found with hookers in the French Quarter, no doubt ministering. Whatever the case, Bourbon Street *survived* Katrina: Brothers and sisters, how we struggle to find a spiritual pattern sometimes. Who can know the way of the Lord?

In the *real* New Orleans community, my co-workers lost homes, pictures, antiques, keepsakes, collectables, and memoirs from their lives and forefathers...irreplaceable. Many lost a loved one...spouse, child, mother, father, friend, or all. Most lost jobs.

On my desk lay a page from the newspaper that had the faces of a 30-year company man, a good man, his 13-year old son, who had not yet even reached puberty, his wife, and his aunt, all lined along an obituary column...all drowned by Katrina. When I spoke with co-workers about their own losses and asked how they were doing, each said, "Blessed"... almost to a person: "*Blessed.*"

"Blessed?" I reflected as I dodged broken furniture and strewn bags of children's clothing in the road while driving to our temporary job sites in Gonzalez and Baton Rouge. Our old job sites were *all* under water.

I recalled Joseph being enslaved, imprisoned, and transplanted to Egypt, only to become a leader by the hand of God. From him, the Israelites were transplanted, embraced, later enslaved, and finally again freed under the staff of Moses *400 years* later. *For with the Lord, a day is as a thousand years and a thousand years as a day.*

As I saw hundreds of thousands of people living elsewhere in America since Katrina, I wondered about the Cloud that guided the Israelites and then moved, them with it, lest they perish. Perhaps Katrina was such a cloud.

Because of it, and because they are "blessed," broken people found communities and homes full of giants with open doors.

With the exodus went New Orleans' cooking, laughter, love, music, and culture. When new restaurants, gatherings, and ministries open across America, it will perhaps bring some of old New Orleans to the mix...simply because they moved with the cloud. Time will tell. Perhaps God's judgment is sometimes diluted by man's hurried context.

Perhaps God *is* God because of his context or attention span. Constantine, for example, was variably haled as wise, selfish, deluded, or political when he *institutionalized* Christianity in 313 A.D. Whatever his motive or vision, with peace, power, and large decorative buildings came the demise of small home worship and intimate churches. Private worship, brought into public, needed washed to look better. Within only a few years, man had diluted the now *free* faith with things like a syncretistic mix of sun gods and crosses...but, hey, people were getting along; we could *improve* God.

Posterity, paganism, piety, power, piffle, and *POOF*: murder, holy wars, persecution, inquisition, reformation. We could *approve* God. Religion has more "isms" than alcohol.

Man adjusts the dials to make things better, never realizing that he is playing with the dials of a principled spiritual universe. Ironically, one can sit isolated and *alone* now and listen safely to the electronic preacher of their choice. Ah, freedom without fellowship. .

AA has a saying: *"Who am I to deny you your suffering?"*

Maybe some persecution has value. Maybe freedom isn't always a blessing. Maybe it takes "a day" or two to see if something has God's hand in it. Scripture is full of places where it took hundreds, or thousands, of years to see the end of a matter. Most scripture is dangerous truth in the hands of a human; better left to God for absolute clarity. Some, though, seems simple enough even for farmers to *ponder*.

Scripture 1: No man knoweth from whence the wind cometh, nor whither it goeth...the wind listeth whither it will.

Scripture 2: The rain falls on the just and unjust alike.

Scripture 3: Judge not lest you be judged, for with what judgment you judge, you shall be judged.

Farmer 101: Shit happens...What goes around, comes around...Cream rises to the top.

Definitions: Preaching down to Job: *Man taking the name of the Lord in vain.* Satan quoting the scriptures to Christ: *Taking the name of the Lord in vain.* "Shit happens"...*dung, simple profanity; sometimes true.*

Chapter 28
let us make man in our image

New Orleans was mentally ill—in fact, most of Louisiana was mentally ill—so, after Katrina, as I became angry, I began to ponder the human race, the nature of man, the nature of *institutionalized* man, and the interconnected "image" of God. I was displaced and thinking to the point of pain.

Since I was programmed, and since I was feeling off balance somehow, I needed to check it. Sometimes, I had learned, I was adequately balanced but just "feeling" something...perhaps an echo or just a "feeling" demanding some attention—nothing to act on. Maybe, however, I needed to change something or some way of thinking or acting...yet *again*.

I *constantly* had to update my thoughts and actions. They had run free for years and served a whirlwind of shit storms to those around me. I couldn't afford that anymore. I *wouldn't* afford that anymore.

Feelings, I had learned...were simply overrated. But, drunk or sober, they *felt* real. Ignored, they would isolate me, and could ultimately make me drink, or worse. Some feelings came and went like rainstorms, others stayed and dug at me...THOSE were the ones that could not be ignored.

I recalled the shrink telling me at a turning point, "There are only so many emotions. They attach themselves to thoughts, and vice versa, and make one believe that this or that is significant when, in fact, it's *only* a thought or a feeling, nothing more. Some things ARE significant. But, if we act-out on them all, the machine cranks up and we're off to the races. We don't have to do that. We can pause. It's a choice...and it goes with every thought and feeling. Choose wisely."

Post-Katrina, and with John A's passing, I again needed to sort the real from the unreal and the tools—given by John A and AA—

were prayer, meditation, and journaling. I didn't know clearly *what* I thought about some things.

If I were starting to like or dislike all of New Orleans, all Christians, all preachers, all white people, all old people, all co-workers, all black people, all Hispanics, all Asians, all Middle Easterners, all people with "other" ethnicity, all of Kansas...whatever, I was *out of tune*. Even analyzing it was *the mask* forming. Some of every group was simply an asshole; some places suck, and some times are bad. That is a fact to stay grounded, as dirt is to soil: *Farmer 102*.

I had to ensure that the people-pleasing *mask of blending countenance* didn't cover my agitation and reanimate with oversimplification or false complexity, just to falsely rest me, or wear me out...then isolate me. It was a liar, connected to the father of lies. Only a taste of truth seemed to *immunize* me against its subtle reemergence—basically, *any* truth.

Since there is nothing new under the sun, and since truth seeks to be found, I hypothesized that truth is hidden like the Eternal master's gold in a mix of new and ancient ways and places. It is everywhere, like a giant garbage dump, and one can sift and take what one wants. For comfort, I preferred to see it as a stream, with branches, where I could float in living waters and drink, when thirsty, of truth.

I would float willingly along a branch of this stream of seeking, asking Wisdom, God's co-worker, where to look and what *They* meant by *"in our image."*

I knew that I had worked diligently to know my *own* nature and "image," but I knew also that I was persistently in danger of dancing with my own reforming reflection. Discomfort was the beginning nature of honest pause. Honest pause was the necessary beginning of prayer and meditation.

I reflected that I had changed many things since my youth, yet knew that my models of "learning" were easily tricked and oft falsely tied to man's glory—degrees, completion, ribbons, awards, success, recognition, *and approval*. Some places I was still a child, others I was a man, others a false man, or a man in diapers. It was all *my* image, but what of it, for me, was still true?

I sought to discover when my ideas about the *image* of man had formed and changed. I knew, foundationally, that I had indeed seen God's image in other people, and that it was accidental intimate human relationships that consistently reprogrammed my heart and mind—not knowledge, training, degrees, or politically correct obligations.

Truth usually changed me unawares. But, I needed awareness to catch-up with it, lest I walk around *not knowing* what I think or believe, or worse yet, proclaiming something that I really didn't know. I had spent years doing that.

I was angry with the preacher. I was angry with New Orleaneans being called "refugees" in towns we had fled to. I was angry about losing John A. I wanted to run and hide, but had nowhere to run to, and nowhere to hide from...myself. AA had acronyms for "FEAR." *False Evidence Appearing Real...Face Everything And Recover...Fuck Everything And Run."* These acronyms spun in my head like a clicking game wheel.

I knew that often in life, to someone's chagrin, I—accidentally, or on purpose—answered a different question than the one asked of me, and gave opinions that were unwelcome. I knew that God sometimes so answered me. I knew that, as with the sled ride, I might seek a truth and receive a different, or an incomplete, truth ungraspable by my human mind, to be settled later—like finally windless dust devils that still had power because they dusted one's eyes in passing.

I hated the journey's pain and experience, but I knew that I had to again chance it. Perhaps it would be better now that most of my days were light-filled.

"...We can pause. It's a choice...and it goes with every thought and feeling," I heard the shrink reminding me.

I began deep breathing and, first, floated along torrent rapids of hot anger, but...finally, into a branch of still water and tranquil sounds. Breathing...seeking...in seeking, accepting.

Overhead, I could see an eagle floating in lazy-eight, infinite patterns on a thermal, and I could hear woodpeckers pecking and red cardinals singing in breeze ruffled cottonwood trees along the banks...I was floating, breathing, floating, drifting...The woodpecker's sound slowly faded into the sound of hammers...I was floating into my past, blending into my memories, drifting into my learning and experience. Anger was vaporizing now, and peace was filling me, with waking slumber and childlike joy...drifting, accepting, drifting, being.

As I drifted, it was not to be revealed as universal truth, only as *my* journey's updating answer from a simple minute of God's precious day. Ah, *breathing*...there was Harry the carpenter...not the President, the carpenter...

<<<<<<>>>>>

Harry Truman Edmondson—whom we called Harry Truman—was a tall man with arms that were obviously disproportioned to his 6' 3" lanky frame. He was Curtis'—whom we called Cat Daddy—brother-in-law and began working with Cat Daddy and I framing houses.

Cat Daddy co-owned the company. Harry and I seemed to be about equally skilled carpenters, dwarfed by Cat Daddy's stuttering brilliance. Cat Daddy was the best framer I had ever seen.

As Harry and I worked together, we began to trust one another and to share stories of our life's adventures.

After months of framing, my anger towards the Bomber Plant was finally fading. I was not yet sober, but was not drinking heavily because I was too tired from framing houses to imbibe the habit at earlier *and later* levels. Harry was sober.

As we worked, I began to realize that, sometimes, I was not aware that he was black. One day, he opened up about some of his adventures and I began to see the man inside.

"I did some prison time for drugs," he said humbly, yet casually. "I remember being knocked down by the police and seeing this young officer looking down at me with a smirk on his face saying, 'You have the right to remain silent.' I know it wasn't the best judgment, but I came up at him with a right cross and said, 'No, *YOU* have the right to remain silent!' He was out cold before he hit the ground. That didn't play out too well for me. Now I avoid bars, and drink Cokes when I'm in one...Did I tell you I'm a boxer?"

"No," I said belly laughing. "You any good?" I couldn't stop laughing.

"Well," he answered, "I'm blessed with these strange looking long-assed arms that eventually deceive an opponent into getting in too close. It'll happen sometime during the fight...I just have to get him tired and play him 'til he makes a mistake. I may not look like it, but I'm a strong little mother fucker when I punch." I had seen that in his tireless, sometimes effortless, handing of studs and plywood up to the second floor and roof as we framed houses. It wore me out every time, but not Harry.

One day, as I jumped into a window well filled with sand, I landed in a gigantic pile of shit. From the embarrassed, yet satisfied, look on his face, I knew it was Harry's. He looked like a dart player that had hit a bull's-eye.

"Harry, goddamn it, you shit in the window well, and I just stepped in it.

"Yeah," he said. "I had to shit." End of conversation. That was my brother, Bill! Asshole.

One day, when we stopped to drink some water, Harry guzzled the orange gallon jug and then handed it to me, as workers had done throughout my lifetime, from the hayfields of my youth on. When I apparently hesitated, he said, "What, you afraid that since I've been to prison I've got AIDS or something?" I knew more about AIDS than that, and I don't know why, or if, I actually hesitated, but I obviously appeared to. He was so straightforward and simple. I would have to find Lisette to find another so clear and direct, yet underlain with goodness. I smiled and drank.

Another day as I was cleaning out an unframed basement, I found an empty 12-inch cube-shaped nail box that had obviously been used as a toilet, filled with Harry's latest shit.

When I *gave him shit* about it, he said, "Nothing ever pleases you, does it? I didn't shit in the window well; I shit in a nice, private box. Or did you manage to step in that too?" He smiled ear to ear and I loved him. There was something conflictingly intimate about finding another man's box of shit.

As I eased along the outside wall of a second story one day, to nail-off remaining pieces of the adjoining roof, Harry and Cat Daddy were finishing the upper roof with a complex triangular piece that had beveled cuts and strange angles.

I could hear that Cat Daddy was irritated with Harry's inability to understand his directions, whereupon he barked, "You don't need to draw me no picture Harry! I ain't some damn *white* guy!"

I recalled Cat Daddy's face the day I asked him how he got so good at framing, and how he had found it to work in Oklahoma before Kansas.

He quickly said, with virtually no description, that he had not been treated well as a black framer in Oklahoma, and that he had to *excel* to even keep his job beside average white carpenters in the 70s. I could see that the pain and anger ran deep. I knew that he would have been treated no differently in Kansas, perhaps only seemingly better. I could only imagine how beer-bottle-boy would have treated him in southern Texas.

I recalled my first sighting of a black man on a trip to Oklahoma with my granddad when I was 13. I mused to recall, though, that this was not what had captured my interest. Rather, it was noticing that, except for a southern drawl, white people in Oklahoma looked and seemed exactly like white people from western Kansas. They should have been different. I had been raised where people from Oklahoma were called "Okies" and were viewed with some sort of general, scoffing, disdain.

I thought them to be lesser people in some fashion. For example, when someone stole another's tools, it was referred to by Kansas farmers as "the Oklahoma discount." I assumed that the white race from Oklahoma was cluttered with low-lives and thieves. Such was my intro to bigotry. Not color...geography. I could only imagine how Kansans received a black man from Oklahoma in those decades. Hispanics and Asians? They almost didn't exit in Kansas back then.

I remembered being told that my hometown had a *"sundown law"* and recalled that I didn't think about it much, considering I had never seen a black person. "Basically," the hired man told me, "the sundown law means that if you're a nigger, you better not stop here and remain after sundown."

I had no context for that as a child. To me, only mean spirited men who said such things were contemptible because of their overall mean spirit, not because of what they said. My daddy was like that, so it went in one ear and out the other as not mattering. Later I saw that it did matter.

I flashed again to my early twenties, and the night that I was stoned with bottles and cans by a crowd of angry center-city St. Louis youth at a City sponsored pool party in Berkeley, Missouri. I recalled how it hurt my feelings that they hated me simply because I was white. I was beginning to see, one story at a time, why they hated me "without reason."

"Hey," yelled Cat Daddy with a sense of urgency I had never heard. "Come here! Harry broke his leg." I came running.

There sat Harry with his right foot lying to one side, like a large toy doll that had been cast aside without life or a caretaker. His powerful, cream-colored, lower leg bone was poking through the skin above his ankle and was jammed into sand that surrounded the nearly framed house. Cat Daddy was tightening a homemade carpenter's tourniquet a few inches above the break.

As I sat, holding the piece of electrical wire twisted by a two-by-four scrap board to keep Harry's leg from hemorrhaging, I could hear Cat Daddy in the distance trying to flag down the ambulance.

I knew that Harry had just been invited to box in Vegas for tens of thousands of dollars per fight and I thought of the incredible unfairness in life's unfolding. I didn't know that this was seeds of hope for later understanding Katrina...but it was.

"Why would God allow such a thing to happen to this good man who had tuned himself perfectly and had turned his life around?" I pondered, with emptiness.

Harry sat there calmly looking at his bone and his limp foot, saying, "Well, I guess I won't be going to Vegas now."

I hurt deeply for my broken friend, Harry Truman, knowing the buck indeed stopped here.

I left Cat Daddy soon and went to work for another employer, but kept in touch with Harry off and on to track his progress. Five surgeries later, he was informed that he would never box professionally again. I felt deep regret for his accidental misfortune.

Time passed and I ran in to him one day at a large commercial construction site where he was now the job superintendent. He and I were, no doubt, both better managers than carpenters.

He still walked with a slight limp, but seemed incredibly happy and serene as he told me that he was teaching boxing to disadvantaged youths at the YMCA. His eyes danced with Godly joy as he spoke of his new avocation.

I instantly knew that his unique story and talent would combine to change the path of blessed kids who were spiraling into America's sustained cast of bigotry, poverty, drugs, and crime. Some would be changed forever because of Harry Truman's *accident*. I affirmed, yet again, that I was simply not God and lacked his patient perspective. *Let the nations know that they are but men.*

"Don't' shit in their gloves, Harry," I ribbed him, as we hugged and parted.

"I might," he retorted. "Depends on the kid. If he's like you...he might need it."

I loved him so and walked away knowing that God had mixed bone, sand, time, adversity, and strong spirit to make pure gold. He smiled, with my brother's smile, as we parted.

I fantasized the hired man telling Harry to be out of town by sundown: A poor choice.

"You have the right to remain silent."

"Be still and know that I am God."

Tomato...Tom-ah-to.

<<<<<<>>>>>>

Breathing and floating...breathing and floating...peace and serenity...peace and surrender...

John A's Toy was 11 when Japanese soldiers herded my blood father, his parents, his Philippine wife, and my older half-sister, Diana, into a prison camp in the Philippines.

They were fed a starvation diet each day, when they were fed, and left the camp at battle's end no longer wealthy Americans with a playboy dream-life, but starved, broken, and bitter refugees.

My grandfather, Claude Russell, had gone to Kansas University where he became an engineer and flirted with having an early KU basketball team. His cavalier sense of adventure took him to the Philippine Islands, whereupon he became a District Engineer and started a lucrative construction and mining business.

My father, Elbert Ewing, was born on March 21, 1915, in Cebu, South Island Hospital, grew up a wealthy white kid, rode horses and browned along the beaches, went to high school in Shanghai, China, and married a beautiful Philippine girl while in his twenties. Their life was ripening for second-generation wealth when World War II sliced it all away.

After the prison camp, their marriage unraveled as they moved to California and my father began his rebellious life as an aspiring artist—against the blessings of his engineer father. Alcoholism, by now, afflicted all but Diana deeply, but my father's charm and arrogant charisma nonetheless glowed brightly.

I would be born of his second wife, a Rosy the Riveter and farm girl from Kansas, who wandered perchance to find adventure in California's Lockheed plant and its surrounding 1940s nightlife.

Her anger would flash when someone used chewing gum to fill a rivet hole and, by *nature* and upbringing, she did not like slackers, cheats, or liars. She had a temper, which my father would later discover by leading with his bottle, his mouth, and his figurative chin.

My father would announce at their first dancehall sighting that he was going to marry my mother, and so he would. He would speak with animation of how man was only a small floating element in the bloodstream of the universe, like a virus, and would charm her with his wit, his art, and his adventures.

She would fall hard for him and bear him two Kansas children, my sister, Dallas and I, before he departed again for California in 1951, a DTs stricken drunk, who had again shared his clever mouth to mistakenly engage Mommy's stern and *giant* farmer dad, granddad Bill, in a Dighton, Kansas, barroom fight at the Corner Tavern. My father would quickly lose.

After he left, Mommy would work hard as a cosmetologist and raise her children, until she found the strength, and security, of John Lincoln Wheatcroft, *aka*/the ole man, who married Mommy and moved us to the farm in 1953.

My sister, Diana, would later show up at our sister, Dallas', first wedding in Dodge City, and then, get back on a plane, before the ceremony, after meeting Dallas's groom-to-be. I missed her by hours, and thus, never got to meet her.

"I will not watch you marry *that* man," she said sternly. The woman had incredible judgment and wisdom. The husband proved to be a violent, abusive, man.

Diana would seek to write a book later in life, but would be asked by my father's sisters and his new wife, "What could you *possibly* have to say?" Indeed?

My father's United States Coast Guard U.S. Merchant Mariner's identification card, issued 2-3-56 from Los Angeles, would show his birth date (perhaps deliberately or wet brained) inaccurately as "3-20-14" and would accurately list him as "5-9, 155," with "light brown hair, blue eyes" and a "complexion: Cauc—ruddy." Beside his thumbprint would be the words "Fireman, Watertender."

A self-portrait, dated 1960, sent to me by him, would show an angry faced man, who looked exactly like me, with the inscription, *"To my son—Douglas Steven, with love, Dad."*

I barely showed it to Suzanne. Leslie would frame, but not hang it, because she could not stand his anger. Violet kept it behind a door in our laundry room. Lisette hung it immediately beside our bed, and offered her gratitude for seeing daily the face of untreated alcoholism.

He would finally reach out to me, but I would never speak or write to him. Though she never asked it, I prejudiced myself as defending my mother's honor, and spoke not a word.

He sent me a letter in 1972, as I neared the end of my on-campus master's work, which simply said, *"Flesh of my flesh, my time is short."* He was dead within a year and I wept knowing that, somehow, I had lost something precious before even finding it.

The educated person in me demands reason and literature to prove what is true and reasoned, but my experience has shown that, in fact, life brings truth to one however, and whenever, it will.

I could again hear woodpeckers' hollow percussion in my meditative, dreamlike state.

"The sum of the parts does not equal the whole," *interrupted* the poet. "Rather, parts find themselves, simply parts, in a whole never spoken."

I could again see the eagle gliding gently on summer thermals.

Questions were frequently answered that one lacked the wisdom and experience to ask. Something glues it together to make stories and relationships unveil complete truth with incomplete pieces. Incomprehensively, one just knows. My mind tried clumsily, and without authorized power, to summarize. It mixed with meditation to make drifting choppy for an instant, but I allowed it.

A white boy, raised by poor farmers, came from the bloodstream of a rich white alcoholic, who ended up gutter-drunk, with nothing but his artwork in the form of some movie stars and an honest drunk's angry self portrait.

Japanese soldiers took booty and left him with an empty wallet, an empty belly, a blurred dream, an empty bottle, and a like-afflicted, war-tattered, "Philippino" daughter...my sister, who was told she had "nothing to say."

Likely, had you been there to share the living room, you would have learned to hate both drunks and Japanese. Yet, you weren't, and Diana didn't. Why?

With the world unfolding, John A's Japanese wife would help sculpt him into the good and gentle sober man that would someday offer a schooled farmer unfathomable, un-repayable, foundations for true friendship, meditative reflection, personal honesty, and lasting sobriety. Would he—or you—have been the same without her? No.

I could hear the red cardinal singing, as I drifted, with the beautiful sound of cottonwoods blowing in the water-cooled, warm summer breeze. The watery ride was calming.

A black carpenter-boxer would first help a white farmer see no color, and would accidentally give front row seats to help understand the universal, bare bone, truth of man living to serve God's hidden grace. Bill would give a second performance of that with his life and death. New Orleans was a global third. Would New Orleans have looked the same without both of them? No. In fact, you would have likely never seen her.

Harry would help a fellow carpenter understand "at" the later gained southern recitation that "...northerners love the race, but hate the individual, while southerners love the individual but hate the race." I now saw that both were true, both were true of both colors, and both were bullshit. True bullshit. With perception and experience, Cat Daddy would remain understandably and intentionally black; Harry would remain understandably and intentionally Harry.

I breathed deeply again, thinking that I was leaving, yet, drifted again to the sound of cottonwoods blowing. And, so, I floated again into summers past. In the distance, I heard Cat Daddy yelling, *"Breathe!"*

I smiled to know that he was yelling at me, because I always held my breath when I operated a nail gun, and it irritated him.

He watched Harry and me like a hawk, working and watching all at once. He was like a big mother. He had a guy-form of being everywhere at once and multi-tasking. He did have uncanny senses. Cat Daddy was such a keen hunter and fisherman that vendors called him "Dan'l Boone," and he used these hunting skills to spot and catch us. He was a kind, yet fierce, mentor to both Harry and me.

I breathed deeply, staying and returning, as I listened to the floating sounds of calm water. I could hear the water bubbling softly as it encountered stones and lapped, with life-giving energies, at thirsty grassy shorelines. Then, I was back on the hot summer jobsite.

As I watched Cat Daddy seemingly *jog* along a second story framed wall, I said, "Jesus, I'm scared to fucking death of heights, and I can barely drag along a wall. I've never seen anyone run around on a wall the way you do!"

"Why do you think they call me *'Cat Daddy,'*" he grinned simply, with an implied bow, obviously pleased that I had finally solved his unstated riddle.

As Cat Daddy watched me set down a running skill saw, and release it while the blade was still spinning, he shouted, "Quit that…you gonna cut yo fuckin' nuts off!"

And so, I nearly did the next day when the saw came back at me because the saw guard did not fully deploy. The saw took off towards me like an angry little toothed-unicycle being ridden by a Gremlin. It stopped just short of my upper thigh.

Cat Daddy stuttered and failed at a King's English, but *damn*, he was experienced, and I didn't have to cut my nuts off to learn it, if I listened. I listened from then on.

"Jesus," he muttered, shaking his head with disapproval, "You workin' me, man! You, ya, ya, you workin' me!" He stood, uneducated, stuttering, muttering, shaking his head and simultaneously cutting complex hip-roof rafter angles that I could not even fathom, purely from seasoned knowledge and a crisp memory.

"…I ain't some damn white guy," my memory recounted.

"No…you ain't." I understood clearly as I watched him work. He was *Cat DADDY*, and he was to wood what Clarence was to airplanes. They suddenly filed in my brain as similar men. "Cat Daddy, Clarence…Harry, my brother. Teachers…friends."

I was drifting now out of a meditative state and back into clarity of thought, without anger. Unlike the sled ride, this time, I had received visitors and visions that calmed the burning fires of limited thought and powerless humanness. Stories calmed my emotions while recollection continued to settle my knowing.

I stared at the ceiling and saw sunlight dancing with shadows as tree leaves silhouetted a natural choreography to never be repeated. My mind began its closing arguments, with calm clarity, rested from daydreaming meditation.

I reflected clearly now that bigotry's antidote was human touch. Colors of people would cluster separately for a while; that is the melting pot of America. Some people found each other though, despite their color, by the grace of God. It came with freedom from fear and hate, as a bonus, and vice versa.

Only individual human relationships could truly breach color's "image" and boundary. Most of us didn't ask the right question. Some men would never know. Bringing New Orleans to them will help. New Orleans quantified the quality of this learning for me; and thank God for something that freeing. Culture is perhaps color in disharmony, creating diversity. Sharing culture is color in harmony, an oft involuntary act of the heart.

I reflected that final wrecking balls for smashing paradigms were felt when I experienced several quick follow-on events that placed man's learning of prejudice and color in perspective. It preceded, but was the same principle as, discovering AA...Life experience, followed by three little tumbler turns to unlock an awakening. It took little time to finally open the *long*-unlocked door and see the lesson that I had always really known by heart.

First, when I was interviewed for a position in a Department on Aging, I was asked if I "...liked old people?"

Still deep brown and clear thinking from working with Cat Daddy and Harry, I answered, "Not all of them."

Hearing it come from my mouth in an interview surprised me, but I knew that I had told the truth. I had simply seen too many bigoted, self-serving, mean spirited, impatient old fucks that I could not stand. They stood in stark contrast to the myriad of good examples I had seen. Some old people never matured, and stayed mean to the bone until God finally delivered them—and us—from their misery. They came in all colors, and at least two sexes.

Second, while working in the Aging department, I became deep friends with a masters level social worker named Anita, and listened with clarity as she described the day she discovered that being black "mattered."

She was five or six, and overheard the word "nigger," as she listened to adults talking in the living room, when her little white friend asked her to stay for supper. As she described it, the pain, still in her eyes, stung me with intensity. I remembered Cat Daddy's description and saw the same flinching principle of injustice.

Third, while attending an "Aging" conference in Atlanta, my friend, Eddy, and I were approached by a street person who had eased into the lobby of the Peach Tree Hotel. He wanted money, and had a good story to go with it, but we had been panhandled for days, even with the *same* good story, so we offered him nothing.

"Where you from?" asked the street guy, seemingly trying to keep us on the line.

"We're from Wichita," Eddy told him in a proud, kind, and rapidly spoken perfect, English, that sounded very broken, and indiscernible, to the unfamiliar ear. His deep black face reflected the lobby's afternoon sun as he smiled vulnerably. He always smiled robustly, ear to ear—always. It was the only smile he had.

With harsh, angry contempt, the African American panhandler stomped off saying, "I don't know where the fuck you from, but you sure as *fuck* ain't from Wichita, mother fucker!"

Eddy's feelings were hurt, though he knew that the draw of the streets was endless and that a donation of money would not change another's heart.

Eddy had come to America from Nigeria after tribal wars erupted and many in his community were killed.

His parents were Catholic and, so, used connections to help him get to the United States, where he became a citizen, joined the Army, soldiered for five years, and then began getting an education.

His sister became a flight attendant. Both lived while trouble passed. To them, prejudice was not recalled as an academic luxury; it wasn't displaced and fanned by generations of racial, social, and economic dance; it had the intense and immediate differently painted, same-colored, face of angry death.

Eddy was brilliant, and hungry for knowledge, so he quickly obtained a masters degree and was working on yet another. He actually studied mathematics and regression economics for fun as a hobby! *Now* he was from Wichita. *No* shade of American prejudice could understand the harsh journey that got him here, and it hurt that he had to endure it.

For me, it was a random moment of colorless truth. His background was no doubt far harsher than that of his latest insulter, who was likely himself simply feeling mocked by life's damaged American experience. Addictions were not lessoning his pain, but might, someday, offer a rebirth from it.

When I came to New Orleans, I found a people who didn't really care what outsiders thought. Black folks, white folks, gays, straights, whatever...they collectively weren't searching for community affirmation or cultural identity.

In New Orleans, it did seem culturally, however, that nearly *everyone* was given "honking" training while still in diapers. The Big Easy was not a place to drive slowly or to sit through a changed green light. **"BLAAAA"** was one of the first angering, and finally humorous, hometown sounds I learned in New Orleans...it was simply hometown Jazz, unbridled by a car.

In other towns, little kids in bright neon plastic car seats with horns were being amused. In New Orleans, it was early *driver survival training*. That likely blew elsewhere with Katrina too. If so, it ain't personal and it sure as hell ain't racial. It's 'cause you are movin' too damn slow for the Big Easy.

"Take what you need and leave the rest; you're welcome here, but we're not looking for your approval," is likely New Orleans' unspoken message. I loved that message, and felt so freed by the slow-simmering, 300-year, spicy, sassy, *nature* of it.

Wichita wasn't yet sure how to package or promote its culture, strength, and beauty, but New Orleans didn't even have to think about it. It just *was*—time refined, community, *nature* and *image*.

In New Orleans, I saw the melting pot in action best when I attended AA meetings, and saw again that the *principles* of alcohol and drugs were definitely blind to prejudice.

AA rooms were filled with people who told stories of once hating him or her, this race or that race, but ending up broken. Chemicals equally took everyone's humanity. What a gift. It leveled the playing field absolutely, and spiritual awakening was one's only hope for recovery. Most awoke color blind. *Everyone* saw the triangular principles of *unity, service, and recovery...or perished alone.* In AA, bigotry is simple: It's a *character defect.*

Black guys sponsored white guys, white guys sponsored black guys, blacks sponsored blacks, whites sponsored whites, different colored ex-cons sponsored one another, Indians sponsored Asians, Hispanics sponsored whites, Middle Easterners sponsored ex-marines, gays sponsored straights, black women sponsored white women, bikers sponsored (*forced*) bicyclists, hookers sponsored ex-ministers...endless combinations melting.

Hell, I didn't even *KNOW* what some of those creatures were that crawled beaten from New Orleans streets...but they *appeared* to be someone's son or daughter, and they mostly turned into *people* over time. I was told that there are beings like them all over the world. Some of them were atheists, or criminals, and participate in *churches* now. A*in't THAT some shit?!*

To quell my anger, a final conclusion rested, and crystallized, clearly: Katrina wasn't God's punishment of New Orleans...It was likely a big fuckin' wind storm that broke sinking, weak levees and dislodged strong people—yeah, and some criminals too—just like everywhere else. Even some criminals came because it was warm in New Orleans, and now they have moved back home, or elsewhere in America—*Land Of The Free.*

Katrina made a second flood hit New Orleans, by the way—Latinos.

Ironically, most New Orleaneans call them "Mexicans." I love that! I hadn't heard that generalization since the early 70s in Tucson. Now, that *IS* culture shock to *"Chocolate City."*

I love watching the melting pot fire back up. Keeps things savory and fresh and, I will bet, the ole town will be just fine when it simmers down and one out of four people are speaking Spanish. That's how 300-year old towns learn...it is nothing new. Ask Spain and France.

Possibly, *as a second option, if* Daniel 8 through 12 and Matthew 24 *are* deploying now, Katrina was the equivalent of a Kansas dust devil going across a random farmer's field—a tremor with other travail.

In this scenario, of course, missiles will fly in the Middle East, a genius flatterer will bring peace, the *"Abomination of Desolation"* will be visible, and then *all hell* will break loose. If so, God help the Earth when her later rains and winds come. It will be a big'n, hittin' a thousand hills, and *everybody* will get to taste the post-Katrina, hold tight to your baby, no food, no water, no shelter, no clothes, no job, no money, no gas, insurance shagged us, low-down, mother fuckin' bluuueessss.

Whatever it was, God will certainly use it for good. That seems to be His *nature*, and those aligned with His nature will be fine. Besides, not much time has passed, really.

I was nine years sober, and it was only days before Lisette and I were to marry, when I sifted through a box of traveling remnants that Violet had saved for me—life's filtered items that I once grandiosely referred to as *"the roots of my soul."* I hadn't realized how true that was.

Among the old yearbooks, poems, and papers, I found a letter from my father that had been written roughly 30-days before I launched my drinking career on the way to KU. It was dated April 22, 1967. I had never read it. I had tossed it unread into a box that traveled with me across time and found me 38 years later, finally teachable.

A gold and black, egg-shaped, *"Russell"* coat of arms was showing through the back flap of the now yellowing windowed envelope, and giant purple letters spelled *"AIR MAIL"* on the upper right face of the envelope.

The coat of arms had a ribbon inscription that said *"che - sara - sara"* and contained a shield with three seashells and a lion. A horned mountain goat stood proudly at the top, above the shield, above a four-buttoned leather breast piece, and upon a mountainous looking, ruffled and draped feathered sash. Both the lion and the mountain goat had their left front leg raised, like proud kittens hunting.

It had 98-cents in postage and said *"Deliver to Addressee Only"* above a giant purple stamp reading *"Certified Mail No. 938679."* It had obviously been sent with some urgency, yet lay nearly four decades with uncaring apathy. The artistic, hand-written, letter would have been written seven years after he drew his angry self-portrait, if I had cared about that. The return address was Cardamine Place, Tujunga, California, 91042. I finally sat and read it:

Dear Son,

I am well aware that this will come as a surprise since it has long, long, been overdue, but I wanted to wait until you were no longer a boy, but a man, a young one perhaps, but I pray a man

nonetheless! I have prayed for both of your good sisters and your good self for many, many years and trust and trust in God that all of you are in good health and don't hate me in any way since I had to force the conclusion because I *WAS* in the grip of the devil himself when I couldn't stop drinking alcohol and it *HAD* the upper hand on me more than you will ever realize and I knew I would only bring shame and disgrace on you all if I stayed around you all any longer than I already had. I am happy to report that I have been away from alcohol in any form whatsoever for almost five years with a few minor incidents, but I was quick to cast it aside and bury it where it belongs so now I am completely healed by the Grace of God and it no longer haunts me. Enough of this for the time being and I wanted to emphasize the dangers and heartbreak it can and *DOES* cause
(Over)
2.
and with all my heart and soul instill upon your young mind never to touch the stuff in any form whatsoever as long as you shall live. Even now, I still worry because you are of the same seed, the same heredity, and the same characteristics as I have. If you study genetics, you will understand what I am saying.

Did you know why I gave you the middle name of Steven? It was your Great, Great, Grandfather's name and he sired 5 sons, 2 of whom turned out to be preachers of the Holy Gospel. You also have a cousin named Steven Russell (my brother's youngest son and a rebel he is). Did you further know that when I was in Shanghai, China going to high school, I used to run the mile every chance I could just to keep in good physical condition, but never ran it in competition? I really ran the 100 yd dash in 10.2 sec., which was considered pretty fair in those days 1931-33. But your Uncle Bob, (my brother) who really excelled in track and field, spent one more year in the school than I did, and was voted the best all round athlete by the school. He went in for the Decathlon events and later won the Philippine championship 3 years in a row.

What is your best time for the mile run? 4 minutes or less? Ha! Just don't get discouraged! It's getting close to the time when you should be ready for college. Louise and I have talked about it a great deal

(Next page)

3.

and although we can't afford to pay for your tuition, we can offer you free room and board with a room all of your own with its own entrance except for the bath room and it has an inside lock if you prefer and you can give it a go if you wanted to for a few years if necessary. There are at least 4 supermarkets in the vicinity where you could pay for your necessities and tuition also. Then there is another thing down in the Valley that may or may not interest you. For a small consideration, you could enroll in a class teaching Judo and Karate, but you would have to observe their rules and that is never to use your newfound strength and skill in anger. I am sorry to say that when I was your age, I would have used it in anger and wrath and lost forever the respect of my fellow man.

Tell your mother all of this is the best I have to offer since I can't work anymore since my last operation. Although I find myself glued to an armchair, I can promise you all of my love and respect as well as Louise's affection. We won't nag you or bother you but only

(Over)

4.

answer your questions the best way we can and introduce you to your cousins Russ & Terry—Bruce & Barbara and let you make your own decisions. You have got a surprise in your cousin Bruce Nelson—he is slightly over six feet tall and weights over 200 lbs., so far my favorite nephew because he has been brought up so well by your Aunt Francis and speaks softly, but with self-assurance.

But enough for now and I hope you think it all over carefully since it could well be the biggest decision of your life, and let me know your likes and dislikes and *WRITE* soon.

I will bet my life on one thing—you can't stand a liar or someone deceitful. It runs in the very blood of our veins.

Give my blessings to your sister, Dallas Lee and her husband Morris (What is his first name?)

All my love & Respect

Dad

I sat feeling a fluid gap between the realities that were and what might have been. I knew that another's words could never have kept me from alcohol, and that if I had moved to California at 17, I would have experienced different mirrors, but would still have repulsed from my own forming reflection. By 17, I was so filled with shame and insecurity that *the mask* was growing deep into my flesh. Alcohol stood inevitable: Kansas's beer, California's wine. I was predisposed to drink.

I reflected on his self-portrait and recalled the words *"EE Russell II"*...I wondered who *EE the first* was. I wondered why he thought 6' and 200 pounds was big...My granddad Bill was bigger than that. Vicarious genetic identity, I surmised, as was *running,* through his brother, Uncle Bob. I understood that incepting weakness; it helped create and feed my mask and ultimately foundered it. Likely, he had deluded himself with similar lullabies.

I wondered, yet already knew, if he would indeed have been able to keep the promise to not *"...nag you or bother you, but only answer your questions the best way we can..."* MY father...or ME? No: What a humble and grandiose idea, though. Five years sober, five years old. Perhaps his wife, Louise, could honor that, but my father? No. He was right, neither he nor I could stand a liar or someone deceitful, yet liars and deceivers we had been.

I recalled a blessed day when Louise flew through Tucson. It was after he died, shortly before she died, and before I had met Suzanne.

Louise called and I met her at the airport where we sat conversing as though we were old friends who had never parted...it was our first and last conversation. I instantly liked and loved Louise. We were immediately friends and I knew that she was the trusted anchor of my father's wayward dreams and visions.

She said that I looked and spoke "so like" my now departed father and we connected in thinking and conversation with a resonance that was eternal. I knew from this mirror that I was indeed my father's son, and that God had blessed him with a soul mate at the end of his journey.

Louise never asked about my drinking, though if she had, it would not have mattered. I did not yet have a drinking *problem*. That would burn slow, then take off like a rocket, leaving Suzanne and the kids to become earthling dots, as they peered upward at my soon to veer, ultimately to crash, igniting and disappearing aluminum bird.

I would get punched in a bar for cloned use of the mouth, but I would never learn or teach Karate or Judo. David would defend me.

I would decimate my life with alcohol, but at nine years sober, would still have less time sober than my father had at death.

I would never be a great miler or work in a supermarket for college money. I would go to college on money provided by Social Security after the ole man died.

I would wait years to know, and touch, the soul of my blood father, and would sadly never know my sister Diana or be introduced to my cousins. Aunt Francis would communicate with my sister, Dallas, building our family history, but then would disappear, likely dead.

If it were the decision of my life, I failed to make it. I didn't know my likes and dislikes. I did better than I might have, because under similar circumstances, we buried Brendan at 17.

"...and WRITE soon." I am writing now.

As I thought of the *"would 'a, could 'a, should 'a"* options, I again looked at the Russell Coat of Arms and immersed peacefully into the words *"che - sara – sara."*

Chapter 29
which they have imagined to do

Genesis 11: **1** ***AND THE WHOLE EARTH*** *was of one language, and of one speech. And it came to pass, as they journeyed from the east, that they found a plain in the land of Shi'-nar; and they dwelt there.* **3** *And they said one to another, go to, let us make brick, and burn them thoroughly, And they had brick for stone, and slime had they for mortar. And they said, go to, let us build a city and a tower, whose top may reach unto heaven, and let us make us a name, lest we be scattered abroad upon the face of the whole earth.* **5** *And the Lord came down to see the city and the tower which the children of men builded. And the Lord said, Behold, the people is one and they have all one language; and this they begin to do: and now nothing will be restrained from them, which they have imagined to do.*

7 *Go to, let us go down, and there confound their language, that they may not understand one another's speech. So the Lord scattered them abroad from thence upon the face of all the earth: and they left off to build the city.* **9** *Therefore is the name of it called Babel; because the Lord did there confound the language of all the earth: and from thence did the Lord scatter them abroad upon the face of all the earth.*

I dreamt and awoke from the *dream within a dream* to see the clock shining *3:11 a.m.*

The little sponsor was standing beside my bed, and whispered, "Walk with me." I knew somehow that I was still dreaming, but arose to dress and follow him. He lit a cigarette lighter and burned it for light. It was an old Zippo. I liked the smell of its fluid, but he spun his hand, motioning to hurry.

As I quickly dressed, it took only seconds for me to be irritated. He was wearing old-man plaid blue, yellow, brown and green golf shorts, with inappropriately swirling 60s looking rectangular mixes of green and yellow neon, a frayed V-necked tee shirt with a fist-sized tear in the right side exposing his belly fat, and a coffee stain on the front; he had one dark blue and one black-patterned sock pulled up each respective leg *completely* to knee height, capped at the bottom with scuffed worn-out deck shoes. He topped it all off with a day-glow orange ball cap that said *"WENDLER AIR AG, INC. Aerial Spraying 316-397-2323."* He was visually puking with tasteless nostalgia. I shivered.

I heard my fraternity brother yelling "PLEDGE, YOU DUSCHEBAG..." but held my tongue out of respect. He wouldn't change. He didn't care. He was brilliant, but simple.

I was pulling on my jeans, tucking in my glow-in-the-dark black, short-sleeved Einstein tee shirt, and was hopping to slip on my shoes as he shuffled away into the darkness.

Lisette lay sleeping and I didn't want to wake her, dream or not. I banged my knee on her antique cedar chest, and again on the futon, as I mentally cussed and groped towards the front door.

I could see the cherry of the little sponsor's unfiltered cigarette burning as he stood outside in the dark waiting. The night was completely black except for the stars, and his eyes glowed strangely like an owl when he drew upon his cigarette. There were no streetlights, no cars, nothing. I was finally turning to lock the front door. "Leave it," he commanded urgently. "Let's walk."

"Why are you waking me from a dream within a dream," I asked, "And, why at 3:11 in the morning?"

He ignored me and walked quickly northward, smoking, and moving with a slight favoring of his left leg. The air was chilled, but not cold, and there was absolutely no wind and no sound, except our walking and breathing. It was like a time and space vacuum. A black cat ran across the street, soundless and nearly invisible.

I caught up with my little sponsor and we walked abreast, me silent and obedient, like a child.

He seemed angry, and I realized, in dream state, that he was remarkably old, but obviously strong, and much larger than I. I was used to seeing him as a little being, small enough to place in a coffee cup. I felt afraid, as when I was alone with the ole man, but I knew this man, and he could be gruff, but he would never hurt me. He never had.

Suddenly he stopped and said, "What do you see?" It startled me because I had been busy just keeping up with the old man, thinking, and studying him.

"I see the old building where the people in my head live," I finally responded—the psychic high-rise."

Folks were emerging or leaning out of their respective windows as they customarily did upon my arrival. I knew most by sight, but had never engaged them in conversation. I realized that I really didn't know them at all. They were like people who populate dreams, nothing more. I felt that I had failed somehow in not knowing them.

"Ever been inside this building?" he asked, with a pensive gaze that captivated me.

I noticed that his eyes were two colors, brown and blue, right and left, respectively.

He suddenly put on scratched-and-bent, oxidized, bifocals and lit his Zippo to read something, pencil-scratched, that he pulled from his right shorts pocket; he then stuck the bifocals back in his left rear pocket and looked back at me. I was quiet, to not interrupt his reading. He motioned for me to answer by swirling his hand. "Soooo…" His eyes were now blue and green.

"No," I responded. "I don't think so. I've never gone inside."

I noticed, now, that one of his eyes was dark brown, the other green, left and right respectively. Perhaps it was the dim and filtered light.

By now, the analytical was walking up and I noticed for the first time, likely because of the reality of this dream state, that he was also taller and bigger than I, perhaps 6' 1", and 220 pounds. He looked out of shape though…almost flabby. I knew I could whip him, but didn't know why I would even think that. He was always meek, irritating, and non-threatening.

The analytical spoke in precise scientific tones, and began to talk *typically* about some bullshit that I didn't care about, to the point of re-irritating me. I was ready to ask him to shut up. It was obvious that most neighbors did not like him. Eyes were rolling everywhere.

"Quiet," said the little sponsor, sternly.

He instantly shut up and I noticed for the first time what a total nerd he was. His embarrassment accentuated it. Goofy, horn-rimmed glasses, owl nosed, flattop haircut and...well, a dork. I wanted to re-dress him as well. He looked like some guy stuck in the 70s. Neither he nor the little sponsor was an acceptable dresser. He had a faded nametag hanging out of a cracked, white plastic pocket protector filled with colored pens, but I couldn't read it. I squinted to try.

By now, the little sponsor was entering a dimly lit doorway in front of the five-story faded brick high-rise. I followed closely, the analytical a few feet behind.

I noticed that the doorway light was a dimming, perhaps 20 watt, bulb screwed into a green rimmed pipe light, best characterized as a bean counter's "teller" hat-looking fixture. It was antique, dented, bent and rusted with time. As I looked upward, I could see chipped, black painted, rusty fire escapes leading to all five floors. There were flowerpots and tomato plants on several of them, while others had clothing, garbage, sleds, bicycles, cheap statues, junk, or nothing.

I could hear the buzzing of yellow and green florescent bulbs as we entered the building and walked down a hallway with pea green, peeling, faded walls.

Brown and cream colored, dirty, lath and plaster were evident behind chunks of missing paint. We were walking on a badly nicked, scratched and yellowing, wooden oak floor. It needed stripped and refinished. There were balls of lint and reflecting strings of loose hair along the edges.

I caught myself wanting to modernize and restore the building, but knew that it was a task beyond my time, skills, and resources. It was probably beyond repair. Hell, I didn't even know what I was doing here, and it wasn't REAL! Shit!

I felt frustration join and displace irritation as we walked. Our footsteps echoed in the hollow emptiness of the building's ugly hallway.

A rat peeked out of a hole in the baseboard, and then quickly retreated. A roach ran from a nibbled breadcrumb along the baseboard and into the hole. I knew that the rat would smell the breadcrumb on the roach and go get it. What a sick thought—but likely, true.

This building was obviously in poor condition, but likely fully inhabited, because I could hear the murmur of people talking through some doorways as we passed numbered apartments on the right: 101, 103, 105, 107, and finally, 109. There were no numbers on our left. I assumed them to be 100 through 108 or 102 through 110. No one emerged and I could not make out words.

There seemed to be different ages, sexes, and ethnicities of people. I could hear one apartment speaking Spanish, another a language that I did not recognize, likely something Arabic.

I could hear faint music playing in two of the apartments, one right, one left. An un-tuned guitar, that needed its strings changed, was being poorly played in an apartment near the back wall. I felt irritation and a desire to knock and tell the guy to change his strings and get some lessons. Jesus! Fuck. It sounded awful.

Being obsessive, I recounted the doors. Yes, there were five apartments on each side, the last of which entered under a stairwell on the left wall at the back. The stairwell went up to a door on the end marked *"2nd floor."* It no doubt led to more of the same, etc., five flights up.

Green, water stained, exposed, florescent-lit ceilings were perhaps 12 feet high, and the hallway was about eight feet wide. It had yellowed oak trim that smelled faintly of seasonal moldy piss, and one of the apartments wafted smells that reminded me of a barroom, the morning after. I fanned my nose, to no one's notice.

The little sponsor walked to the back door, past all apartments, and opened it into, what I thought would be, a hallway or another set of apartments. It opened into a dark alleyway, which confused me about the stairway on our left...where did it go? Perhaps in the rear, the second floor and up were overhung in some fashion? If not...The analytical obviously knew the building and didn't, for once, enlighten me. That irritated me. Normally I couldn't shut the fucker up.

"Come here," said the little sponsor, lighting another unfiltered Camel.

It was pitch black. When the door shut I couldn't even see my feet. I could, however, see him lighting the cigarette, then the orange cherry in the black night. I carefully moved toward him. It was perhaps fifteen feet. He was opening a cellar door. With my eyes adjusting, I could now see a small flickering light in a hole, perhaps twenty feet to my right, and I could hear deep breathing, tapping, and digging sounds rising from it.

"Ssspppppptttt," little sponsor said, in a snakelike tone, projecting his hiss down the musty cellar stairs. My eyes were fully adjusted now, and I could see something glimmering, like a single candlelight, six limestone steps below.

I heard an owl screech in the night, perhaps three blocks away, and I watched a small snake slither into the side of the stony cellar. Out walked the sociopath.

"Want some *toads*, **DICK**?" he taunted me as an ambush, making me flush with unanticipated attack that dug as reflex into my childhood shame. "I've got *plenty*," he smiled evilly.

He emerged with an upright slithering fashion, his snakelike eyes darting back and forth with calculating glee as he scorned me.

"Quiet," said the little sponsor, already reopening the back door to the brick apartment building. "Come on." He stood holding the door while the three of us passed—the analytical, the *deliberately* slow-moving sociopath, then I.

I noticed that the sociopath looked skinnier than even I had recalled him, and that his hair was longer, grayer and stringier than before. He was substantially less than five feet tall, but walked cocky, proud, and defiant, nudging the ole sponsor to irritate him as he passed. The sponsor ignored him, as with a misbehaving child, which I could see stung a bit. I was glad that my little sponsor treated others that way.

As we reentered the buzzing green hallway, the ole sponsor knocked at the door where the irritating guitar playing had been, and to the door came the poet. I was shocked and felt mean for some reason.

"Shit," I said amazed. "Your playing sucks. Stick to words, man. If not, at least get new strings and tune the fucking guitar."

He looked hurt and covered instant tears, gulping and smiling like a young child.

The sociopath grinned and winked at me as though I had taken the words right out of his mouth. I felt ashamed. The little sponsor looked at me to see if I had learned anything. I shrugged, embarrassed by my behavior. The sociopath slapped me on the back and cackled like a laughing chicken I hated him, and I hated his approval.

"One last stop," said the little sponsor, knocking lightly on one of the doors with music. As the door opened slightly, I heard that the music was a fox trot from a 1912 Edison wind-up record player, akin to one I had cuddled for minutes, hours, weeks, months, and years as a young boy. An eye so brown that it lacked pupils peeked through the open cracked door, and there stood the ole man's mother—my Grandma Dot! I stood gasping, breathless with joy.

She looked *exactly* as I remembered her when we were sweetest friends, before I compartmentalized her, long before she died. She was beautiful. Her eyes sparkled and her pure white hair was rolled into its familiar tight round bun—prim, brilliant, beautiful.

I moved to hug her, but the little sponsor held out his arm and stopped me with caution. She did not recognize me at all. It was as though I had never existed in her life. She only knew the little sponsor and the poet. They hugged and laughed playfully. She looked at neither the sociopath nor me. It was as though we were invisible to her. She seemed to recognize the analytical, but ignored him. Knowing her, I understood why.

I looked at an old neon clock that hung on the wall and, although the second hand was moving normally, the clock continued to indicate 3:11. I assumed it was broken along with the rest of the building. Its neon green was pretty, though, functional or not. I could see that the analytical was also fixated on it, and that it bothered him. He wanted to fix it as badly as I; perhaps more...but ironically, we didn't have time.

The little sponsor was ascending the stairway and motioning to us with his right hand and arm. "Come on," he said, seemingly hiding a surprise. Perhaps he had seemed angry to throw me off-guard. Though now, trying to look stern, he was obviously about to smile ear to ear.

I followed the procession and walked up the yellowed old stairs, last in line. They creaked as we stepped on each of them. It made a strange song.

The little sponsor opened the door, and held it open, with his strong right arm, reaching in, as we each passed in turn. I wasn't ready for what was next.

From the open door rushed a smell that I had never sensed before. It was like a four-dimensional "new car" smell, but stronger, powerful, spiritual, and indescribable. I felt young, wise, new, full and relaxed all at once. I was overcome with peace and serenity. My mouth watered as an involuntary response. I felt the emotion and a thought-stream that I had first experienced on my Tucson living room floor, but *vastly* more powerful; tears formed without reason.

My mind was keen beyond sensing, my sensing keen beyond reason. I felt as though I had no body, or as though I were becoming a floating giant. It felt as though I were pure energy, contained only by an aligned *External* Will, lest I vaporize.

I looked searchingly at my little sponsor. His eyes were smiling with a cloudy mixing calm of purple, pink, black, brown, yellow, green, and blue. It was like watching crisp three-dimensional clouds pass in an Arizona or Kansas sunset. His eyes began to alternate turning pure brown, blue, black, green, or violet in color. It seemed strangely natural, as though he were forming, and reforming, in a timeless eternity.

I somehow felt that time meant nothing here. Space was apparently iffy. The light that surrounded us was something beyond spectrum and gave everything a changing hue—yet it was so subtle that one could not sense changes with simply physical sight.

The old wooden door, marked *"2nd Floor,"* had opened into a giant structure of some sort.

We entered like a special museum tour, in awe and absolute humility. It was obvious from the faces of all that NONE had been here before...except the little sponsor. We may as well have been entering an alien spacecraft, though even that might have been more definable. We had entered a large egg-shaped lobby area with marble floors and walls that slowly changed colors. There were eleven evenly spaced doors around the lobby. I turned to notice that the *"2nd Floor"* doorway had disappeared entirely.

Our tour guide stood silent, allowing the absorption, as we tried to grasp the ungraspable. We were mute and speechless...All, even the analytical, *especially* the sociopath. He stood twitching, with some sort of painful discomfort, until the little sponsor put his hand on Soch's shoulder and said, "Relax, son. It'll be alright." He stopped twitching and had the first look of trust or humility I had ever seen on his face. I knew that it was caused by fear.

"You're supposed to be here," comforted the little sponsor, patting Soch's drooping shoulder. "You're all supposed to be here." Soch caught himself, and jerked away defiantly.

We were intuitively standing as a perfect circle. The poet was sobbing with joy. Soch re-straightened his shoulders and looked around to see if anyone had noticed his accidental body language. He intentionally looked cocky to the point of fake.

"What IS this," I finally asked with a grain of sand effort that made the owl story a sub-proton. "What is this...umm, this...*place*?" I was standing with tear filled eyes and complete awe still barely able to speak. The poet was patting me in an empathetic, comforting motion.

"It's *you*," the ole sponsor said calmly. "Loosely stated, it's the *you* God created in us all. This particular one happens to be...well, *you*...powered by hope, loss, joy, and a few other little natural forces. We're all part of it, but it's all part of us...it can't really be explained in human terms. Let's walk some more. That'll help you see."

We followed like school children, hand in hand. The ole sponsor led, then Grandma Dot, then Soch, Analytical, Poet, and me.

Soch and Analytical were quite uncomfortable holding hands, but were too afraid to break the human chain.

"Bear with me," our sponsor said, smiling.

He touched a floating purple neon dot and an elevator seemed to appear from nowhere. It didn't really "appear," we just knew it was there and entered "it"...there was no structure, no "ding," no opening door...just a rush of sweet smelling air and, poof, we were entering an invisible round elevator near the center of the lobby. It *felt* "round" and it felt safe, though we could not *see* it.

"Oh, before we go," I interjected, "what is that antique, etched, brushed green, copper and gold marking in the center of the floor that has compass-looking brass arrows and the letters "**S, U, and R,**" each pointing in a different direction?"

I was fumbling since I still lacked context *AT LEAST* for the building's shape and size. I had been too busy "feeling" it. The analytical looked completely baffled. The poet was still weeping with joy...patting me and weeping. Others simply stood listening.

Little Sponsor laughed aloud. "Bear with me," he chuckled. "Just remember what you learned early in New Orleans and *forget* the idea of north, south, east, and west. These things are all more like...well...*ALL* 'true north.'"

Just then a door flew open and three four-year-old girls ran, chasing one another in circles, through the lobby and out another door. A wobbling two-year-old toddler girl was following them closely. "Why, that's..." I gasp.

"Yes. That's your daughter, your sister Mary Ellen, and your daughter's daughters." finished the little sponsor.

"But they're...and..."

"Don't try to understand this place," he responded before I finished. "It'll get clearer, but you'll never fully grasp it. Let's go."

He chuckled as we rose on what felt like a cylinder of windless floating air. Despite a fear of heights, I felt completely safe. I had no concept of our size. Perhaps we were giants, normal size, or shrunk to fit in a thimble. It didn't matter, but I wondered.

We rode for perhaps five seconds and stepped onto a floor that looked *exactly* like the one we had left. I wondered if we had moved at all, yet knew that we had. Green plants and waterfalls appeared around the lobby as we "exited" the "elevator." Walls felt as though they were moving, but got no closer to us...perhaps the entire floor was rotating. I didn't know.

"How many floors up did we go?" asked the analytical, with an obsessive need to know. He looked proud to have formulated *any* rational question.

"None," responded the little sponsor, "But we're in a different place, a higher place, if you will. Floors here don't have numbers as you've learned them. Rather, they have, well...umm...follow me." He shrugged with lack of words, spun like a top and headed "**U**."

I could hear muffled voices and laughter, in what sounded like an AA meeting, in the direction of **"R"** as we shuffled along behind the little sponsor.

We walked toward the sound of carpentry. I knew that wonderful sound. Hammers, skill saws, nail guns, boards dropping. Men were laughing and talking. As we neared their voices, I could see that the interior structure was being built and that men were building it. One of the eleven doorways was framed, but still missing its door. This felt foreign somehow to the *structure* I had seen thus far. The rest of it had felt more like a glassy, stone, spiritual, translucent...*membrane.* I looked at the little sponsor and he smiled back already sensing my question.

We walked into the room and there were three men working— Cat Daddy, Harry, and my brother, Bill! Bill! They all dropped their tool pouches and walked toward us smiling. I was again wordless.

"What's up, Bro?" said Billy, as though we had just stopped a conversation moments ago. He was smiling with the old familiar, attack chicken, shit eating, rub-your-face-in-it grin. "You seem surprised to see me?" he said, looking puzzled. Harry and Cat Daddy reached out to shake my hand, but then, each grabbed and hugged me.

"What IS this place?" I gasped again, seeking an answer to the unanswerable.

"Well," answered Harry, "It may not look like it yet, but it's going to be a giant dining hall."

They didn't have a clue what I was asking.

"Oh," I responded. "It's looking good. I notice you're trimming it in oak, Bro—only wood you love."

Bill didn't seem to know that he was dead, and neither Cat Daddy nor Harry seemed to know it either. Then again, how could they? Grasping for understanding, I surmised that it was because they had never met in life and Bill had died after I met them. They only shared my memory in common. The sponsor looked at me as though I were close to the reason, but far from the truth.

Harry hugged me, kissed Grandma Dot on the cheek, shook hands with the analytical, fluffed the poet's hair, and patted the sociopath on his shoulders as he deliberately eased off an audible, greasy, Harry fart. I knew that smell. It sincerely stunk, even in this environment. He stood waiting on a response.

"You FUCKER," exploded the relatively tiny sociopath in a *dangerous* tone! "You're the bastard that shit in my cellar, aren't you?! I'd know that smell anywhere! *You* shit in my cellar!" He was wiggling his rat-like nose like an embittered shit connoisseur. We all snickered silently, easing into belly laughs. I waited knowingly for the reply.

"I had to shit," Harry answered. End of conversation. He and my brother slapped hands and laughed insanely. We joined in.

The sociopath burned red with anger as he gawked up at the 6' 3" boxer. I could see that he wanted to fight, but then Harry leaned over and hugged him for an uncomfortable amount of time. Suddenly he looked like neutered nutria.

"No hard feelings, I hope," Harry smiled. "You ain't the first." He winked at me with unspoken knowledge, and that familiar wink that only he and Bill could do.

"Hey, Dad," echoed a familiar voice from the common area. "How long before we're gonna eat?" In came Brendan, covered with the smell and residue of gasoline and freshly cut grass.

"Soon, Bee," answered Bill lovingly. "Soon as we finish this one little run of trim. Go wash up and we'll see you at home."

Bee smiled at me, as though we had just parted, and said, "Hey, Uncle Doug!" His green eyes twinkled. I could hear his *steps* walking away. He didn't know either.

"Come on," prodded the little sponsor. "Time to go see something else."

As we turned to leave, I hugged Bill, Cat Daddy, and Harry and knew somehow that we were never parted, only paused.

I could see their reflections in the seamless inside "glass" of the exterior "building" wall. Bill was black, Cat Daddy was white, Harry was black. Each of the reflections were 3-D, looking indiscernibly like the image being reflected. Unlike the others, Harry's reflection seemed to flutter, and so, as I looked closer to perceive it, I saw the hand-sized sub-reflection of dozens of playing children. I knew now, *partially*, what I was seeing. I looked to see our own reflections, but noted that the little sponsor had none. No reflection?

"Catch y'all later," I said, waving as we attempted to regroup and shuffle off.

The sociopath had returned from red to his normal gray, and the analytical was poking his finger at the exterior "glass," as though he believed that he could actually understand it. Grandma Dot was holding and smelling a freshly cut scrap of beveled oak. The little sponsor was leaning, smoking another cigarette and watching us think. The poet was laughing and crying simultaneously, mock-waltzing with his reflection and sniffing at the air.

Everything, smoke or not, smelled NEW...that indescribable multi-dimensional smell of *new*. I no longer cried in its presence, but I loved it as a perfume still unborn. I smelled a faint waft of cedar and oak, then the scent of freshly cut grass as we departed the area.

As we reemerged in the "lobby" I again saw the etched compass-looking antiquity saying "**S, U, and R**." I looked at the sponsor, but I didn't ask. The little sponsor smiled at me and remained silent on the topic.

His eyes were now a calm mix of brown, gold, and green, like the changing autumn earth. I had gotten used to these changes, but knew that I never should. It was this adjustment that transformed children into adults and adults into doubting cynics. I never wanted to "know" such things again. I prayed for help to not know too much and raised my eyes for a final look around the area.

With a bang, a wiry middle-aged fellow with a farmer's tan, rubber boots, a bent tan Stetson hat, and a filthy, sleeveless tee shirt walked out of one of the side doors carrying a dusty lantern and a shovel, both in one hand. He looked very intense, head down, walking fast, talking to himself in muttering tones, waving his free hand in the air, and cussing rhythmically, perhaps every five steps.

He was obviously not a social being and was covered with dried mud, dirty sweat stains, and raw dust...much like a farmer who had been rained on briefly while disking a field, all day, on an old open-cab tractor.

He muttered across the room, saw us, looked up irritated, and exited through another door. He seemed to be made of sweat and gristle, held together by stains, fragments of dust, anger and determination...not a big man, but obviously gritty and mule-strong.

"That's that bastard that digs all night near my cellar," commented Sociopath, with an angry resentful look and tone. "Just when I finally get used to the goddamn scratching and thumping noises that carry through the ground into my walls, the bastard sets off a stick of dynamite, then it gets fairly quiet for awhile, and thump, thump, thud, he's back at it again. What an irritating son of a bitch. I've tried to talk to him about it when he's down in that hole, but he ignores me. I even kicked dirt in on him one time. I don't think he has any eardrums left and, probably, less brains. Farms all day and digs half the night. Stupid fucker."

"The well digger," I thought. "The man who hand-dug the wells on our little farm. Jesus, how odd."

Just then he reemerged with an identical, head down, muttering walk and look, but now with two sticks of dynamite in the same hand as the shovel and the lantern. I felt knee-jerk, academic gratitude that the lantern was not burning. He stomped back through the same door, and his cussing and muttering died off into an echoing distance.

Damn, I respected that man. He had to be Sahara Gary and Cowboy on super steroids. No wonder he had ignored Soch. Even *if* he could hear, he would not waste a minute or a word on that pesky little fuck—too focused on digging a hole and farming. Good for him!

"He better not steal any more of my cellar's stones for this well like he did last time," Soch complained scowling. "He better not. Ah, fuck him. I've got a friend with endless supplies of sulfur. May take awhile, but I'll get him again—just like last time." He hissed his evil snicker and stood up straighter, cracking his neck from side to side and rolling his shoulders with arrogance.

"Let's go to the top," the little sponsor *suggested,* smiling as though he knew all of my lingering thoughts about the well digger and Sociopath. "This will answer a lot of your questions." He looked at several of us as he spoke.

I was overloaded with information and concepts. The entire crowd looked drained, except Grandma Dot. She looked childlike and happy. I felt tired, but every other emotion was intermixed and confused. I was ok with this state of being. I was serene, awe-filled, peaceful, and indescribably happy to have seen my friends, my brother, and Brendan.

The purple neon light appeared again and the Poet said, "Can I push it?!" He danced in place like a child, shaking clenched fists.

"Sure," said the little sponsor, patting him gently on the shoulder. "Go ahead...push it."

He did and, again, we entered an invisible, yet now known, cylinder of...something...and it carried us upward on a cushion of motionless air. We emerged atop the "structure" onto a **GIGANTIC** triangular terrace, sculpted with flowers, trees, waterfalls, and singing birds. It was like a Garden of Eden. There was nothing like it in my memory…nothing even close.

"This may help you," the little sponsor offered, walking toward the nearest edge of the edifice, somewhere midway between **"U"** and **"R."** "This may help you see and understand, though, anything you perceive will be your adaptation of what's really here. There's no way you can really *know* it; trust me."

I was drowning in sights, sounds, and smells. It was far beyond breathtaking.

"Let's start with the basics," he instructed. "I know you're afraid of heights, but here you need not be. It's inside you and your *'appointed* hour' is not now. Trust this as you join me in looking over the edge."

I trusted him completely. He had never lied to me or let me down—ever. I felt the same vicarious courage as when my Uncle Don talked me into jumping off the diving board for the first time at the Dighton swimming pool when I was 6. I had also loved and trusted him completely.

We paraded toward the edge, but people began to drift off as they found something to distract them. Grandma Dot, for example, began to smell flowers and found that, by touching them, she could change their color.

She sat on the edge of a fountain surrounded with flowers and changed the color of the water and, then, the color of the flower, playing with contrasts. I knew how she loved that. She smiled at me as though she suddenly recognized me, and I knew that no hug or touch could compare with the look that we had finally exchanged. A red cardinal landed on her soft blue cotton dress and she picked a berry to feed it. All was healed.

"She'll be staying here," said the little sponsor. "It's her time to stay. She's done living in your high-rise. That was your place for her and many others who touched you along the way, strangers, enemies, friends. She must leave there now. She'll be eternally happy here. Trust me." I did.

As we neared the edge, the little sponsor put his hand on my chest to stop me and to reassure me. His eyes were bright green now, encompassed with a ring of gray-blue, encasing giant, focused, black pupils. He gave me something with that look that could never be captured, encrypted, or spoken. It just was. I felt as safe as an eagle. *Fearless.*

"You need to put on the eyes of *"simple"* now," he spoke softly. "S-I-M-P-L-E. Don't try to think when you look at this...just look and allow yourself to perceive. Thinking will follow."

He climbed up and looked over the edge. I followed, but stood looking back across the veranda, roof, forest, zoo, aquarium, terrarium, garden, umm...place. Poet was right in *this* context. "...Parts find themselves, simply parts, in a whole never spoken."

Only the sociopath remained with us and he began jumping to peek over the stony edge. He was shrinking as we ascended. He was perhaps under four feet high now, and frankly, looking paler gray than ever. He was obviously frustrated by his predicament, but was no less defiant or proud. I could tell that he wished he could be in the cellar, but I knew that his treacherous curiosity would want to feed on this new information to use it against others and me. I helped him up the wall.

The wall was wide and guarded oddly by an oxidized railing that resembled the fire escapes below. With all the other "construction" I had seen in this building, worn railing made no intuitive sense, but the sponsor had told me not to think, so I wouldn't.

I grabbed the top railing, which was about chest high and realized that it was made of copper. Someone had tried to paint it brown at some point, and the paint was flaking off, resembling rust, but it was *copper,* brown and greening *copper.* I pulled out an AA coin and looked at the triangle. It said "Service, Unity, Recovery...ahh...**S, U, R.**"

The little sponsor smiled and winked at me. "Made it out of the pennies you wasted and never earned getting drunk…not bad, huh?"

I peeked over the edge for the first time. I was silenced mute with renewed, humble, awe.

We were indeed standing on the edge of a triangle shaped edifice, but it appeared to be **HUGE**, *much* bigger than I would have expected.

The bottom courtyard and building foundation was a continuous unit, glassy and clear looking, and the edges of the triangular building were resting on it, running completely to the edge at each end to touch *a circle of "glass"* that both surrounded it, and served as its foundation. The circle of glass that we rested on was just that…a *perfect* circle, with geometric, downwardly tapered outer edges.

The building itself was practically invisible, and despite its size, would likely not even appear to casual passers by because it, like the inside wall, reflected everything around it with 3-D perfection. Some things were different colors, but they seemed to simply run into the building as visual clones. The rising sun had no reflection—none.

The circle's carved, tapering, outer edges sloped downward and then blended into green earth and blue waters beyond, where the earth then fell off in the distance, becoming a sunlit early morning horizon that was speckled with colors and shapes, as when one is looking down from an airplane. Houses were dots; people were less than ants, and fields were like postage stamps in the distance.

"Thoughts…Questions?" offered the little sponsor, finally, looking totally wise and filled with love.

"Yeah," chimed in the sociopath, who was now peering between upright copper railing bars. "This is all *cute*," he scoffed cynically, "but what's all this got to do with *me*?"

Of course it was about him. Jesus. I swallowed hard, with disbelief. Had he seen NOTHING?

"I'll answer that in a minute," said the little sponsor with surprising patience and kindness. Then, he turned to me.

"Why do the edges of the foundation and courtyard refract light like a prism," I asked? "And, why would someone build something this big on *GLASS*. By the way, how big *IS* it?"

The little sponsor chuckled at the analytical nature of my questions, but answered them succinctly, nonetheless.

"First," he responded, "the edges refract light because they are indeed prisms, and they are prisms, because the entire building is sitting on a *diamond* approximately—in human terms—nineteen city blocks across, though that is a rough snapshot in time, and not really accurate or relevant. It can change by multiple powers of 10 in microseconds, and *everything* inside it proportionally. It's like atoms and time simultaneously moving, both slower and faster than normal. Eeeeeeh...It's complicated. You may have felt this inside in the form of changing colors, varying ages, size, and the illusion of moving floors and walls?" I had indeed.

"A diamond," I repeated, pondering to grasp it.

"Yes, to be precise...forget the size and karats, that wouldn't mean much to you...it's Israeli...a round, brilliant, VS1 clarity, nil graining, color grade I, with 62.4% total depth, 58% table width, 15% crown height, 43% pavilion depth, medium, faceted girdle...*very good* polish, *excellent* symmetry, cutlet...none. Whew. I knew you'd ask that, so I had to review my notes in front of your mental high-rise—hard to see by Zippo. I worked on it for *days*." He chuckled with pride at his near flawless recitation. "I've never seen it smaller than 1.21 karats, by the way. Never. I have seen it *much* bigger than nineteen city blocks, though." He looked like a professor.

"Gees, I'm impressed. Why VS1? Why not *flawless*?" I asked, as though I had a right to question utopia.

"Because *you're* not flawless," he responded, without pause. "This is built around *you*. Everyone's is different."

The sociopath looked at me, and snarled, as though he wished *he* had delivered that crystal reckoning. I noticed that he was growing, nearly five feet tall again.

"Oh," I said softly...answered, refocused and re-humbled, with the sponsor looking peaceful, and the sociopath looking holier-than-thou.

"Look out in the distance," little sponsor *suggested*. "Point at something that interests you."

I looked for a while, and then pointed at a small white airplane that seemed to be doing long *lazy-8s* across a green field several miles away.

"You were always partial to airplanes," he said. "Point at it again." I did. "Once more," he said. I pointed yet again.

Suddenly the entire scene...plane, field, everything, was perhaps 300 feet below us, as though we were standing directly above the field. All else was blinded from our sight, except the field.

I realized that the plane was not doing lazy 8s; it was spraying the field. As the white aircraft zoomed toward the building and turned, the little sponsor took off his orange *"Wendler Air Ag"* hat and waved it at the pilot. Then, as the pilot turned, instead of reengaging his spray, he circled, flew parallel to us along the railing, and dipped his wings as a wave. Then, he realigned, reengaged his spray, and sped off into the distance. The entire scene retook its place among the distant fields and scenery.

"Wait a minute," I said, looking at a man who already knew my question. "That was old man Wendler, and *he's* dead! Besides, a hired pilot, who died when it burned, crashed his little baby, the white Pawnee, that we just saw. This stuff works out *here* too?"

"Yeah," said the little sponsor rolling his hand as though I were slow. "And..." He kept rolling his hand waiting for me to catch on; he began whistling the Jeopardy theme. I felt stupid. But, I was, after all, a B-student learner...creative sometimes, but not always quick.

I blushed at my "thinking"..."SIMPLE, right," I repeated.

He was nodding, and exhaling smoke, exactly like my brother had done when we once talked about tall weeds and a someday pond.

"Simple, yeah." I said to clarify that I was getting it. We spoke it simultaneously.

"Now, your question," he said, gazing downward at the sociopath. "I've been waiting to answer this for a loooong time." He looked like a cat about to eat a canary. "I'm glad you asked...'*What's all this got to do with MEeeeee?*'"

"You know all that stuff we've kicked around about the nature of man, the image of God, etc., etc.? Come on, now...you were listening, and trying to influence our thinking. Well you are, plain and simple, made head to toe, bone to bone, and gristle to rat-like bristle of *his* character defects." He motioned towards me. "Always were...always will be."

"You are pretty much a bottle opener. A church key, if you will—a necessary evil. You'll like this...Analytical, is just that, analytical. Poet...he's a poet. But you...you're a *complicated* piece of work." Soch shuffled, being labeled both complex and necessary.

"You are composed of the seven deadly sins and all of their thorn tree, festering, pythonic outgrowths. I don't like you even a little, and neither does anyone else—not that you'd care. I even have one of you in me, but I can't simply *WILL* you away, and neither can he...you'll be with us till the day *we* leave this planet." Sponsor glared at the little man that gawked upward. Sponsor's eyes were now red beyond flaming.

"You have a right to exist, and only God can drag you into the true light, and trim you down one little piece at a time. You are a self-centered, mean spirited, chicken shit little fuck, but you *will* live until the day they kick dirt in on this man's coffin. That, by the way, will be the day that everyone else moves from the mental high-rise into this ambient thimble. *YOU*, however, *won't* be moving. Period. Enjoy your remaining days, and watch yourself shrink in your cellar...or grow again in the gutter." He looked at me with clear concern.

"Oh, don't fuck with Harry, by the way...He'll kick your ass and you'll *feel* it, cause you can't be killed, but you are a form of flesh. It'll hurt badly, because you're ironically sensitive and a whiner when it comes to pain...It'll hurt *real* bad. A little shit's the least of your problems." He stood gloating like an old woman who had just beat and cornered a rat with a broom.

Soch was now about 18-inches tall, skinny as a milk jug and red as a beet. He was lambasted speechless, powerless, and *some* pissed.

"Let's go," said the now bigger little sponsor. "Let me help you down, Sonny," he said putting his giant hands around the doll-like, angry, defiant, and humiliated being. "Want to nudge me now?" He concluded, sitting the baby down at below knee height and reminding him that the nudge at the high-rise back door had not gone unnoticed.

"Wow, a resentment," I thought, watching Soch grow by about three inches, now looking absolutely like a pale nutria.

"Let's walk," said the sponsor. "Oh, here. You're efficient, so you can take this *express* route home," he chuckled, as we passed a garbage chute. In a tai chi swoop he bent, grabbed, raised the lid, and dropped Soch in the hole, feet first like two milk jugs tied together.

I heard the little scorned one rattling and cussing with a tin-can-like banging and echoing sound, fading as he swirled stories and stories and stories and stories to the bottom.

"He'll come out in the alley, half a block from his cellar," the little sponsor winked.

"Don't worry, he's pissed at me, not you...he'll only take it out on you a LITTLE. I wouldn't let him grow too much, though, if I were you. Watch your choices." He laughed uncontrollably, knowing that I would be paranoid and cautious for some time to come. "God removes character defects, but *he's* the splinter that makes you feel 'em...so, be humble." He chuckled some more at the little firecracker he had lit.

A helicopter was circling as we walked **"S"** from the compass. This compass was etched in a sunken fountain on a garden floor. As it sat down near a flower arrangement on the veranda, I noticed that Jeff Wendler was getting out of the aerial spray-rigged whirlybird.

"Jesus, Jeff," I said, running up to shake his hand, "I thought you...were...umm, were...on the outs with your dad...so, umm...working alone?"

I was recovering from what was about a major blunder. His dad had shot at him once, to scare him, when the defiant youngest went into business, buying a helicopter sprayer, and competing with his old man. Worse yet, however, Jeff had stabbed a knife into his heart, in a fit of depression and rage, and killed himself. It was tragic. He was SO talented and brilliant.

"Na," he said, with his dad's eyes sparkling. "He and I are spraying together now. I'm doing a field **"S"** while he's doing one **Uish**. We get along nowadays." He walked slowly towards the sound of someone playing a guitar *poorly*...I knew that sound.

"Can I see it?" Jeff asked politely, with his blue eyes as peaceful and clear as an angel.

"Sure," said *Poet*, smiling like a big child.

He embarrassed me sometimes, but was so nice. Jeff tuned the guitar and began to show him some chord patterns. As they handed the guitar back and forth, I could actually see Poet getting better. Jeff didn't let him make mistakes any more than his brothers, Lain or David, had me in the early days. I had no questions this time for the little sponsor, who grinned.

"Oh, look here." The little sponsor turned, pointing towards a bricked area.

The bricks suddenly turned a neon purple and a pair of old folks floated out of them. They, however, did not stop on the veranda as I had expected. Instead, they continued skyward until they were balloon sized and, then, invisible. They kept going up.

"Wow," I said without formulating a question.

He turned, faced, and studied me carefully, as though he needed me to see the continuing unpredictable, physics-defying *nature* of this "place." He could see that I did.

"Let's move over here," he coached, with a concerned look crossing his face. "Poet, Analytical and I will find our way back, but there's only one way for you to return, and I'm going to ask you to trust me like never before when I show you it." He had compassionate tears in eyes that were now violet gray. "There's no easy way to say or do this." I felt his tone and, thus, felt deeply anxious, but I remained still.

A green toad, half the size of a basketball, jumped toward us as we began to walk. I picked him up and carried him perhaps twenty feet **"S"** to a garden area, where I sat him down. It had a cold white tummy, and pissed on my hand predictably as I escorted it. No amends could overcome what I owed the toad people. *"Remember not the sins of my youth,"* I pondered unspoken. "...la imortalidad del sapo." I spoke aloud.

"Es en el corazon," affirmed the little sponsor with a sad, still comforting, gaze. "It's in the heart."

Now the "not so little" Sponsor continued slowly toward the corner that said **"S"** and I followed. The morning sun was at our back, and shadows were forming from large, thick bushes and trees as we walked.

I found myself suddenly encountering chest high grass as we got perhaps 100 feet from the edge. I turned when I heard people, and saw Suzanne and Leslie talking and laughing with other people that I did not know. I was shocked to see them together, but knew not to question things with reason here. Things just were.

I noticed Violet, looking rested and small, reading a thick book and sitting beside a fountain near the tennis courts, and across from a sculpted stone wall. She looked so happy and content. She looked up, and directly at me, but obviously did not know who I was. It hurt, but I knew again that things here were not mine to calculate or control. If only I'd known that years ago. I accepted it as inevitable now.

Leslie spotted me and waved heartily, whereupon Suzanne looked as well, but she obviously did not know me anymore than Violet had. How I wished I could have played out all my lives perfectly, but I could not...I did not. I felt love, gratitude, and hope for each of them, with a companion knowing of joyful remorse.

"Come on," said the little sponsor, with a sound of urgency. "We have to complete this visit...now. Your time here is over." I followed him, finding it easier to move the grass aside after he had trudged it.

He again climbed up on the wall...this time the **"S" and "R"** wall, near the **"S"** corner, and extended his hand to pull me up. My eyes caught the horizon and I *greatly* didn't like what I saw. I instinctively recoiled with acrophobia and vivid instinctual flashbacks of demise.

This side of the building was *absolute* darkness, as dark as the other side was light. Worse, however, several hundred feet below, was the eternal wafting aurora of intermixing lights that I had seen once before from my fraternity sleep state. There, the lights had wooed me from the wooden porch of the old house where my father and his friends were having a séance of fellowship. I jumped then not knowing the real life consequences of trying to awaken from it. I knew and recalled those consequences clearly now. That night, in reality, I nearly died.

These lights were identical, moving as dry ice gas, stirring, dancing, eternal, endless in color and size. I flashed back, with physical and emotional horror, to diving, then suffocating, then *begging* to remember my name, too weak to move my body, ultimately barely awaking to survive that *dream's* near death power drain. Here it was again.

I felt like a child and I cried, begging and trembling with fear. I huddled behind my little sponsor and clung to his arm like a two-year old.

"You can only return this way, Doug. There is no alternative. I wish there were, but this comes down to acceptance and faith. You *have* to jump into the lighted abyss of **"S" and "R"** or you *will* die here without waking. You *have* to jump." His kind brown eyes made me know that I was blessed; his strong arm made me know that I was not alone.

"If it helps," he added softly, "I'll tell you now that this side is dark *above*, but lighted *below*. Jeff wasn't spraying in darkness. The refracted light of the morning sun is coming up through the diamond and making these prismic lights. Now it gets a little harder to comprehend." He smiled gently again, communicating pure understanding and hope. Each eye had a deep, deep, deep brown ring around black pupils the size of nickels.

"What if he's a demon, tricking and luring me with all of this to my death," I paused with a faithless thought. "No, *'by their fruits shall ye know them,'*" I pondered, knowing that he was the kindest, sternest, yet most loving, being I had ever known. "Besides, this time, I'm ready to die, even if he were lying—which he is not. He is all that's good in me, personified. He's honest, faithful, real—like an innocent childhood friend."

"I'm glad you're clear on that," he affirmed, seeing my thoughts. It's tricky business, this human stuff, huh?" He then turned and pointed across the lights.

"The lights are refracting, reflecting, and intermixing with a human cloud. Yes, I said *'human'*. The cloud is human vapor...souls. Remember in *James* when it says, *'for what is your life, it is even a vapor...?'* Well, this is where it *'vanishes'* to." I recalled Suzanne's son, David, quoting that at a Sunday dinner table—radiating wisdom.

"Often," the little sponsor continued, "someone reformulates, as a dream specter, and then walks around this building, or the little high-rise that's attached to it. Sometimes they even move-in for a while. Some are curious; some are compelled to. They are the people you may or may not know in your dreams. They accompany memories and perceptions to become one big, well..."

"This cloud is that veil between life and death, breath and breathlessness, death's sleep and life's dream, truth and truthfulness, you and others, you and yourself, you and the eternal. It's one's last breath mixed with God's first breath, if you can comprehend that. It's as real as your physical life, but totally omniscient, without conflict or fear; it's...well, it's peaceful. All souls are interconnected here as one, yet remain purely, and I mean *purely*, themselves. This vapor cloud runs through all living things and always has...always will—the Alpha and the Omega."

"A poor job, but that's about as close as I can describe it in human terms. Yes, it can absorb you. Yes, it nearly did that night in college, for reasons you'll understand later. Yes it could now, but as I've told you, it won't. It *will* not. Tonight's about faith—knowing its power—like college was about power, knowing no faith. Ultimately, it will absorb you, and on that day, we'll go together. *I'll* be there with you then. I promise." He put his hand on my shoulder, and in the myriad of lights, I somehow realized, for the first time, that he was black.

God, his eyes were so full of love. I trusted him completely with my life, and all fear left me. I cried now, not from fear, but for joy. I knew fully that angels live within and without. Of course, they are likely a part of the inconceivable lighted cloud, a cloud, perhaps, that moved with Moses across the Sinai into Canaan, before and beyond—the *image* of God.

"I have a stupid, even irrelevant, question," I said, like a first grader. "But the *analytical* in *me* needs to know."

He smiled as though he welcomed it, and motioned to ask, with his palm opened toward me.

"Why are you black when I'm white? I'd have thought that my mind would have created you as white, almost without thinking about it, just because of my background?"

"Hum," he paused. "Interesting observation, but remember Lisette's answer to why she owned a short legged dog?" I nodded and blushed simultaneously.

"We definitely overworked that," I affirmed.

"This one's not *as* obvious, but is as *simple*," he responded. "There are two answers to why I'm black. First, *you* didn't create me, as you did Poet and Analytical. I watched over you as a child, and entered your heart, when you were 23 years old, at *your* invitation. You didn't even notice my arrival for 24 more years, whereupon, you began to conceive of me as your 'little sponsor.' You were too busy quoting scripture. Simply put, I was sent to you as a *comforter* and as a *teacher*. Second, I'm black because *I AM*."

"*What* is your name," I asked, gasping and barely grasping that he was not a part of me like Analytical and Poet.

"If I told you," he gazed lovingly, "You would try to change me, and that's what you've been running towards, and from, your whole life. Let's just say again that *I AM*." His eyes retained giant pupils, but began to match the dancing lights below, and his breath appeared for the first time as though it were cold.

"Did you ever notice how a baby in a womb, someone bowed in *humble* prayer, or an old man, pressed earthward with time, are like frail commas," he whispered? *Live* and *be...those* commas." He suddenly shined, then flickered, and shone brighter, as pure, ancient, timeless, innocent, wisdom. I instinctively stooped with goose bumps and involuntary awe.

I suddenly knew fully who he was. I knew when he came, and why he lived within me. Sociopath was his polar spirit, molded—and modeled from me—but demonic, carved from my character defects, glued together, shaped and nurtured by *spirits* indeed, and by choices, breathed in *by* me like a fragrant virus, once willingly...and maintained, however desperately, for the rest of my life now by hell's appointed little creature and its father of lies. We really did battle *powers and principalities*. Little sponsor was the Holy Spirit.

"I hate your outfit," I said jokingly. "It's just not *You.*" He patted his gut and then kissed me on the cheek. He hugged me with a hug that warmed me completely, and forever.

"Take a final look; then go," he whispered.

I paused to look back across the triangular garden veranda and saw my Grandma Dot, far away now, handing flowers, one by one, to my four year old daughter, my four year old sister, their four year old daughters, a four year old Brendan, Brendan's grown sisters and a four year old Beau. My sister, Dallas, her children and Mary Ellen's son, Dylan, were all waving at one another and approaching the *flowering festival*, growing younger with every step.

Beau was pulling a baby girl in a little red wagon, with a frayed rope handle, and she was blowing purple bubbles. People were joining the group from all around the veranda, and beyond, yet, somehow, the group did not become a growing crowd. As I saw more cousins, lovers, enemies, and kin, I knew that I knew *nothing*.

I looked back at the prism cloud below, then turned for a final look, with the dancing lights behind me.

I saw my friends Anita, Kat, Karen, and Carol chatting with Lisette and our Best Man, Dean, beside a golden statue of Athena—wiggling 59 toes in a pool of sky blue water. They arose, turned in choreographed unison and smiled at me. Dean bowed, they curtsied, and then they all joined, laughing, and blew *me a kiss.* They were so beautiful and I loved them so. My spirit drank them in as eternal friends.

The kiss joined a blue spotted butterfly, and collected a small breeze, becoming a six-part harmonious heavenly sound as it came towards me, and as it passed. The little sponsor faded to invisible, and kissed me, joining the breeze as a seventh sound.

"Tell that clumsy ole John A, 'Hi,' for me," I heard in my spirit, without words. I smelled the *new* smell that filled this heavenly place. For a moment, I hated to leave.

But, I deeply breathed-in this passing eternity, spread my arms like an eagle, and dived into the infinite, churning, beautiful lights.

I fell, and then slowly glided, weightless and clumsy, as when I flew in random dreams. I smelled eternity, and gained power, as I touched the lights. I sank into them, joyful, with a willing heart, fulminating with acceptance and immeasurable gratitude. I became a spirit, *afire illumine.*

Love was my final feeling. "Faith," was my final thought. "Jesus" was my final word. Lisette was my final desire.

I awoke as though I had been whispered to by the New Orleans night. It was *3:11.* The small, cold fingered, beautiful French woman—as was customary, without explanation—sensed my awakening and dragged her mountain of covers across the bed to put her leg across me...returning, undisturbed, to sweet slumber.

I struggled to remember a dream that I had awakened from, but comforted myself that dreams find their own place in life's unfolding. Whether I knew or recalled it today or ever was mute. All I knew, and all I dreamed, remained tucked in some eternal hope chest of the heart and mind along with spirits and people who touched me. They gave of their life, and we gave one another to eternity and, ultimately, to the crystal mind of God. By living a day at a time, and by resting at night, I could do my small part, as a grain of sand in the human ocean. I knew, suddenly, and certainly, that no more was expected.

My soul felt unexplainably full, beyond measure, and I lay my hand upon my chest to feel the fullness of it. I recalled days before when it ached with dark loneliness and dragged me helplessly nowhere from within and without, injuring sojourners and beloveds. Tonight, my heart felt full and warm.

"Thank you God for my life," I whispered, feeling small and humble. *"Forgive me a sinner."*

I suddenly smelled a waft of lighter fluid, and thought it odd. I *loved* that smell.

I breathed deeply and inhaled the warmth of my wife's sweet breathing. I began counting backward from 7,777 to return to sleep, but then giggled as I instead counted Lisette's warming devices— One golden flannel sheet for us both, one cream colored down comforter that we share, one doubled over cream colored down comforter on only her, one blue electric blanket, unplugged and doubled over...only on her, one doubled over white knit blanket, only on her, one doubled over blue, flowered comforter on only her, one pair of Lisette's mismatched red and gray socks, one pair of gray long johns...one ...of something else...*one*

"I'm *c-c-cold*," she whispered shivering.

Without waking, Doug put his arm around her, and snuggled her beautiful face against his chest, moving her hair back gently to keep from sneezing.

"I love you, ma' Boo," she whispered, kissing Doug gently on his sleeping lips.

Doug was dreaming of a day when kids played in perpetuity and pressed small, warm handprints into the cool, fresh concrete of a hand-dug well.

"I love you too, my pet," he whispered, smiling.

Eplogue

As they slept, an open Bible lay on a 300-year old French nightstand, which had passed carefully and lovingly through Lisette's generations.

The Bible had protected the antiquity from water which dripped through the white-tiled ceiling during Katrina, and drops of water *marked* words, seemingly randomly, seen only in the orange and purple hue of nighttime's gently moving oak leafed silhouettes and filtered streetlights.

None could see the now dried dripping patterns by day, but heaven smiled sweetly as it looked through the curtain's veil at words unspoken and unread. To the watchful eye, drops of water had left a living pattern of watermarked letters and prophetic words:

2 Corinthians 5:11

17 Therefore if any man be in Christ, he is a new creature: old things are passed away; behold all things are become **new**.

18 And all things are of G**o**d, who hath **r**econci**l**ed us to himself by Jesus Christ, **an**d hath given to u**s** the ministry of reconciliation.

19 To wit, that God was in Christ reconciling the world unto himself, not imputing their trespasses unto them; and hath committed unto us the word of reconciliation.

20 Now then we are ambassadors for Christ, as though God did beseech you by us: we pray you in Christ's stead, be ye reconciled to God.

21 For he hath made him to be sin for us, who knew no sin, that we might be made the righteousness of God in him.

CHAPTER 6

We then, **as workers together with him**, beseech you also that ye receive not the grace of God in vain.

SALVATION HAVE I SUCCOURED THE:

Behold, now is the day of salvation.)

3 Giving no offence in any thing, that the ministry be not blamed:

4 But in all things approving ourselves as the ministers of God, **in much patience, in afflictions, in necessities, in distresses,**

5 In stripes, in imprisonments, in tumults, in labors, in watchings, in fastings;

6 By pureness, by knowledge, **by longsuffering, by kindness, by the Holy Ghost, by love unfeigned.**

7 By the word of truth, by the power of God, by the Armour of righteousne**s**s on **t**he right h**a**nd and on the left,

8 By honor and di**s**honor, by evil report and good report: as deceivers, and yet **true**;

9 As unknown, **and** yet well known; as dying, and behold, **we live**; as chastened, and not killed;

10 As sorrowful, yet always rejoicing; as poor,

2 (For he saith, I HAVE HEARD THEE IN A TIME ACCEPTED, AND IN THE DAY OF	yet making many rich; **as having nothing, and yet possessing all things**. 11 O ye Corinthians, our mouth is open unto you; our heart is enlarged.